Wish You Were Here

Wish *You* Were *Here*

Love & Longing in an American Heartland

Zachary Michael Jack

American Midwest
Truman State University Press
Kirksville, Missouri

Copyright © 2016 Zachary Michael Jack/Truman State University Press, Kirksville, Missouri 63501
All rights reserved
tsup.truman.edu

Cover art: Mayer, Merkel & Ottmann Lithographing, "Angel of Midnight Seed Corn," from *Joseph Breck's Annual Descriptive Catalogue of Seeds*, 1886
Cover design: Lisa Ahrens

Library of Congress Cataloging-in-Publication Data

Names: Jack, Zachary Michael, 1973- author.
Title: Wish you were here : love and longing in an American heartland / by Zachary Michael Jack.
Description: Kirksville, Missouri : Truman State University Press, 2016. | Series: American midwest series | Includes bibliographical references.
Identifiers: LCCN 2016026477 (print) | LCCN 2016043816 (ebook) | ISBN 9781612481708 (pbk. : alk. paper) | ISBN 9781612481715
Subjects: LCSH: Middle West—Social life and customs—21st century. | Middle West—Social conditions—21st century. | Jack, Zachary Michael, 1973- | Middle West—Civilization.
Classification: LCC F355 .J33 2016 (print) | LCC F355 (ebook) | DDC 977—dc23
LC record available at https://lccn.loc.gov/2016026477

*To Edward Lee
and Michael Allen,
who taught me that Stayers
can also be Dreamers*

"There ought to be a book written about me, that there ought! And when I grow up, I'll write one—but I'm grown up now," she added in a sorrowful tone: "at least there's no room to grow up anymore *here*."

—Lewis Carroll, *Alice's Adventures in Wonderland*

"I had the feeling that the world was left behind, that we had got over the edge of it, and were outside man's jurisdiction. This was the complete dome of heaven, all there was. Between that earth and that sky I felt erased, blotted out. . . . That is happiness, to be dissolved into something complete and great."

—Willa Cather, *My Antonia*

"The talented youths who, in the expansive era of unlimited prosperity, were carried away on waves of enthusiasm for projects of various sorts, wanting nothing so much as to get away from the old things of home, now, when it all collapses, come back solidly to the good earth."

—Grant Wood, *Revolt Against the City*

Contents

Preface
Wish You Were Here

We 70 million rural North Americans are tuned to lonesome places. Maybe this explains why we often work best left to our own devices, or why we choose to spend our days—or dream of spending our days—in America's Big Empty, the sprawling region in the center of the country whose silences many urbanites find positively unsettling.

The fashion when writing about the great American Middle— flyover country, as it's sometimes called—is often to portray us as graying and evangelical. We're imagined to be stoical types, balding and pitchfork-wielding, or else lone-wolf cowboys, embittered, in either case, by what writer Carol Bly in the 1970s called our "sexual chill" and our subsequent alienation from the rest of an urban, sexed-up, screen-time nation.

Each year I make my home in two such intensely rural places, bookending the traditional Heartland from north to south: Iowa, where the number of acres planted in corn exceeds by 10 million the total number of people, and the remote timberland of southeast Missouri, a state with more live trees—an estimated 8.2 billion— than people living on earth. And I'm far from alone in making the difficult choice to spend my early middle age, my young at heartland, unfenced and unbridled. Statistics show that thirty-somethings and early forty-somethings are returning to the Big

Empty to roost in ever-increasing numbers. In northern Montana, for instance, Toole County experienced a 25 percent increase in the thirty to forty-four age group from 2000 to 2010. Likewise, in frozen Minnesota, sixty-one of sixty-seven rural counties experienced a net gain of thirty- to forty-four-year-olds from 1990 to 2000. They're coming, many of them, to build nests. They're coming to live a sweeter, simpler life, though the living here is far from simple. Like any class of pioneers, they find the going sometimes harder than they thought, and begin looking for others with whom they can share their experience.

Like them, I don't see our country's hinterlands and hinter*loves* as chilled or empty. Instead I see immense love and longing in the prairies and plains and grasslands of the nation's midlands, as well as great hope and participation, earnestness and vision, fostered by a life lived along the horizon-line. Where some see stultifying ritual and repression, I see romance born, as romance so often is, from the distance between ourselves as thinking, dreaming, yearning beings and the difficult visions we, month after month, year after year, create and sustain, each in our own unlikely places. Allowed to stew, sweeten, and mellow, our hinter*loves* often take on an erotic quality, a keening and a pining born organically from the country places where we choose not just to sharpen our axes but also, and importantly, to hang our hats and feather our nests.

These bittersweet distances we court and ultimately befriend are the very things, in the end, that make us pine. They teach us that from love comes longing. Distance is the secret ingredient that enlivens and enlightens the plaintive wail of Bill Monroe's bluegrass tenor, for example, or Slim Whitman's high lonesome yodel. It's what lends the Mexican *corridas* and *rancheros* their powerfully nostalgic pleadings. Distance long-stoked cannot help but create the heat and fire that sometimes cause us to throw open our windows at night and yap in the starshine along with the coyotes.

As its title suggests, *Wish You Were Here* consists of pieces and *pensées* from an American hinterland, championing and sometimes challenging what was once well understood as "the romance of open places." These essays and explorations and expeditions offer a slip of how we navigate the twenty-first-century American Heartland, how we long, how we love, how we live, leave, and sometimes lose here: not Lonesome Dove, but lonesome love.

Introduction

Your True Regionalist

"Your true regionalist is not a mere eulogist," the Heartland's most iconic painter, Grant Wood, reminded his followers in the throes of the Great Depression. Wood was forty-five years old in 1936, at the height of a career that nearly every one of his most-trusted advisors said would be better spent in New York City or Paris. "Seven years ago my friends had sincerely pitied me for what they called my 'exile,'" Wood recalled. "They then had a vision of my going back to an uninteresting region where I could have no contact with culture and no association with kindred spirits."

Throughout my late teens and well into my middle twenties, I had heard similar get-while-the-gettin's-good messages from friends and well-meaning mentors and colleagues until, a few years shy of thirty, I decided to strike out against a sea of geographic troubles, hoping to end them. I wanted to make manifest Wood's claim: that to love the rural and small-town Midwest didn't mean leaving it, only to mourn when it inevitably died for the absence of my very demographic, but to vote with my feet and become partner to a regional solution. I didn't want to go quietly into that good night, so I contacted a handful of public meeting halls and civic organizations, told them about my beef with the brain drain, and barnstormed my way across what proto-regionalist Hamlin Garland once called "the Middle Border" (from Minnesota to Missouri) to

1

let the pollsters and census takers and academic sharpshooters know we were out there—we educated, twenty-, thirty-, and early forty-something lovers and fighters—and that we choose to put a very personal plug in the brain drain, attempting to find life and love right here in the midlands. Before I knew it, the *Des Moines Register* and state NPR affiliates had gotten wind of my trek, splashed it across their front pages and headline news, and spread it around the Corn Belt. Almost overnight, the voice of an oddball brain retainer had reached potentially a quarter million midwesterners.

But there were other, more sobering numbers motivating my trek, a slew of which had been released as demographers digested the 2010 census data. By July of 2011, the Associated Press reported rural America's share of the total population at just 16 percent, its lowest ever, alongside the macabre headline "Rural US Disappearing?" In March of 2014, PBS's venerable *NewsHour* followed suit, splashing the headline "Is Rural America a Thing of the Past?" across its national topics webpage. Rural America, the AP reported, had reported its first-ever population loss. From 2011 to 2012, census estimates showed a net loss of 40,000 people from non-metro areas. Globally, the news wasn't much better. In its *World Urbanization Prospects: 2014 Revision*, the United Nations projected that by 2050, 66 percent of the world's population would be urban.

Back in the Heartland, newspaper and radio services picked up my story in part because it told the unlikely tale of the stayers, the holy grail population desperate Midwest policymakers target in their efforts to staunch the out-migration of young professionals. I couldn't claim that my story was typical of my age group and education level—after all, it was my demographic outlier status that had powered my interstate trek in the first place. Still, I hoped that those who were young and similarly wedded to rural Middle America, or those who once were or who cared passionately for someone who is (or was), would recognize the tune and dance to it. Despite the gloom-and-doom statistics documenting our historic losses, globally there were still 3.4 billion of us rural-dwellers, roughly 46 million of us in the United States alone. The real story is what it meant, and what it means, to be young, or young at heart, in America's great graying middle, to be deeply rooted in a place demographers wouldn't think to find us, having long since given us up for dead. It's about sinking roots and laying down one's welcome mat in a region where, since the Great Depression, successive generations have been told to leave while there's still time, to leap from tall-corn and tall-grass hometowns cast and castigated as sinking ships. It's about the good folks who have somehow found the courage not just to stay afloat here, but to fight the good fight, and even sometimes to thrive.

A decade earlier, when I'd returned to the rural Midwest with a freshly minted degree in hand, I found myself in the exact place and at the exact age about which the panic over departed "brains" had reached a fever pitch. At the advent of a new millennium, the Associated Press newswire hummed with the bummer news that a third of Indiana residents left the state after graduating from college and that Nebraska's top performers on the ACT exam were increasingly out-migrating for their four years of university. The gloom and doom on the AP wire soon found other smaller newspapers piling on to augment and amplify the blue note. The *Toledo Blade* reported that the more education its citizens had, the more likely they were to move, while the *Cedar Rapids Gazette* asked with a note of desperation, "Is there any possible regional solution to the brain drain?" Lacking a panacea, the paper urged its readers to "talk to friends and relatives who have left. What made them leave? What might draw them back?" Pining like this, it seemed to me, amounted to a lover's lament over a courtship gone south, where one party—the abandoned—rehearses over and over what went wrong.

My home state of Iowa, by virtue of attracting so many young brains to its affordable universities, suffered the worst of the population hemorrhage after graduation. The IRS tax return tracking service showed that Nebraskans were the only Heartlanders more likely to move to Iowa than Iowans were to leave for neighboring states. As a relatively recent graduate of Iowa State University, the state's agricultural land-grant university, who came home to serve as a section editor for my county seat's small-town newspaper, I found myself once more the recipient of a supposedly maudlin inheritance, a curious specimen at the ground zero of a problem now making national headlines. Suddenly, being a young, rural, highly educated professional in a state like Iowa or Nebraska or South Dakota had acquired a weird kind of cachet. Like being born the son of a West Virginia coal miner in an era of widely publicized mine disasters, fate had conspired to make of my midwestern peers and me unwilling poster children for an ugly demographic problem that now answered to a soul-sucking name: brain drain. The negative attentions stung us stayers, the only consolation being that fate had at least seen fit to provide us with some kind of experiential credential or calling card—made us both by birthright and by circumstance an expert in at least *something*. It was as if Bad News U. had granted us an honorary PhD in demographic death and decay by its School of Hard Knocks.

We rural young at heartland had become an endangered species—"famous among the barns," as poet Dylan Thomas had it—rare coinages of a reputedly dead currency unspent and middling while the real human capital flowed elsewhere. By then my own hometown of one thousand souls had itself been called out, by name, as a "rural ghetto" in a popular book on rural decline and denial.

—————➤◦◄—————

Look closely at the satiric brushstrokes in *American Gothic* and it's evident Grant Wood was no simple or uncomplicated booster of his homeland; he believed the regionalist could, and perhaps should on rare occasion, be what he called a "severe critic." Nevertheless Wood swooned over the Middle West even in an era when outmigration from the nation's midsection was nearly as steep as in the digital age. "Occasionally I have been accused of being a flag-waver for my own part of the country," he confessed in his little book of 1936, *Revolt Against the City*. "I do believe in the Middle West, in its people and its art, and in the future of both—and this with no derogation to other sections. I believe in the Middle West in spite of abundant knowledge of its faults."

Like Wood, I would have ample reason to reject my native Heartland, should I wish. I would have bones to pick, born of longtime, hard-fought experience as an unmarried rural "young person" awash in alleged brain drain: I'll admit I am at times lonesome for my long-gone demographic peer group, who ghosted our home region long ago. I write my earnest wish-you-were-heres to friends in places like Ogden, Utah; Minneapolis, Minnesota; and San Diego, California, while I stew and simmer in a place where beer cans decorate the roadsides in greater numbers than brown-eyed Susans; where thieves grow audacious enough to enter the homes of the elderly and swipe petty cash while the widow of the house does the dishes; and where hog barns confining thousands (centralized animal feeding operations, or CAFOs for short) spring up a mile or two upwind of our hobbit homes without so much as a public notice in the local newspapers. Granted, I occasionally fall victim to the woe-is-me recitations endemic to the diehard regionalist still young enough to be reminded that they have "better choices." There's no "good" coffee here, I'm constantly reminded, no prospects for a date, no major university within fifty miles. The Internet, when it's working, is slow as buttermilk through a straw; and it's paradoxically difficult to procure a fresh tomato in the middle of the world's lushest vegetable monoculture. Many of our small towns have turned into food deserts, lacking so much as a hometown grocery store.

In the end, I live here because I love here. It's too easy, in my view, to be a simple eulogist, the regionally bereaved, the long-distance lover with sincere regrets—to be that mourner who, upon hearing of a death in the larger Heartland family, flies in for the weekend from Lincoln or Chicago, St. Louis or Minneapolis, with a sad face and sad words for a person and a place they knew once way back when, and who pulls into some remote farm town in a flashy rental car with their best funeral clothes hung with care, and sits summoning their courage to get out from behind the wheel as they watch old farmers in bib overalls whose names they can't quite recall shuffle past, heading for the wake.

Young at Heartland

Part I

Hinterloves

"I can't tell you how many people I've spoken to who have said, 'I would love to live in x or y small town but I'm single and I *just can't*,'" Stephanie Larsen of the Center for Rural Affairs tells me when I call her to ask what prompted her move back to the Great Plains from Washington, DC. After enduring a forty-five-minute Metro commute during her days as a nutrition and food security legislative advocate in Washington, DC, thirty-something Larsen and her partner bought a twelve-acre parcel, dubbed it Thistle Root, and rooted down outside Lyons, Nebraska, a town of roughly one thousand located forty-five miles south of North Sioux City, South Dakota.*

Already Steph and her partner find themselves conspicuous outliers in a town where the population is older (just 5 percent of the population falls in the eighteen to twenty-four bracket) and profoundly homogeneous (in excess of 98 percent white). Life-partnered, the impressive pair has chosen for their home a place where well over half of adults are conventionally married. So I ask the prairie-enthused Larsen why more of her thirty-something peers haven't followed her road less traveled.

"If I didn't have a partner, I probably wouldn't live here either," she confesses. "Especially when you're doing something different than everyone else around you. It's really hard to have the strength completely within yourself without someone who's in it for the

*Since the time of this interview, Steph Larsen and her partner have moved to a twenty-acre ranch in rural western Montana, where they graze sheep and cows.

long haul with you to say, 'You know what, we're gonna be these weirdos; we're gonna do that crazy thing.' Because you get it from all sides. There's your neighbors, who are like, 'Organic, what's that? That's dangerous. That's a threat to me. I don't like it.' And from urban friends, who say, 'You wanna go *where*? Why would you choose *that*? Can't you just go to the farmer's market and be happy about it?'"

Larsen, who grew up a professor's daughter in the university town of Eau Claire, Wisconsin, says the credibility issue for young urbans who choose to live in the region's agrarian hinterlands can be a daunting one—the struggle sometimes boils down to how to get farm and ranch people to recognize that you're something other than a snot-nosed, fresh-faced kid from the city with high-falutin' ideas about how things ought to be. "I have advantages because I have fresh eyes," Larsen maintains. "I hear a lot from people who grew up on farms, 'Oh, it's such hard work. I would never go back to the farm. It's dirty. It's stinky.' Quite frankly, I don't find those things to be true."

In a sense, Larsen's sentiments reflect both the answer and the problem for young 'uns with the nerve to move to the nation's brain-drained midlands, where demographics dictate that the highly educated young will be a conspicuous minority. Larsen's not a wimp or a prima donna, as her comments make plain. And yet the citizens of this rural town on the Plains might recognize in her assessment a certain kind of naïveté . . . after all, working a desk job from nine to five and coming home at night to a dozen acres with a handful of laying hens and a large garden is a world apart from the dirtier, smellier, more visceral world of farming and ranching many of them grew up with by necessity. Even the idea that Larsen considers herself a farmer, and writes about it, rankles some of the natives to these fathomless grasslands.

"It is hard work. It's not for everyone and I respect that," Larsen says. "But I think where it's important to me is to listen to and respect the experiences of people who have done this for a lot longer than I have. And at the same time it's important for them to respect the questions that I have, because sometimes you're so close to the problem you can't see the obvious solution. That's where having some fresh blood and fresh ideas in a rural community can really be a benefit."

Here again, the decision to live young and in love in a land associated with gray-haired staidness and puritanical repressions (picture the man and woman of Grant Wood's *American Gothic*) can create an identity crisis similar to the one experienced by college students who, for example, leave their native inner city for an affluent suburban liberal arts college. Such students routinely report that when they're speaking to administrators or professors or classmates, they feel the need to be one kind of person, and when they're back home for weekends or holidays, they feel the need to be something completely different, that the two worlds are seemingly mutually exclusive.

Larsen's life embodies that dichotomy. When she occasionally writes for the local hometown newspaper, she can't completely be herself there, sticking to safe topics that are homey and, at best, gently challenging. But when she blogs for liberal, post-feminist websites on the West Coast, she revels in playing the role of provocateur. Should a mix-up occur—for example, should one of her post-feminist blogs accidentally get submitted to the *Lyons Mirror-Sun*—the results could be either catastrophic or comedic. It's a *The Importance of Being Earnest* dilemma, wherein the charismatic, identity-riven Jack splits his personality by necessity, explaining to his pal Algernon, "My name is Ernest in town and Jack in the country."

"There's definitely some challenges associated with insularism and the fact that I don't know people's names," Larsen admits. "They are sometimes wary of outsiders. . . . It's taken me several years and a newspaper column before people really know who I am. . . . I know there's much less agreement among my neighbors about the way I choose to think about things than, say, in an online community. . . . Here we have place in common; [online] we have a subject area in common. And so there are certain topics where I'm, like, 'I'm not so sure I want to put this out there for people who've never met me.'"

In the main, Larsen's cautions are well-grounded, evidence that, like any good writer, she's considering her audience before she puts pen to paper, finger to keyboard. At the same time, her challenge—how to be herself in a place where demographically she's an outlier—evidences the dilemma faced by many modern back-to-the-landers, who often find a closer intellectual kinship online with folks halfway across the country than they do with the folks down the road, a difference that sometimes results in a bunker mentality. It's a tough row to hoe—a metaphor that transcends mere idiom in places like Lyons—but an important row, because rural America has the potential to make up in ideological diversity what it might lack in racial or ethnic difference.

Just as Bill Bishop's 2004 *The Big Sort* reminds us of the dangers of the nation's young professionals' segregating themselves in like-minded, urban communities, writer Carol Bly sees a role for young contrarians and pariahs bold enough to be entirely themselves in homogeneous communities. Of the potentially combustible mix in her own Plains town of the 1970s, Bly wrote in *Letters from the Country*,

> We know, for example, that somewhere in our town of 2,242, there live people who believe that the preservatives sodium nitrite, sodium nitrate, and BHA variously threaten future health, and also in town live the local staff of the Agricultural Extension Division, who have just published an essay saying the advantages of these preservatives outweigh the disadvantages. Yet these two sets of people don't meet each other on open panels, and scarcely at all even privately.

Bly's solution? Host "Enemy Evenings" as a remedy for long-repressed "years of chill and evasive tact." An Enemy Evening, in Larsen's case, might mean serving up that fiery post-feminist column intended for the advocates and activists on the West Coast right alongside the latest from the Lyons Women's Club.

As much as Larsen enjoys her office days on Main Street, where her primary policy interests lie in achieving affordable health care for the rural Midwest's self-employed, she also enjoys her evenings and weekends at Thistle Root Farm. She wouldn't give her urban peers the hard sell that regional think tanks and governmental commissions think is needed in the quest to bring the nation's young back to what was known in the nineteenth century as the Great American Desert. But what she does expect of her peers is empathy, true open-mindedness regarding the exceptional demographic choice she is making.

"I wouldn't ever try to convince someone that this is the life they should lead. This is the life *I* choose and I love it," she says. "I've never really lived in the country before. . . . I get this a lot with Nebraska because people say, 'Ugh. You live in Nebraska . . . Why? It's flat. It's ugly. There are backwater people.' My reply is, 'Have you ever been there?' Because until you actually are here to experience with your own eyes as opposed to taking everyone else's word for it or judging Nebraska from what you've seen from Interstate 80, you have to think about how unable you are to judge."

I mention to Larsen my personal hunch that the future of the Great Plains may in fact be bright, if history rhymes, as Mark Twain claimed. Throughout the Gilded Age of the 1880s and 1890s, when late twenty-something Theodore Roosevelt moved from a privileged life in East Coast high society to experience the rough-and-ready life of the cowboy in North Dakota, the rate of urbanity was quietly tripling in America. And yet, weirdly, Americans' reactionary interest in farm country deepened even as they left en masse for the metropolis. The same paradoxical phenomenon, I theorize to Larsen, might be happening today. How else does one explain contradictory trends toward radical depopulation of farm and ranch country on the one hand, and the dramatic increase in interest in organics, food security, farmer's markets, and sustainable living on the other?

Larsen agrees that the dynamic relationship between city and country goes back to what she calls "urban-rural linkages." "There has historically been, even when people live in the city, lots of peo-

ple who have country homes. They have cabins. . . . They have some
kind of connection to rural areas. I've spent a lot of time in Latin
America and that's even more so there," she explains. Larsen brings
a geographer's perspective—the subject of her master's degree at
the University of Wisconsin—to the problem, avoiding the pitfall
of viewing rurality reductively.

Years ago I too had the opportunity to live among and study
indigenous cultures in the proud colonial town of Pátzcuaro, Mexico. Within the first week of my months-long residency, I met an
indigenous translator/cheesemaker based at one of the old colonial
hotels on the city square. Francisco offered to take me into the small
agrarian villages ringing the sacred Lake Pátzcuaro, where each settlement was known for the production of a distinctive, traditional
craft that bolsters the local economy. As we moved from house to
house, having conversations over tea warmed over open fires, what
shocked even me, a citizen of America's empty quarter, was how
deathly quiet were these villages, where women sat at their looms
so wordlessly it positively unnerved. And what surprised me most
was the almost complete absence of men, a gendered emptiness so
complete it seemed as if an alien ship had beamed all the young
and middle-aged males up to the mother ship. Francisco explained
that virtually all of the men of working age had, post-NAFTA, left
to earn wages in the United States. They had, in effect, shipped out,
whole armies of them, and, like soldiers, they would send letters
and occasionally money back to wives and daughters and mothers
charged with keeping the home fires burning.

More than a decade later, that unforgettable crystal-ball look
into rural life proves revealing not just of Mexico, but also of my
Midwest, where the departing young leave often as de facto economic refugees compelled to make their living in more prosperous
geographies. In effect, Heartland youth enact a first-world version
of the Mexican man exodus—taking their brains and beauty to
more lucrative markets, often never to return except for the briefest
of visits. While such a liminal back-and-forth gifts a generation of
geographically displaced with conspicuous omniscience and even

cosmopolitanism, it also severs generations-old ties to the land that can never be rebuilt.

"Because fewer people are living in rural areas . . . they're losing some of that physical connection," Larsen confirms. "I think they're starting to see it more in their food, and trying to grapple with that connection by reaching out to farmers. In part that's why there's this explosion in farmer's markets. People are wanting that connection. . . . They don't want to be completely urban . . . even as they don't feel they want to live in rural areas, but most people have never even seen a small town, so their opinions of what it's like come from the movies and country songs, which may not necessarily portray an accurate depiction. . . . It's not all sparrows and rainbows. There are challenges, of course, but there are challenges to living an urban life too."

Larsen maintains that her experience in Lyons underscores the assumption that "if you're smart and talented you need to go to the city." When rural people look around at the few educated young left in their community, she says, they do so with the unspoken questions, "Well, why are you here? What punishment is this for you?" Any answer to self-defeating queries like these, Larsen thinks, must involve the recultivation of a sense of place and community. "To me there needs to be some pride that says, 'You know what, I *choose* to be here. This is not a punishment. I was not banished. I choose to be here. This is a great place to be'—really taking pride in the rural, and not in some false or chintzy way."

Larsen sees affordable health care and direct marketing for young rural-based entrepreneurs as key to coaxing the region's youth back from the cities, and she thinks technology has a role to play too. Having recently remodeled her farmhouse with mail-order hardware and fixtures, Larsen is convinced that living and loving in the farthest flung corners of the Heartland become doable with a high-speed Internet connection. "I've said to myself I feel like I'm going back to the days of the Wells Fargo. . . . I do most of my shopping for non–food related things online, because it comes right to me," she says, citing plumbing she recently purchased on

Amazon.com. "I think that technology is the other answer. If you can buy a sink online, you can date online," Larsen claims, while she concedes that "the population of thoughtful, educated people with a college degree or higher is very small in rural communities."

━━►•◄━━

I opt for a second opinion of what it means to be young in the small-town Heartland from Luke Gran, director of the Next Generation program, an initiative of the Practical Farmers of Iowa (PFI), based in Ames, that focuses on encouraging young people to return to farming.* Up until 2009, when he assumed the post at PFI while still in his mid-twenties, Gran had been single and had come close to moving to southeast Iowa to start up a consulting business. "Quite frankly it scared the bejesus out of me to think of myself as having no prospects for dating. . . . I had this apprehension that this rural county . . . would be filled with no one to connect with. It was definitely a concern in my mind."

Instead, Gran, a 2009 graduate of Iowa State University in forestry and international agriculture, took the first halting steps into setting up an environmental consulting business based in his hometown of Newton (population just over 15,000) where he stood to benefit from existing networks of family and friends and where a half-hour commute would take him to metropolitan Des Moines, ranked nationally as a best-buy for singles. "I could do the most good in the community that I was from," Gran says of his decision to stay home after graduation. "So I hunkered down in central Iowa and started a little consulting business until this job jumped up." That job has, in many ways, been an education for Gran, whose father was a white-collar worker at the Maytag Corporation in Newton, not a self-employed maverick. "I come from a well-educated family," Gran says, adding that his grandparents on

---

*Luke Gran and his wife now run a small CSA on their acreage outside Ames. Luke is also self-employed as a forestry consultant.

both sides went to college. In fact, Gran's closest familial link to a
Heartland farm is some two generations removed, via his grandfather, a Pocahontas County dirt farmer who somehow wrested a
living from eighty acres.

After marrying and beginning his post at PFI, Gran and his
wife moved into an empty family farmhouse a short commute from
Ames, where they work. Ames, located about a half-hour north of
Des Moines, is home to Iowa State University and shows up on
lists of Best Places to Live from *Money* magazine to *Sperling's Best
Places*. Though they live close to what in the Midwest qualifies as
a utopian community, their rented farmhouse, three miles beyond
the nearest small town and a mile from the nearest neighbor, gives
them a taste of some of the on-the-ground realities of a life lived in
the rural Heartland. "There are no other young people in our lives
around us," Gran confides. "We have to go back to Ames for all our
relationships. I think it's a huge issue, the lack of young people. It's
very disconcerting."

Gran and his wife have family in the farther flung rural town
of St. Anthony, population just north of 100, a forty-five-minute
drive from Ames. In St. Anthony, just beyond the commuting ring
from Des Moines, the Next Generation director reports, "I do not
see young people. *Period.* People there are beyond the age of having
kids. And their kids have moved away and live somewhere else, and
they don't see themselves coming back to that place.... They don't
see a future on the farm, man or woman."

Like many young people who, in order to make the difficult
choice to remain, locate within a short commute of one of Middle America's university towns, Gran wills himself to hopefulness,
transitioning abruptly from talk of economic and cultural despair
in the hinterlands to positive mention of towns like Decorah in
northeastern Iowa, home to Luther College and seat of Winneshiek County, which, despite being remote, are "pockets of social
opportunity." Gran feels lucky to work in Ames and live near the
amenities of its enlightened university community, but he says a
college town alone isn't the panacea it's made out to be. "Quite

frankly, just because Ames has young people doesn't mean they're young people I want to know," he tells me. "Farm people want to know other farm people. That's where the interesting challenge is. We need to have enough young people and young businesses that are sustainable and profitable to create a community."

Like Steph Larsen, Gran ascribes almost limitless potential to the Internet as a way to make living in the midwestern sticks less socially alienating for the educated young. To that end, PFI regularly hosts online webinars for its members, allowing them to fruitfully interact without driving long distances. On another positive note, he reports that a friend in his immediate peer group recently raised sufficient capital to purchase a small rural acreage, a foothold that means Gran, his wife, and other youthful singles and couples interested in growing food can potentially collaborate, subletting an acre or so of land that they might visit and cultivate on long summer nights or on weekends.

As for the prospect of one day raising a family on a few acres in a distant town like St. Anthony, Gran doesn't think that's the choice for him. "If we lived on the farm and farmed on the moon and no one else was in our age group, that wouldn't make us happy. Even if we were incredibly profitable and everything else was great, a big part of why you farm is to share it with people who understand. You can share your concerns and challenges and successes with other people and that's what makes life really exciting. . . . We need young bucks. They bring so much energy and enthusiasm. I feel . . . I've already lost some of that youthful exuberance, and we need that to keep things sustaining."

In some ways, I'm learning, the problems of being young at heartland boil down to scale. Boomers I interviewed who grew up in the rural and small-town Midwest of the '50s—before the layperson had ever heard the phrase "brain drain"—spoke of locating legitimate courtship opportunities literally right out their school bus or farmhouse window. But today, the chance of spotting a twenty- or thirty-something educated mate while canvassing the countryside from your Toyota Corolla amounts to a statistical bolt of lightning. And even if you do spot someone of the right age and background, it may be hard to reconcile your needs and wants and dreams, if none can be located in your zip code, at least according to Eric Fynaardt from Searsboro, Iowa.

When interviewed for a 2006 article in *USA Today*, Fynaardt pointed out that in his town of 160 people, 10 are single and only 2 are women. Here is one of the young bucks Gran conjures as a possible cure-all, but the young buck himself reports that many women think of him and his ilk as "hillbilly hicks tied to our land. Girls say, 'I don't want to date him. I don't want to go back to the farm. I want to explore city life.'"

Fynaardt's sentiments were quoted in the article "Web Levels Dating Fields: Site Matches Single Farmers," which highlighted as a possible cure the only high-profile dating website devoted to rural singles, FarmersOnly.com, a site I myself tried several years ago. The brainchild of Ohio adman Jerry Miller, the novel project is a publicist's dream, though its mission—to match far-flung singles committed to rural life—is as old as the county fair and the gingham dress.

Miller's role as the founder of the site, in addition to his day job as the publicist for the Alpaca Owners and Breeders Association in Beachwood, Ohio, has taught him plenty about what's vexing Middle American courtship. "One farmer told me the story of her frustrations in trying to find her match," Miller writes on his site's home page. "She thought trying online dating may be the answer and joined some of the big national online dating sites. What she found was that the city folks that dominated these online dating sites couldn't relate to her lifestyle. They wanted to meet at 9:00 p.m. for a cup of coffee when she would typically be preparing for the next day, which started at 5:00 a.m. Caffeine at that hour was the last thing she needed!"

My own experiment with FarmersOnly confirmed my demographic suspicions. Nearly all of the half dozen or so viable options returned by the search function lived in the nearest university town, an hour-and-fifteen-minute drive from my own Wobegon in Jones County, Iowa. Of the few distant prospects, only one actually lived on a farm or ranch. The rest were a mix of graduate students in the sciences and young professionals living in the nearest university town, from whence they expressed an interest in agriculture from afar. In his message Miller reminds potential users that his site is open to anyone "who can relate to the rural and country lifestyle," including those who "raise or breed alpacas, horses, cattle, chickens, dogs, goats, rabbits, sheep, grow crops, or if you're an organic farmer, student farmer, cowboy, cowgirl, or just a farmer wannabe!" But what I found was a site dominated by wannabes with only an academic interest in rurality, but with neither the willingness nor the ability to live out that fascination beyond the city lights. Of the few viable options within a ninety-mile radius of my home farm, more than half had not checked their account in the last month— par for the course on a site like FarmersOnly that courts fence-sitters with free trial memberships.

Reviewing the previous press archived on Miller's site, one senses in the coverage not an empathetic understanding of the heart and soul of an agrarian region, but jaded journalists' nudge-nudge, look-what-the-yokels-are-up-to-now curiosity about the down-home. The tagline for a CNN story concerning Miller's launch reads, for example, "They can plow a field, punch them dogies, and think tractors are sexy . . . and now they can find love online." Likewise, the host of CNN's *News to Me* program segues, "Do you spend more time talking to chickens than people? Is the nearest Starbucks a time zone away? Do not despair."

"A lot of people that hear about the site think it's a joke until they find out it's real," Miller tells the host, who asks in reply, "Do you find that country girls kiss on the first date?" Undaunted by the needling, Miller continues, "On FarmersOnly one of the favorite pastimes or hobbies is going mudding . . . a lot of city people ask what's mudding. That's when you get in your four-wheel drive, ATV, or truck and just go out and drive through the mud. . . . Instead of lipstick you get a little mudstick on the face."

Word of the site reached MSNBC's *Countdown* host Keith Olbermann, prompting the show's producers to invite early subscriber Blain

Newsome on as a guest. Newsome, an attractive twenty-something from rural Tennessee whose online profile read in part, "any man who thinks I would like a fancy supper over four-wheeling in the mud is definitely crazy," embodied the site's novelty. Though Newsome, then a master's candidate in agricultural communication at Ohio State University and a onetime equestrian coach there, gave a serious interview, the tone of the conversation turned needlessly (but predictably) punny, with Olbermann, who himself earned a communication degree at ag-centric Cornell University, ascribing various jokey handles to the romantic wants of his winsome guest, such as "Blain Newsome, who is looking for no hat, all cattle."

Olbermann asks Newsome whether the country values she's looking for might instead be resident in a city guy—whether her search need be geographically and culturally bound. Newsome's reply is telling. "You know, for me personally, yes. I mean, because if he's a city guy, he's much more concerned about what kind of bar he's going to go to or what he's wearing or his hair. And I'm not trying to stereotype everybody. I'm just saying all of the city guys that I've met are like that. And that's just not the kind of guy I'm looking for."

The interview is a compelling tête-à-tête, featuring a rare moment of airtime for a rural, educated, choosy young woman allowed to advocate for her own likes and dislikes within an urban-driven dating market. Without the least bit of irony, the fresh-faced Newsome defends her own persnicketiness, saying, "You know, I'm already kind of a picky person anyway. . . . My friends back home in Tennessee would always tease me because I always told them, 'You know, I'm not going to date somebody unless they're agriculturally oriented in some way, form, or fashion.' And this site lets me be really picky. And there's all kinds of people with all kinds of interest in agriculture."

By 2010, Miller's website already boasted in excess of one hundred marriages. The barrage of media attention engendered by its 2005 launch quickly elevated Miller's brainchild from a fringe concern of 8,000 members to over 100,000 registrants. That number, however, may be somewhat misleading. While the number of "active" members (which includes those whose trial memberships lapsed, preventing them from logging in to delete defunct profiles) is high, the actual population of dedicated, practicing members nationally at any given time is probably closer to the population of a small midwestern city like Mankato, Minnesota, or Manhattan, Kansas. In any case, the registrant numbers on the rural site show it to represent a small niche, predictably paling in comparison to outfits like eHarmony, where industry analysts have reported membership in excess of 30 million—roughly the population of Canada.

In the end, if you're single, live (or want to live) in a rural place, and are seeking the love of your life through an online dating site, even FarmersOnly.com, you join at a huge demographic disadvantage if your bottom line is meeting the love of your life on the great American prairie.

<hr />

I call Miller at his exurban home to ask what Middle American courtship trends he sees that may have the potential to turn the Great Plains and Mountain West back into seedbeds for romance. "Remember, out of 300 million [in America], basically 60 million live in rural areas," he says by way of context. "That's 240 million [in urban areas]. A lot of the most successful [romantic] relationships are now work-related. They work at big companies with a thousand employees. They just meet someone through work. But again, if you're in a rural area, you're not working for a company with two thousand employees. I think FarmersOnly gives a chance to the people who don't go off to college, who are stuck in an immediate area, who otherwise are not going to go to the next city or community over, or who are not going to go to the next county fair and just hope."

Miller tells me that while there's plenty of nostalgic interest in the agrarian Heartland among the tens of thousands of small-town or rural baby boomers he sees yearly at national farm and ranch expos, he doesn't see as much enthusiasm for the lifestyle among young people. "When you live in a small community out in farmland, most of the people that you socialize with are from the small rural area," he says. When he thinks of the aging demographics of the nation's hinterlands, Miller is not so much worried about the consequences to first-wave love of high school sweethearts, or even the second wave of college kids who meet and move out into the world together. He's concerned, instead, with the third wave, the folks who went through the first two waves and are now either unmarried or divorced, who are committed to living in non-metropolitan America, and who, after a decade or two of fruitless searching in their lonesome local communities, might up and leave if they don't find love around the next bend. "The first wave naturally happens when you're a teenager in high school. Some people just find that spark. . . . Couples just naturally are attracted to one another when they're fifteen, sixteen, or seventeen years old. . . . I'm talking about the people who just never find that person from their immediate community. I think it's a sad situation. There's just a lot of lonely people who never really had a chance."

I press Miller not on the philosophy of his site, but about the ultimate effectiveness of it. Sure, a few dozen certified marriages might come from it every few years, but in the grand scheme of things such modest numbers risk statistical irrelevance. And even for the lucky few romantic sweepstakes winners who meet and get hitched to their Heartland sweetheart online, what of the legions of other frustrated lovers who, even with an assist from the Internet, still find themselves driving an hour or two, or six, to meet a like-minded soul? In effect, these digital pilgrims have solved one problem (the difficulty in locating potential mates) while accepting another (the proportionally longer distances required to meet and date that potential mate).

"I think online dating could be very effective in keeping the [agrarian] culture going," Miller insists. "You have more experience than me, but as far as living in agriculture in a rural area, when you're young, basically all the people I interviewed knew the people from their immediate area. If you aren't compatible with anyone [nearby], what do you do? I find people going to singles parties in larger cities and hating it. I think with this site, you come on and put on your profile and all of a sudden you realize, hey, there's someone thirty miles away that you would have never met."

What Miller is building toward—and he wants to grow his successful start-up further—is a critical mass of online daters in Middle America, a quorum that would allow a would-be suitor to find a viable prospect within 30 miles, for example, rather than 150 miles. In an era of lengthening workdays and chronically over-scheduled young people, he believes the convenience factor is key in making the American hinterland viable again for lovers of all ages, and especially so for young people looking to start a family and thus ensure the next generation. "When people first started on the site, relationships were building 1,500 miles away," Miller says, chuckling at the recollection. "My first marriages were between, like, someone from New York and Texas, or California and Tennessee."

Of the site's early adopters, Miller remembers a midwesterner named Margaret, who at sixty-seven years old faced a number of dating obstacles. Early on she'd called Miller up to complain, as he retells it, "'I'm really lonely. I need a date. I don't know anything about computers.' Then she calls me a couple of nights later and asks how to put a picture on the site. So then maybe two weeks later she calls up and says, 'Yeah, this is Margaret in Ohio, and I just got married!'" Seems she had met a North Dakota rancher who just happened to be trailering a truck down her way that weekend. He'd decided to stay the weekend, a breathless Margaret had told Miller, and after he'd passed that first test with flying colors, she reciprocated with a trip up NoDak way. Miller picks up the fairy tale there. "They said, 'What are we waiting for?! I'm seventy-six, you're sixty-seven. They called up the preacher and got married.

I think that's amazing. They are so happy together. I talked to her years after that. They're, like, perfect."

Dating in the hinterland—quantifiably more rural and less educated than in other parts of the country—is unique, Miller argues. One encouraging difference he finds in the less-populated, less media-saturated markets in which his site thrives is a greater tolerance for unconventional body types. "I was at the county fair here [in Ohio] recently, and I was just watching the crowd," Miller recalls. "There's like ten thousand people walking by and I'm saying, 'You know something, there's not even less than ten people out of this ten thousand that Hollywood would consider attractive.' They're just real people of all shapes and sizes. You see girls who weigh 300 pounds with guys who are six [foot] eight and 110 pounds, and they're walking through holding hands. That's great."

But while dating in America's sparsely populated frontiers may require being more aesthetically open-minded, Miller claims the number one barometer for the desirability of any potential Internet mate remains what he calls the "barometer of Hollywood." Once in a blue moon, the site's founder reports, he'll get a girl or a guy posting a pic and profile that comes close to what Miller calls a "Hollywood ten," and they're quickly overwhelmed by the response volume. Miller recalls one young model who reached the Hollywood standard, and who had joined his site due to her long-standing interest in horses. Within days, he reports, she called him up to say, "'Jerry, I just wanted to tell you I signed up for your site, and I had to take my profile down after two days . . . I had something like five hundred e-mails in my inbox waiting. I don't have time for that!'" On the other end of the spectrum, the rural romance guru says, are the men and women who received so few responses they call him up just to confirm their account is working. "Now I think that's a shame," Miller says. "That's one of the most painful things for me, but it's normal. . . . It's probably been that way for ten thousand years."

Miller sees the nation as a whole, at least the boomers and older, leaning more "libertarian . . . more fiscally conservative but liberal social," in other words, leaning toward quintessential Heartland values. He believes many people, young and old, would choose the agrarian lifestyle if they could only make a living in farm country, and like Larsen and Gran before him, he sees a ray of hope in technology. "With emergence of Internet you can live in the country and still experience the business world if you want to. . . . You can be sitting out in the barn and put on a suit and look like you're in the boardroom."

In the end, however, Miller sees what most demographic scholars see—while the region's baby boomers, many of whom grew up on Middle American farms and ranches, may be compelled by nostalgia to return to their roots, younger people who came of age after the agricultural crisis of the 1980s seem destined for the cities. "To sum it up, I think because of television and the Internet young people get exposed to the idea that the normal lifestyle is supposed to be that corporate rat race, Hollywood-type environment. I think that's what kids look up to. I think that's the biggest danger. . . . When you look at the most successful Hollywood shows, whether it's *Sex in the City* or *Desperate Housewives,* they're depicting the family falling apart. . . . It's pretty much sunup to sundown exposure to media. That's what's really changing everything."

As a generation of small-town and rural Middle Americans comes of age without fair-minded representation of their native culture in movies and television, they have no choice but to imprint on other more urban models, Miller says in closing. "Now your model, your peer, is Lady Gaga. That's more normal than Donna Reed now. That's what I think is dangerous."

Recalling my conversation with the founder of FarmersOnly has caused me to wonder if it's not the miles between urban "oases" that account for the out-migration of hinterland young, and perhaps not even the added degree of difficulty implicit in finding a mate, but

older, more reductive conceptions of aesthetics. Miller had called
it the "Hollywood barometer," suggesting that the young lions and
lionesses on his site found themselves buried by solicitations and
RSVPs. Perhaps the real culprit in the romantic downgrading of the
Heartland, then, isn't geographical but aesthetic.

There's good evidence to suggest this may indeed be the case.
In a broader Heartland, encompassing naturally scenic areas like
Jackson Hole, Wyoming, or the Black Hills of South Dakota, or
even the temperate Branson and Springfield hills of the Ozark
Plateau in southwestern Missouri, populations have grown significantly over the period from 1980 to 2000. Mapping the population loss of non-metro counties with net out-migration of 10
percent or more during that same twenty-year span, writer Richard
E. Wood describes the overall magnitude of the exodus from rural
America as "shocking," the bright spots tending to be "suburbs-in-
the-waiting . . . or places close to recreational attractions such as
mountains, lakes, and oceans." A map from the U.S. Department of
Agriculture's Economic Research Unit shows one of my two home
counties, Jones County in far eastern Iowa, surrounded by counties
marked with the foreboding black that indicates an out-migration
of 10 percent or more. Elsewhere in the Midwest and Great Plains,
we see that South Dakota—with the exception of the far eastern border counties near Fargo, the state capital of Pierre, and the
wider Black Hills metropolitan region—is almost entirely shaded
black to indicate the gravest of demographical losses. Nebraska too
evidences a hemorrhaging outside of the counties adjoining the
Lincoln-Omaha-Sioux City corridors and the counties paralleling
Interstate 80 as it points westward past Grand Island and Kearney
to North Platte, west of which out-migration again reaches double
digits.

In some ways the depopulation map may be read as an atlas
not of people but of their professions; the counties experienc-
ing the steepest losses almost without exception are those where
farming and ranching dominate. And yet, given reasonably high
commodity prices, it's not farm economics so much as farm aes-

thetics, or lack thereof, that appear to have turned off the region's upwardly mobile young. Conventional, chemical-intensive production of large-scale commodities like corn, soybeans, wheat, and livestock no longer strikes generation X and gen Y as a romantic occupation and, as the places where such harvests happen tend to be flat, thoroughly cultivated, and largely devoid of forests, major lakes, and mountains, they appear to lack the requisite aesthetic appeal. By that eyes-minded equation, it's no surprise that Iowa, which boasts the highest percentage of ground under cultivation of any state in the nation, has experienced one of the worst net out-migrations in the country.

Increasingly, as Steph Larsen intimates, to be young at heartland is to be mired in what much of the rest of the country considers "the flatness," a great geographic mundanity that elicits not a come-hither look, but an averted glance—the broad swath of flyover country that offers the indiscriminate passerby (or passerover) little if any eye candy, and that the region's out-migrating young professionals tend to associate with ugliness, which in turn is symbolically yoked with conservatism, age, and decay. While young people's demographic rule of thumb might once have pointed them to places populated by beautiful people, new marching orders seem to be taking them to places that are themselves beautiful, and that therefore draw the beautiful people.

In the final analysis, this monoculture of taste—the sexed-up impossible-to-reach beauty standard—is not so very different than the monoculture of "corn and beans, cows and sows" that has dogged the rural Heartland for generations. Just as Miller and other managers of pioneering dating sites have learned that the most beautiful men and women attract a disproportionate amount of attention, a parallel trend manifests itself geographically. Extending the analogy and personifying it, Denver would be especially dateable, as would Branson, or Wisconsin's Door County, or Chicago on the lake, or Park City, Utah. But Marshall, Minnesota, or Sac City, Iowa, or Kirksville, Missouri, or Liberal, Kansas, might not fare well in the geographical version of *The Bachelor* or *The Bachelorette*, to say nothing of the more bereft, less-educated farm communities that encircle even those relatively well-endowed college towns.

If anything, the changing demographics of the Big Empty throw down a gauntlet, challenging the young at heartland to find beauty in unlikely places and through unorthodox lenses. While the Midwest and Great Plains have long been saddled with reputations as flat and featureless flyover country, seen a different way, their "camouflage," as writer Michael Martone puts it in *The Flatness*, may help those who love the Heartland enjoy it as deliciously and intimately as a best-kept secret: "Let altitude then be the best defense and let the midwesterner wear the mantle of 'the Flyover.' . . . Down below I'll be waving, waving, glad to see those rush by, taking with them those streaked mental snapshots they've recorded from their cramped coach seats." More than that, however, residents of flyover country must let themselves be won over again by native subtleties. "Most strangers," farmer-poet Michael Carey laments, "zoom by on highway, lured by the siren call of the big-breasted mountains. . . . But that's like saying you can't love a woman if she's not Sophia Loren."

Symbolically at least, it is precisely this magnetic capacity that stands the potential of captivating and keeping the country's enterprising young as once it did, but if and only if the young at heartland are sufficiently self-aware to recognize that what they choose to see in the great midlands from Manhattan, Kansas, to Milwaukee, Wisconsin, is in fact what they will get. If, gazing into the looking glass prairie, they ask the narcissist's question, "Who's the fairest in the land?" they will forever be disappointed and frustrated, prone to seek their fortunes in more buxom places. But if native beauty is what they seek, when, gazing into the chest-high sedge, they see themselves reflected in a stable future and rooted in a deep, worthy past, they stand to fall in love with their homeland all over again.

The Perfect Community

"Your book felt very conscious-raising . . . to know that my place was a place worthy of study, that someone had taken the time and care to write about it, and to raise questions that at that time, as a twenty-year-old kid, I had never even thought to ask."

I am confessing all this to Osha Gray Davidson, author of *Broken Heartland: The Rise of America's Rural Ghetto*, chapter 1 of which—Exhibit A—featured my hometown of Mechanicsville, about a half hour from Cedar Rapids and with a population of about 1,000. I can hardly believe the laudatory words—unbidden and unrehearsed—coming out of my mouth. "I think in some ways it put me on the path of knowing that it was proper to write about the people that were immediately around me . . . that to write about a place you're intimate with is another way of writing about lots of people who are intimate with the places that surround them."

The sentiments are true, but it's also true that I resent Davidson's too-true exposé of my hometown. Like so many writers of the rural experience, Davidson quickly moved out of town after exposing the ugly truth of the rise of our "rural ghetto"—moved out of Dodge long before his book hit the shelves in 1990, moved back, in fact, to the nearby university town of Iowa City from whence he came.

I had steeled myself for the call to Davidson at his home in Phoenix—needlessly shaming myself into thinking that in speaking with him I was, in a way, sleeping with the enemy. It wasn't *his* grandparents and great-grandparents, after all, who lay buried in

29

Rose Hill Cemetery, troubled and turning over the shared fate of their hometown and its heirs, not *his* grandparents who shopped at Jim Cook's hardware store—places and people laid bare in his narrative of rural decline. In reaching out to interview him, I had hoped for some kind of connection if not closure—like phoning a black sheep member of the family after many years of estrangement, or an ex with whom one had, many moons ago, undergone a difficult breakup. Perhaps speaking with him more than twenty-five years after his book first shed light on the abject poverties of my home community, and communities like it all around the Midwest, would help me close an ambivalent chapter in my life—a chapter about a chapter—*his* chapter, damningly titled "Decline and Denial." I'd felt haunted, in many ways, by those two words, spending much of my time growing up on a farm outside Mechanicsville. "Others may object to using the word 'ghetto' to characterize rural communities," the author wrote in the preface. "But the word 'ghetto' is, I believe, far more helpful in characterizing and analyzing the state of today's rural communities than it is misleading. It is my hope that the evidence contained in the following pages bears out that claim."

Sadly for me and my family, the evidence did bear out, and after reading the case Davidson made in chapter one of the paperback edition my sister brought home from a college sociology class one day, I felt robbed of my innocence, as if I could never again look at my sullied hometown in quite the same light. And yet now, listening to Davidson tell me what he remembers about the three good research-and-writing years he spent living in Mechanicsville, I find myself unable to summon the intended bile. It turns out we know people in common—Everette Ferguson, Forrest Johnson, the Cooks, to name a few—and that during his stay in town he lived less than two blocks from the home where my maternal great-grandparents lived after they left the farm to "retire" in town.

For three years Davidson raised his two daughters as a single father just a few blocks from the school building where my grandparents attended middle school and high school, and the gas station where, on Sunday mornings later in his life, my grandfather would pick up his copy of the Sunday *Gazette*. To his credit, Davidson is perhaps the only nationally prominent contemporary writer who has spent more than an afternoon in my hometown, let alone lived there. No matter that he lived there only as long as his funding from the Ford Foundation held out, or that he never again wrote a book on the plight of rural Americans, he'd still made an effort to meet us where we live; this fact and others make us, in a strange way, brothers by circumstance, and not so far removed. So I ask him now whether he still believes, in his heart, in the Jeffersonian model of a robust patchwork of small rural towns serving as the backbone of a nation.

"Oh yeah, nothing's changed my opinion of that. I mean I live in the sixth largest city in the country now. And so I'm more attuned to urban issues and the positives and negatives of urban life. But having lived in Mechanicsville, I grew to appreciate what small towns have to offer. I realize that it wasn't for me at that time . . . though for three years it was. I was ready to leave. There can be this idea that if you leave a place it must be because you don't like it, instead of the reality that there's so many different factors . . . so many different facets . . . of life in small towns and large cities."

Here again our conversation resembles the kind a once-jilted lover might have with an ex about why they moved on. A deeply articulate man, even Davidson grows sensitive, and a bit defensive, when explaining why he packed his leaving trunk. "Where you choose to live is based on so many things," he explains. "It isn't a rejection of one or another in order to choose one. You only have one life . . . and I knew at that time it was important for me to move . . . for me and for my daughter. But there are qualities in small towns that I think are tremendously important that I don't have here in Phoenix. Overall, it's worth it; the trade-off I've made to live here, but that doesn't mean that I love Mechanicsville any less. Obviously, to live there for three years; I wouldn't have been able to do that if I didn't love the place too. . . . I also know that there are tremendous problems with small-town life. I think Mechanicsville actually improved after I left. I can just hear the people saying, 'You think that's just a coincidence!'"

Davidson laughs heartily at the notion of his legacy with the people he lived with and left in the late 1980s. He misses the self-effacing and essentially leveling brand of humor townsfolk once relished directing his way—the kind that ensures no one gets too high on themselves, nor too low. As an example he cites three men who used to sit out in front of the town's post office, commenting on everything in their purview like a Greek chorus. When Davidson, all dressed up for his citified work, would stop off to pick up his mail on the way to the university town, they would unfailingly tease him with the line, "Who died?"

Egalitarianism, Davidson calls it. "I remember one professor that showed us slides of cemeteries in small [rural] towns and one in a larger place. In the semi-urban cemeteries you could tell people's statuses in life by the size of their tombstones, which include these great big monuments. Then in the small-town one, even though it turned out there were some very wealthy people buried there, their tombstones were almost all identical in size. He used it as an example of how [in small towns] you don't want to stand out or make it look like you're doing better than everyone else."

But what Davidson notes as egalitarianism cuts both ways, meaning that it can also mute or otherwise obscure important differences and distinctive talents. Egalitarianism often fails to trumpet what is good and right about a community to young people all too tempted to leave. "Like most small towns, Mechanicsville always had trouble holding on to its young," Davidson writes. "Many felt stifled here, their possibilities too limited, the pace of life too slow. And so every year, one or two of these ambitious young men and women left for the bright lights of Des Moines or even the brighter ones of Chicago, Minneapolis, St. Louis, or beyond."

Striving for journalistic objectivity, Davidson's book mentions at least one person, then–hardware store owner Jim Cook, who, when he got out of the military as a young man, returned to his small hometown despite the flak he took from fellow servicemen who thought he'd gone off his rocker. Davidson, who came to fear Cook's rampant hometown boosterism as well as to respect its genuineness, quotes Cook as saying, "I looked them right in the eye and said, 'I've been every place I could be, and Mechanicsville is no different than the rest of them. It's just as good as Carmel, California, or Timbuktu. Every one of them has their faults and if I'm going to have faults, it's going to be with the people I know.'"

I volunteer to Davidson that I feel similarly, in a way, about my home place, and although I don't live within the city limits of my ancestral hometown proper, I do live just down the county road and over—on a farm a few miles across the home county line where my family has been a rural fixture since 1855. "That's one thing I've always appreciated about small-town living," I say once Davidson gets me talking. "Everything feels more manageable. I know where the town begins; I know where it ends. I know who to talk to if I want to get something done. I think even ideological differences are more manageable because you're looking at a scale of moving the hearts and minds of 800 people, or inculcating a vision in 800 people, versus 800,000 people."

My decision to live so near to my family's ancestral home has been a professionally contentious one, for sure—it has cost me professionally and personally in more ways than I can count. And it's the battleground nature of a place like Mechanicsville—the intense tug-of-war its young people feel, the should-I-stay-or-should-I-go-now dilemma—that, Davidson readily admits, first caused him to choose my natal place as a national case study in the first place.

"That's why I chose Mechanicsville, because it was up in the air as to what its future would be," he tells me. A respected environmental journalist and blogger these days, Davidson hasn't formally researched rural demographics, poverty, or inequity since his book came out back in 1990, so he's careful to qualify his comments with the admission that he hasn't keep current in the field. Still, he says, "The things I did read about drugs in small towns . . . that really accelerated after I left . . . make me think that the grim future that had been predicted by some seems to be coming true. . . . As to the problem of brain drain, I haven't heard anything about that changing. In fact, I hear about it continuing."

"The creation of rural ghettos is a complex process," Davidson wrote of Mechanicsville, quoting the owner of our then-solvent local newspaper, the *Pioneer Herald*, as saying, "I don't know what's going to happen here. In the past six months we've lost ten businesses in the three towns we cover. Maybe somebody ought to come in, buy the whole downtown, and just tear it down."

For all its belated revelations and badly needed circle-closings, my opening Q and A with Davidson leaves me feeling unsatisfied. I haven't for the moment answered what is for me an equally pressing question, or more accurately a mystery, of what has been sufficiently compelling about this place—my place and, for a brief period, his—to cause seven generations of my family to fight to remain here and hereabouts. And if a journalist's job is to raise difficult questions, as Davidson did all too well in *Broken Heartland*, as well as to leave town for the next story before the tough questions can be answered, what would a fair job description be for a writer like me who stays near to home in order to find answers? And does my own stubborn rootedness here really make the kind of on-the-ground difference I hoped it would—the writer on the farm determined to write the rural plight and perspective, but skeptical that his words, or anyone's, have the power to change persistent demographic realities?

———➤●◀———

Not more than two generations ago, my own hometown was not unlike the onetime farm towns that would become the well-to-do western Chicagoland suburbs of today. It was a blessed and prosperous place, called the Pork Center of the World by town boosters and fortuitously located on the Burlington Northern line and the famed Lincoln Highway, the nation's first transcontinental interstate road, connecting New York City to San Francisco via the Heartland.

Mechanicsville had treated my farming family well since my ancestors, the Pickerts, first arrived in 1854 from Waterton, New

A hometown calling card.

York, and they loved the town for what it gave them. In the 1940s, my great-grandfather Walter took breaks from farming and the penning of books on more serious subjects like soil conservation and sustainable farming to write cheerful odes in praise of the burg where he sold his field corn, purchased his liquor and lumber, and picked up his groceries. One of Walter's praiseful ditties went like this:

> There's a great day coming in Mechanicsville,
> It'll do you more good than a vitamin pill.
> Mechanicsville is located on a golden strand.
> The finest place in the great land.
>
> It merits no star on the maps given out
> By filling stations hereabouts;
> But gee-u-gosh just come and see,
> What's in store for you and me.
>
> The Lion's club and the Legion, too
> Have a lot cooked up for me and you;
> And that vacation trip of your fondest dreams,
> Will be incomplete to us it seems,
> Unless you plan your itinerary
> To the greatest town in the greatest state.
>
> The preacher says that we must die
> To meet the Lord up in the sky;
> But come and see him at your will
> For his address is Mechanicsville.

We're the home of Colby and his livestock mart,
Without him we could hardly start
A stock show with a worthwhile frill
For the Pork Center of the World is Mechanicsville.

A generation before Great-Grandpa penned his blush-worthy verse, hometown merchants Irving Taylor, J. R. Grunder, and H. D. Scott had joined forces to donate fifteen dollars (roughly $200 in today's money) as a prize for the young community member who wrote the best letter singing Mechanicsville's praises at a time of clashes between rural traditionalism and the urban Jazz Age culture. "The name of the author of the first prize-winning letter, and the names of other prize-winners, will be announced from the bandstand during the band concert in Mechanicsville on Wednesday evening, June 18," the town's burghers announced. "All young people who submitted letters in this contest are requested to be present."

A day after my great-aunt Mary Puffer mounted the stage to receive her award, her letter ran in full in the *Pioneer Press*. Beneath a banner headline stretching the breadth of a broadsheet—"This Letter Won First Prize of $15.00!"—trumpeted the announcement of the contest winner for those who hadn't made it to the band concert the night before: "Winner: Miss Mary Puffer, Daughter of Mr. and Mrs. Everett Puffer."

Prize-winning letter-writer Mary Puffer around 1926.

"She mounted the platform and received her prize—$15 real money," the newspaper gushed. "Naturally, she was happy, not so much because of the amount received, but the consciousness of having accomplished something worthwhile, something that would have a permanent influence on her life and her desire for education. She was profusely applauded by spectators." The Contest Committee duly noted that "it had a bunch of good letters to read" and that they had carefully considered each one. "The following letter," the *Pioneer Press* explained, "indicates a keen mind, close observation, and a fine mental attitude toward the home community. And it was a young person who wrote it."

Beneath the committee's introduction was Aunt Mary's letter, entitled "A Perfect Community."

> In the first place, a good community and one that wants to progress should have its citizens behind it. If everyone is complaining and doesn't want this and that because it costs too much or isn't needed because they always have gone without it before, how can a community expect to progress or modernize? It may be done against these persons' wills, but isn't it lots easier and you feel ever so much more conscience-free if you know that there are and will be no complaints after it is done. It often happens that someone, or as likely, several do not vote or give any suggestions when things are brought up. Then, when everything is over with, they start complaining and tell what should have been done and what they would have done if they had anything to say about it. A real thrifty, interesting, progressive community does not like to have such citizens. . . .
>
> Loyalty is a great help to your community. Everyone appreciates loyalty. Anyone who is loyal to their country is honored—and why not? The author shows his feelings by putting them in words; the painter, by putting them in pictures that express his thoughts and impressions; the sculptor forms figures that give like impressions, and we

can show our feelings toward community by loyalty which is easier than the others.

However, one who is loyal must want to be loyal and try. There is nothing in the world like trying. But the author and the painter must have character if they wish to impress other people and become popular—really popular and famous. So must the citizen and town have character if they wish to progress and be known and honored. It must be clean, industrious and wholesome. Its homes should be well-kept and attractive. Its citizens should be enthusiastic and willing to work, eager for a good community; they should be interested in everything concerning it and have a good clean character themselves. Then the community cannot help to be just like them. Instead of bouncing around in springy sedans, they could start up the idea of paved roads, give a helping hand and it wouldn't be long till you could ride with ease and satisfaction and there would be less springs broken. Instead of going to a local church or to the opera house for our common community and school gatherings, we could all chip in and help with our hands, heads, and capital and erect a community house. In this way, if we all help, we can come nearer to having something satisfactory to everyone. And everyone can contribute either labor, ideas or capital—all are necessary.

The youngest generation should be just as interested in their community as the older folks, for they are the future citizens of our town. They ought to be given a chance, just as they are in this contest, in all affairs of the community because they are the ones who will get the use of them later on. Young folks have ideas and should develop them and try them when they are young. Experience is the greatest teacher.

Young citizens should start their own life several years before they enter high school instead of after school or college. It is just like developing your mind. You must

start young. Before you are in high school you should see
that you get more independent from your elders each day,
that is, depending less on them for your support. Helping
to support yourself is the stepping stone of supporting
others. I believe that is the cause of so many bad results
of young people today. They start too late in life to depend
on themselves. You should learn to live for yourself first—
experiment on yourself. Mother Nature is very wise, but
failure to understand her in time has meant failure of
many fine young lives. So, girls and boys should begin to
take interest and help in their community early in their
life, and I promise you it will pay.

One year before my great-aunt Mary penned her pro-
Mechanicsville letter in 1924, the Agricultural Experiment Station
at the state's land-grant university conducted a survey of Mechanicsville's host county, Cedar, under the umbrella of their rural
sociology division. When researchers George H. Von Tungeln, E. L.
Kirkpatrick, C. R. Hoffer, and J. F. Thaden analyzed the data sent
them by county residents in 1923, they found a landscape as seemingly ripe for the young at heartland as my aunt Mary claimed in
her letter. Unlike today, the farmers were relatively young. Approximately six out of every ten farm owners, the survey says, were
between the age of thirty-five and fifty-four, and nearly half of
them had owned land by age thirty-one. Debt was largely unheard
of, with nearly half of all owners claiming to have no debts at all,
and forty-two of the farmers surveyed reporting "no misfortunes"
of any kind having befallen them.

Agrarian folkways were equally intact among farm wives and
daughters. In Cedar County in 1923, farm women were more
likely to have some college education than their husbands, with
nearly 5 percent reporting some college. In fact, the farm wives'
parity with their city counterparts in terms of educational attainment was significantly greater in 1923 than in the census year
of 2010, back then coming within 1 percent of the overall rate

of college educational attainment among all women statewide. Indeed, a statistically significant number of women from town and city had *opted* to leave the bright lights for the hard work of farmyard and feedlot. "Women who are total strangers to the farm," the study declared, "are more likely to go to the farm than men of the same class." There were also, the questionnaire concluded, "more professional men among the wives' fathers than among the husbands' fathers."

In the Jazz Age Heartland, farmers' sons more than held their own in attracting mates whose level of education exceeded their own. Their brides were younger than they were too, four years on average, and 96 percent of their farm wives set out a garden to keep their families healthily fed. Of the more than two hundred independence-minded farm women responding to the College of Agriculture survey, 83 percent were earning income outside the house, while only 13 percent joined their husbands in the farm fields.

Today's numbers in my brain-drained home county tell a strikingly different tale, and one much less hopeful for the young and the restless. According to the 2007 Census of Agriculture, the average age for the female farm operator was then approximately fifty-five. The size of the farm had nearly doubled to 331 acres and the farmer and his partner had grayed considerably. In sum, the numbers demonstrated that meeting and marrying a farm daughter in my Heartland home state was significantly more difficult in 2007 than it was in 1923. If today's farm woman is old enough to run a farm, she is, the statistics tell us, almost certainly already married and, on average, in her mid-fifties.

Just over a half century after my aunt Mary penned her letter advocating a more thoroughgoing community spirit, and the scholars from the Agricultural Experiment Station threw in their two cents, Mechanicsville celebrated a centennial of a sort. Perhaps it was the very absence of teamwork that the extension agents had long ago pointed out, but for whatever reason, McVille had forgotten to celebrate its one hundredth birthday on time in 1955.

In 1975, Hugh and Kathryn Lamont decided that kind of forgetfulness wouldn't stand, and came up with a spin to rival any Manhattan ad agency—they would celebrate the one hundred years plus twenty more and call it a Rip Van Winkle Centennial, after the Washington Irving character who took a twenty-year nap before returning to his rural village. The informal booklet prepared to commemorate the event contained no explanation for the peculiar celebration beyond a poem by Lillian Nie entitled "Why 'Rip Van Winkle,'" whose last two stanzas read,

> Today Mechanicsville is close to poor Rip's side.
> Mind you, we weren't sleeping, we were preoccupied
> With bringing our city up to par,
> Our eyes intent on that distant star.
>
> So engrossed with our labor of love were we,
> "Centennial Year" slipped past surreptitiously.
> Now you know why we are twenty years late—
> At least our city is "up to date!"

In the centennial pamphlet's opening pages Mayor Thomas Railsback observed, "Over the years many things change, but one thing that has always been outstanding is the community spirit." Letters rolled in from high places to commemorate the eccentric event. From President Gerald Ford came a letter addressed to the citizenry that read,

> The first settlers of Mechanicsville brought with them tremendous enthusiasm, determination, and cooperation, along with an abiding faith in God and in themselves. Your birthday provides an opportunity for a rededication to those values and ideals that have kept our nation strong. I know you can be counted on to take the best of your past—and build on it in a way that will reflect the vitality and spirit of your people.

Indeed, despite being too busy or too preoccupied to celebrate its proper centennial, by 1975 the community had, in part,

The Jack farm in rural Mechanicsville, circa 1970.

answered its critics. A study conducted by the Iowa State University Cooperative Extension Service in 1980 entitled "Mechanicsville Community Attitude Survey" found that 90 percent of respondents now believed their neighbors would help in an emergency. In fact, after the death of the town's longtime doctor in 1972, residents had come together to create the Pioneer Medical Center and The Pioneer Terraces (subsidized housing for senior citizens), and had recently approved a $600,000 health care facility that would "enable families to have their loved ones closer and receive the finest care."

Sponsoring the Rip Van Winkle Centennial booklet were a local pharmacy, a lumber company (Koch's and Stanwood Lumber), a dance hall, two hardware stores (Koch's and Cook's, phonetic doppelgangers), a couple of auto garages and body shops, a clothes store, a car dealership, a combination funeral home and furniture store, a feed store, a motel (the Rustic Villa, whose motto read "For the rest of your life"), an oil and gas company, several feed and grain centers, a few cafés, a farm implement company, a farmer's co-op, a telephone company, a newspaper, and the usual mix of home-grown insurance companies, beauty salons, gas stations, and banks. "People born in urban areas," Hugh Lamont wrote on behalf of the

Centennial Corporation, "relish moving to a smaller community so long as that community can provide the necessary services and maintain the tranquility and quality of life we enjoy here."

Governor Robert Ray chimed in too, writing that he was "pleased to offer [his] congratulations on the observance of the Rip Van Winkle Centennial" for a "colorful, vigorous history." The state's chief executive opined, "As we enter a final generation of a waning century, we increasingly prize the partnership of land and people. . . . By the same token we know that continued change will be necessary in the future to preserve the fundamentals of the way of life we prize." The governor seemed to hint at some as-yet-unforeseen seismic shift awaiting my then-prosperous hometown, some harbinger of calamitous times ahead, and in hindsight his words proved prophetic.

The governor's implied prophecy came to pass less than ten years later when the farm crisis hit Heartland communities like mine with unprecedented force, so much so that by the late 1980s Mechanicsville had become Exhibit A in Davidson's *Broken Heartland: The Rise of America's Rural Ghetto*. "Even for those few adventuresome souls who pull off the interstate and head into small farm towns like Mechanicsville, appearances are deceiving," Davidson wrote. "The disaster that is sweeping through the Midwest is not like a tornado or a flood that leaves a trail of rubble and washed up cars in its path. For this reason the rural crisis makes for poor film footage and so doesn't rate a spot on the nightly news. . . . If you look carefully at downtown Mechanicsville, you will notice that although the buildings still stand, a majority of them stand empty." When Davidson asked resident nonagenarian Everett Ferguson—our good friend and neighbor—what was happening to Mechanicsville, Everett repeated the question with, as Davidson put it, "a scorn reserved for those who ask the obvious," and proceeded to tell the reporter that his town was, to put it bluntly, dying.

By 1990, only 6 percent of the residents of Cedar County were between the ages of twenty and twenty-four. The number of people living in my home state's urban areas eclipsed the number living in rural areas by a half million. By 1990 the number of females living in Iowa metropolitan areas was more than double the number living in non-metropolitan areas. Statewide, there were fewer than 100,000 females ages twenty to twenty-four—fewer than the total population of a single booming west Chicago "technoburb"—Naperville—in that year.

An out-migrating twenty-two-year-old of today might barely have been a glimmer in her grandparents' eyes in Mechanicsville's Rip Van Winkle year of 1975, but her grandparents would have been full of youthful vigor then, no doubt lining up proudly on Cedar Street to parade from the school to the sale barn. They would have square-danced on John Street on Saturday, mussed Mombo the Clown on Sunday afternoon, then boogied the night away at the dance and 1950s dress contest on Sunday night. On Monday night—Memorial Day—they would have watched the Big Free Variety Show on the park stage featuring the Sisters of the Swish Centennial Costume Style Show and the Brothers of the Brush Centennial Beard-Judging before the closing ceremonies at 8 p.m.

In 1975 Mechanicsville could afford to take a break and party; commodity prices were soaring, with corn topping three dollars a bushel. Many if not most of the founding families, including my own, had found Mechanicsville compelling enough to stay a century or more. Beneath a picture of a mucky, unpaved Main Street circa the late nineteenth century ran this tribute to the village's original clans: "It has rightly been said we 'grow on the back of giants.' The men and women who chose our land to people, were pioneers, giant types ... on the occasion of our hundred and twenty years ... we salute some of those pioneers." Included in the list were my paternal grandmother's people, the Puffers, and a complicated, almost biblical family tree whose last paragraph ended in my sister and me: Natasha and Zachary.

The lineage laid out in the Rip Van Winkle Centennial booklet reminds me both that we are all children of a *place* as well as a people, and also that we products of places like Mechanicsville have been downgraded, having lost our mojo and mystique in the eyes of the majority who prefer hybrids to heirloom seeds. We are homely and homey, we Tashas and Zacharys, branches of a tree declining not so much by fate itself, but by the fate of our outlier circumstance, our acorns and chestnuts now cast to the four winds when once they rooted close to the paterfamilias. Of the long list of my paternal first cousins named in the pioneer history, I am the only one with a four-year degree who remains here living rurally—a stalwart stayer or an existential coward, I'm not sure which. Either way I'm going further out on a limb even as I feel the limb giving way beneath me.

We have a habit where I live of cutting off our histories at the exact moment when the accounts seem to grow less flattering, the way pictures of the black sheep of the family seldom appear on the entryway wall alongside all the others, and if they do, it's a photo from the black sheep's innocent youth, before the things-that-won't-be-spoken-of went so badly wrong. Perhaps this explains why even the more thoughtful, history-minded men in our community eagerly tune in to Civil War documentaries on PBS or World War II specials on the History Channel, and why so many of our farm families still watch Lawrence Welk reruns on Saturday night. These same good folks don't want to relive Nixon's Watergate, or the farm crisis of the Reagan years, or the bling and blather of the digital age's tabloid "entertainment journalism," and who can blame them? For them, and even sometimes for me, the history worth remembering stopped, for all intents and purposes, with the glorious heroisms of the Normandy invasion in 1944 or the sweet sixties love songs crooned by Sissy and Bobby while outside the picture windows illuminated by the ambient blue glow of their TV screens, the taillights of the community's brightest young people can be seen lining up to leave town, like the final scene from *Field of Dreams*, only in reverse.

What became of our hometown during and after Osha Gray Davidson labeled us a rural ghetto is not my favorite history either, but it's mine all the same, just as much as it is his. And just as our gas tanks need topping off and our coffees need warming up, our histories could use some catching up.

⎯⎯➤•◄⎯⎯

In Middle America, talk of brain drain comes and goes according to the latest, bleakest report spun from some underfunded governmental agency staffed, as irony would have it, by many of the same underpaid, geographically displaced brains who left their home region to launch their careers in the first place. In 2000 the panic over departed brains reached a fever pitch across flyover country. Iowa, by virtue of attracting so many young brains to its affordable and uniformly excellent universities, suffered nearly the worst of the population hemorrhage post-graduation, according to Internal Revenue Service tax return tracking. "More Iowans, younger Iowans, and better-paid Iowans" became the rallying cry for the administration of Governor Tom Vilsack and Lieutenant Governor Sally Pederson, who answered with yet another citizen commission to study the problem. Vilsack meanwhile hosted receptions for former Iowans in San Diego, Los Angeles, New York, Chicago, and Minneapolis, efforts that, in sum, coaxed a reported one hundred ex-Iowans to return to the Hawkeye State. But even the program's greatest champion, Lieutenant Governor Pederson, had to admit a degree of Sisyphus. "Some people say it's just ebb and flow," she said. "But if the trend lines continue the way they are. . . . They'll be much worse, and they'll be very, very difficult to turn around. Now is the time to take action." And take action Pederson did, penning editorials in a number of Iowa newspapers, among them the *Opinion Tribune*, where she conceded, "We still have a tremendous brain drain. This brain drain results in Iowa ranking 40th in the nation in the percentage of employees with college degrees." Pederson put it bluntly: her state needed to "entice bright young people."

Still, the generation Pederson and Vilsack most hoped to court mostly turned a deaf ear to the governors' whispered sweet nothings.

In 2000, the *Cedar Rapids Gazette* did as it had earlier encouraged its readers to do, contacting natives who had moved to neighboring states to ask why they'd broken things off and whether they'd ever consider coming back. Des Moines's Tony Davis, a senior at Augsburg College, had found his fiancée in the Twin Cities, along with a plum internship, and wouldn't be returning any time soon. "When you weigh the pros and cons right now," he said, "it's just not as appealing as Minneapolis. . . . I've always lived in the city and I don't imagine living in a rural area." Meanwhile, Cedar Rapids native Chuck Tomasek, thirty-seven, confessed, "At this point, I don't know if I could come back and stay busy enough to keep myself happy."

Over the next year, the *Gazette* doggedly followed the cold trail of the cultural and economic refugees with successive news stories and editorials that seemed only to add to the desperate plight of the rural and small-town Heartland. In 2002, the newspaper reported that 60 percent of the graduates of the state's flagship university moved out of state after graduation. Four years later, Grinnell College biology major Jason Cook wrote an op-ed piece pointing out that those who stayed behind in the Heartland faced not only bleaker job and networking prospects, but also a far steeper college debt load than the national average. In short, Cook's numbers suggested, Iowans who preferred to stay behind to seek mates and jobs would have to go into disproportionate debt to follow their hearts.

By 2008, even the optimistic *Gazette* had to admit that leaders had been "wringing their hands over Iowa's brain drain for years" while it had continued unabated. "Enlist the young to grow Iowa," the *Gazette's* op-ed read, while documenting the net loss of nearly two thousand college-educated residents in the five-year period leading up to the 2000 census. Nationally, the prognosis for the Heartland's ability to attract and retain young people proved equally disconcerting. The census showed a shift away from the older, colder states like Nebraska, the Dakotas, and Iowa (where children five and younger were outnumbered by people seventy-five and older) to sexier states in Dixie. In Richard Florida's "Human

Capital Map" published in 2008, America's Big Empty amounts to a sea of counties where the percentage of people with a bachelor's degree per square mile does well to top 20 percent regionally, but for a few high-density "smart cities" like Chicago, Minneapolis, and Kansas City. "Increasingly, the most talented and ambitious people need to live in the means metros in order to realize their full economic potential," Florida concluded.

To illustrate the on-the-ground effects of Richard Florida's "Human Capital Map," suppose today's Cedar County farmer's daughter opts to jump in her buggy and follow the Lincoln Highway east for three hours to far western Chicagoland, where she hopes to learn what change in fortunes driving 180 miles along the same line of latitude might bring. She is precisely the kind of young person Osha Gray Davidson had written about: the ambitious young women (and men) who "left for the bright lights of Des Moines or the even brighter ones of Chicago." She is twenty-two, the granddaughter of couples who merrily danced the night away during those Rip Van Winkle days of 1975. She is educated and still in the age demographic most likely to relocate, and yet possessed of a deep and abiding love of home.

East she drives into the rising sun, pulling off the Illinois Tollway when her tank registers three-quarters empty, just as her farm father always advised. "No use tempting fate," he could be counted on to say—the fatalist father's way of reminding his talented and ebullient daughter of the necessity of planning for the worst. She has entered what is now Illinois's fifth largest city, Naperville, a booming technoburb, winner in the sweepstakes for the region's educated young and a 2006 *Money* magazine runner-up finisher among the Best Places to Live in America. She notices that the streets are newer here, the schools nicer, the downtown bustling even on a weeknight, with people of many races and ages mingling on the generous footpaths along the carefully groomed and dammed DuPage River. She's not yet come to the heart of Chicago, but landed in an "edge city," just twenty miles or so farther east from some of the fattest and flattest farm ground in the world in DeKalb County, Illinois—land that reminds her of home—and thirty miles from the Magnificent Mile on Chicago's glittering North Michigan Avenue.

On the Farmer's Plaza on Eagle Street just south of the riverwalk, she's stopped in her tracks by a curious site—a vintage John Deere Highlander plow mounted on a marble pedestal, its inscription reading, "Dedicated to the Farm Families Who Pioneered the Naperville Community." And the pamphlet she picks up at the Napier Settlement historical museum reads, "In a setting of restored and recreated structures housing period-appropriate collections, a bygone era comes to life through cultural, recreational, and educational programs depicting the life and customs from Naperville's founding in 1831. . . . The Settlement's tranquil atmosphere provides a visual and personal experience, offering a contrast with the major urbanization and suburbanization rapidly engulfing the area."

She had sensed, growing up on her family's midwestern farm, that her way of life was endangered, but here it seems to have passed already into the realm of history, family farmers remembered in plaques and plazas as if they were as distant as the founding fathers in powdered wigs. She is intrigued by this place on the affluent western edge of the Rust Belt, a short road trip from corn country and yet economically and culturally so different from the Heartland she knows. A banner strung over the public library entrance declares it to be the best in the nation, so she ducks inside for a moment to consult the census. She's startled by what she finds. The household income of this once-upon-a-time farm town is more than two and a half times the mean household income of the folks back home, less than three hours away. The rate of vacancy is half here what it is there, where empty storefronts and even abandoned homes have long vexed the city council. The rate of disability, too, is less than half. But the most striking discrepancy of all is in education; here nearly 65 percent have earned a bachelor's degree like hers. Back in her Heartland hometown the percentage hovers just north of 10 percent. Her farming father always said college degrees, more than anything else, predict the future of a place, and she believed him—

believed him enough to get a practical four-year degree in nursing at her state university.

Her parents taught her, too, to celebrate diversity, something she experienced for the first time when she went off to college. Naperville, she can tell at a glance, isn't the most diverse place on earth, certainly not like the Chicago Loop where she had been once on a high school field trip. But here she sees plenty of Asian and Indian faces, accounting for nearly 15 percent of the population. She remembers the last time census takers canvassed her hometown and found only three Asians and two African Americans among the nearly two thousand people who shared her zip code. And the number of single men here by comparison with back home . . . well, there's no comparison. She remembers joking with her girlfriends the last time the census came out about the five unmarried men, aged twenty to twenty-four, who had shared her home zip code. Naperville's not exactly a singles' haven, this she can tell from the many proud owners of oversized wedding rings parading past her on the riverwalk, but the census numbers say there are forty times as many potential dates in her age bracket as exist back home in her tall-corn hamlet.

On her way back to the car she passes the plow in Farmer's Plaza again before stopping at City Hall, where a clerk hands her a brochure explaining the town's many calling cards. She reads that *Money* magazine ranked Naperville a top-five place to live numerous times in the last decade, and consistently rates as one of the best places to raise a family—something that she'd like to do in the not-too-distant future should the stars align. There are eight colleges or universities within the city limits, and two more just a few miles beyond that.

It will be expensive to live here, though. The average rent hovers around a thousand dollars a month, twice as much as she'd pay back home to rent an entire house or even to pay for a monthly mortgage. Yet if the people make more money here—and they do, two and a half times as much—the investment in herself, in her future, would be worth it. In fact, the City of Naperville alone employs as many people as live in her entire hometown, and several of the top ten employers—companies offering steady jobs in gas and energy—are located just a few miles away along the Illinois Technology and Research Corridor. The school district employs several thousand people. The city's largest employer is a hospital employing four times the number of people as live in her little hometown—perfect for a young nurse.

Less than three hours after pulling her old clunker out of the Naperville parking garage she's back home again, driving down a ghostly main street feeling a melancholic kind of change come over her. It's not yet six o'clock, but nothing is open in town save the bars and the Casey's convenience store. The old brick buildings seem shabbier now, the people older and whiter and slower-moving than those back in the boomtown. The scene makes her restless heart ache. When a few minutes later she pulls down the long lane to her parents' farm, she's no longer as certain of her previous hometown boosterism or even of the surety of her natal stars. Naperville seems a long way away—a dream from which she must will herself to wake. Her grandpa always said, "you dance with the one that brung ya," and this—this corn town—is the place that brung her.

For her twenty-second birthday her parents had bought her a DIY book written by a Midwest farm girl like her who left for Seattle. Her parents purchased it, she thinks, partly as a tease and a goad, knowing that she's never canned peaches or sewn a quilt or baked cornbread or acquired any of the other quaintly bygone skills the book promises to teach her. While she may not have quilted growing up, she helped her mom do the farm accounting and she knows plenty about returns and dividends, thus she knows that if she moved to Naperville tomorrow and found a mate of similar education level and a job of about average pay, as a household they would stand to make on average about $60,000 more per year than a couple would back home. Over ten years that would amount to $600,000 more—merely by moving a few hours from home—more than enough to offset the significantly higher rent she'd likely pay over the same period.

Weary but strangely giddy from her trip, she joins her mom and dad at the dinner table to find them regarding her with a mixture of curiosity and concern. Politely they ask about her odyssey, gently ribbing her about the gas she'd burned in her jaunt. She's glad for their familiar banter, but she feels like she has a secret burning inside her now, one that they would surely understand, but that would frighten them or, she fears, wound them deeply. So she keeps the conversation light, noncommittal. But inside she's dreaming.

If, in that *Back to the Future* moment, the Mechanicsville-born grandparents of our twenty-two-year-old Heartland daughter had stopped their Rip Van Winkle celebrations long enough to consider, they would have been amazed that a little community like theirs could get up to so much fun, and that a town as proud as theirs could forget a thing so essential as a centennial and still somehow manage to land on its feet. And they might have been still more amazed, and chagrined, to imagine that two short generations later their future granddaughter would face such a stark economic choice between continuing a life as a young, single, educated woman in a Heartland farm community that lacked a family doctor, a café, an in-town newspaper, a true grocery store, and a sale barn. They would have turned morose, no doubt, at the thought that pragmatics would all but dictate to their granddaughter-of-the-future that she leave her hometown of multiple generations and become a suburban pioneer in a place as prosperous and hopeful for the future as their own beloved Mechanicsville had been in 1974.

And if in their loss and their grief, such good-hearted, even-tempered, and eminently reasonable grandparents as these were to become angry—privately at least, for they are not of the sort, or of the age, to succumb to angsty displays in public or even to write editorials—their anger, long felt and otherwise invisible, would be understandable. If that anger didn't first turn into quiet retreat in the face of long odds, it might indeed be righteous and even fierce—the anger of a mother whose children and home are threatened along with the health and welfare and future viability of her family. Such a mother or grandmother might well be circumspect, fully cognizant, and even empathetic of a daughter's plight—in a moment of supreme honesty she might even urge that daughter to leave—but inside she would be hurting. It would not be an over-statement to say that she might feel as if she had suffered an invasion of her home—a *home invasion*, though the culprit in the violation of her home would not be the kind of thug she could simply shoot with a rifle.

⸻ ⬦ ⸻

"I see it a little bit differently now after talking with experts back then," Osha Gray Davidson tells me. What I had feared might be a contentious phone conversation ending in a hang up or a kiss-off has turned into a compelling back-and-forth, now well into its second hour. "That part of the [brain drain] problem is not just the town. It's unfair to present it as a problem with the small town itself. The kind of education universities engage in guarantees that people will leave their small towns. They're not able to take their new skills to small-town settings. . . . Most university programs don't prepare students for staying within their home community. The idea is that if you are successful you are going to have to move. And I think that's too bad. . . . I think people have to fight to stay."

Fight is right. I don't tell Davidson, but that's exactly what it's so often felt like to me, as a highly educated, younger rural resident, to remain where I was planted: a fight for an irrational choice, a choice made against self-interest and professional advancement, a fight to remind myself on a daily basis of the reasons I'm willing to suffer the slings and arrows of demographic outlier status and an unreasonably long commute, and at the same time, as a recitation and rallying cry of why, despite the difficulties, it still seems worth it to me. But sometimes, in more hopeless moments like those I experience on my punishing commute, I forget what, and whom exactly, I'm fighting for.

"I didn't supply answers [in *Broken Heartland*]. I just raised questions," Davidson cautions. "That was a conscious decision. I didn't think I was qualified to answer the problems of small towns." He senses, I suppose, that as we move toward conclusion I am looking for answers from him that he doesn't have—that I'm treating him more like a guru than what he is: an award-winning journalist. "If I spent my time trying to answer the problems of rural communities, I wouldn't write as much or as well about the problems that I saw. . . . It was more of a journalistic snapshot of what was going on in that time and in that place."

As we settle into the delicate pas de deux of two people who, ostensibly at least, have vastly different worldviews, not to mention current geopolitics, I'm finally feeling as if the man has come out from behind the machine. All these years, as it turns out, I had nothing to fear from Osha Davidson, or any particular reason to be upset with him. His book had been so thoroughly neutralized by my home community that it had required my sister's taking a class at the university forty-five minutes away to bring it, however belatedly, to my attention. And Davidson, I learn, didn't leave because he had anything against us per se, but because he had never intended to stay once his book was finished and his grant was up. He was nothing more or less than what his profession—journalist—dictated he should be.

Still somehow because he had written about me—or rather about the place that was such an integral part of me and of mine—he had loomed larger than life in my young adulthood, like the Grinch must have for the Whos in Whoville who had never seen him come down from the mountain, but whose over-watching presence shaped their village life all the same. Davidson would go where the story was—mercurial after the fashion of his trade—documenting the wound without necessarily having, or even aspiring to have, the bedside manner to heal it or even to take its pain on as his own. A journalist would be a fool to become emotionally involved with his ailing subject, not to mention run afoul of his profession's unspoken creed. In other words, in interviewing the Grinch who stole

Mechanicsville's innocence, I find he's not a Grinch at all, but a highly decorated, eminently likeable, down-to-earth public writer and scholar very much engaged in the environmental fates and fortunes of his adopted hometown of Phoenix, Arizona.

Finally, I work up the courage to ask Davidson the question I would have asked him straight out of the box had we indeed been two old flames conducting an autopsy of a failed relationship: How did you know it was time to go? On the other end of the line, he pauses in a way that tells me both that I have posed a difficult question and that our discussion is moving toward its inevitable denouement. "Well, for one thing I got . . . married. . . . Up 'til then we had been commuting to see one another. When she wasn't staying at my place in Mechanicsville she still had her place. . . . So that's quite a drive. Actually, I was still living in Mechanicsville when we got married, and then moved to . . . where she could commute from. . . . I think more important is that the reason for moving to Mechanicsville was to write the book, and once that's done there really isn't anything holding me there. And I missed the amenities. . . . I really missed university libraries . . . I could ride my bike there . . . do research, see movies, and go hear lectures, stuff like that. The urban kind of thing was ultimately more my experience."

And there it is again—the importance of the environment on which we imprint as children—that brand loyalty and expectation-building that develops between a place and its patrons. Davidson grew up in a Midwest metropolitan area, a university-endowed city, with a father who held a PhD from NYU and who was a well-known business professional and a respected leader in Des Moines's Jewish community. His son no doubt imprinted on the same cultural amenities his father came to enjoy and to expect, at a time (the fifties)—when metropolitan living proved the exception rather than the rule in the Midwest, and a true rarity among the citizens of states like Iowa, Nebraska, and the Dakotas.

When, two decades later, the elder Davidson's son attended Iowa's flagship university located in its most cosmopolitan city, the son enjoyed more of the same—a vibrant local food scene, a famously tolerant community marked by racial, ethnic, and religious pluralism, and a rich and long-standing arts culture—and he moved further up the amenity scale even than what he had known as a child. The urban imprinting Osha Gray Davidson received in Des Moines only stood to deepen in his adopted college town, as it does for most students attending university. Indeed, demographers have demonstrated that what young people acclimate to in their twenties, when for the first time they are allowed to choose for themselves an amenity-rich environment, becomes a de facto gold standard for them thereafter. Moving, demographer Richard Florida points out, slows down with age: "this does not bode well for cities and regions that seem to believe they will be able to re-attract young people who have moved away for fun and adventure once they have hit their thirties and decide to settle down and start families." Places that lose their young people, Florida continues, "will never be able to catch up, since moving slows down with age. The winning places are the ones that establish an edge early on, by attracting residents in their mid-twenties." Add to this disadvantage the marked paucity of young, college-educated singles in their twenties in Heartland small towns, and my Mechanicsville and its ilk find themselves swimming against an increasingly powerful tide.

As we say our good-byes, Davidson tells me, tongue partly in cheek, that he really knew it was time to leave Mechanicsville when, one night late in his time there he found himself acting like an old person even though at the time he was still in his thirties. "I joke that I knew that it was time for me to leave when one night we were there watching TV at ten o'clock at night, and I heard a car pass outside, and I immediately went to the window and pulled back the curtains to see who could be driving by that late at night. . . . And I thought, *Oh my God it's time to leave here.* I'm checking to see, 'Who's that out there, and what are they doing?!'" We laugh together at our mutual recognition of the archetype he is conjuring as he channels the voice of an elderly busybody in her curlers and nightgown. The humor is good-natured, self-effacing, and more revelatory than it might at first seem.

To truly staunch the brain drain, young people in their twenties and early thirties would have to come to see such pervasive "eyes on the street," as well as the utter lack of anonymity and mobility such omnipresent supervision brings, as good things. Paradigms would have to shift. By some cultural transformation, the parting of curtains at a car driving down the street past 10 p.m. would have to be seen as an appealing manifestation of a rare civic-mindedness. After all, the "perfect community" my great-aunt Mary imagined nearly a century ago in her award-winning letter could only happen, she warned at the time, if young men and women began "to take interest and help in their community early in their life."

The trouble is, too few young people want to get to know the woman at the window and fewer still want to become her; she's an archetype they associate, to paraphrase Davidson's subtitle, with decline and denial. But the woman at the window is also the force that kept the region's small towns sustainable, sanguine, and safe for generations. Meanwhile, the car driving by at 10 p.m. may not be the local ne'er-do-well slinking home after hours—not a rabble-rouser or troublemaker requiring small-town sanction or suspicion—but the twenty-two-year-old educated farmer's daughter returning from her reconnaissance trip to a boomtown like Naperville, Illinois, a tear in her eye at the scary thought that it may indeed be time to leave, a realization dawning slowly on her now as, over her shoulder, she sees for the first time the concern in the face at the window watching her as she goes.

Prairie Sweethearts

Hours after setting out in a chilly dawn I reach the outskirts of the meatpacking town of Denison, Iowa, not far from the South Dakota border, on a whimsical pilgrimage I am calling, for lack of better, a prairie sweetheart tour. My intention in driving over 1,200 miles is to see three childhood sites of iconic country girls, stopping in two separate midwestern states while nearly touching a third and in so doing, to pay homage to the retro crush of my college years—Donna Reed—and the heartthrob of my rural boyhood—Laura Ingalls Wilder (or at least the version played by Melissa Gilbert on TV in the 1970s).

Before me now the welcome sign announces Denison's Donna Reed–inspired motto: "It's a Wonderful Life." Turning north on South Main, it's evident the town's burghers and boosters have not forgotten their town's most famous daughter. The cheery, cinematic slogan appears on every street sign, while larger placards dedicated to *It's a Wonderful Life*–style virtues such as charity decorate nearly every downtown street corner. Pulling to the curb in front of the 1914 Germania Opera House, now the Donna Reed Performing Arts Center, I open the door to a typical midwestern county seat scene—a bustling main street consisting of a grain elevator and packing plant, courthouse, jail, and a pleasant mix of storefronts selling small-town staples. Before me is The Male Stop men's clothing store and behind me, the Thrifty White Drugstore.

Inside the Opera House, I find volunteer archivists Pam Soseman and Jerry Peterman waiting for me. I'd written in advance to request that they dig up Donna's senior picture for me, and as I shake hands with Jerry, a kindly, bespectacled man who's lived in Denison since 1964, he hands me the goods—an oversized copy of the graduating class of 1938.

"Can you pick her out?" Jerry asks me, grinning.

In the same way lovers inexorably lock gazes, my eyes drift into the upper right-hand corner of the spread, to Madonna Lorzen and James Bruce, who appears to be giving the fish-eye to the divine thing beside him: Donna Belle Mullenger. Certainly, the 1938 Denison High senior class was no slouch in the beauty department. There was Ila Bledsoe with her big, Claudette Colbert eyes, and saucy Lorena Mahoney with her eyebrows raised and Irish head tossed back all devil-may-care. There were the blonde Ecklund twins, with their Doublemint Twins good looks. Still, none approached the understated elegance of Donna Belle Mullenger, who, though she had finished runner-up for the title of Miss Denison one year earlier, rightfully stole the show and wore the tiara as Denison High's Queen of May in 1938.

Pam tours me around the recently restored 550-seat Ritz Theater where young Donna Belle gawked at Hollywood icons whose ranks she would one day join, and the adjacent candy store (now a café), Reiney's, where she and her pals would load up on sweets before the movie. I sit down with the small group of dedicated souls who keep Reed's memory alive in the town that "brung 'er." Joining Pam, Jerry, and me in the old lobby of the Ritz is Tim Tracy, managing director of the Donna Reed Foundation. Above us, photos of some of Reed's favorite leading men—John Wayne, Robert Montgomery, Randolph Scott, Mickey Rooney, and others—appear to cock an ear toward our conversation. I begin by asking Jerry, who's lived in Denison for nearly fifty years, what Donna Reed means to the community. "For the people in Denison," he says choosing his words carefully, "The one thing I have seen happen is that they play off *It's a Wonderful Life*. . . . On every corner you see *It's A Wonderful Life* on the street signs." Jerry didn't see *It's a Wonderful Life* until about twenty years ago, he confesses. "I hadn't heard anything about Donna Reed until I came to town [in 1964]. Then I would see things in the newspapers. I think things have changed in Denison. . . . There's a lot of people here that didn't grow up with the story of Donna. . . . Occasionally we'll have someone come into the theater and start telling stories about her . . . but for the average person in Denison, I think a lot of people don't even remember the history."

Managing director Tim Tracy interrupts to say he sees things a bit differently from where he lives, thirty miles west of here in the town of Carroll. "There's a little bit of star-envy that there's someone famous from [Denison]. . . . We don't have a movie-star presence in Carroll. It's true in Iowa that you have icons like John Wayne and Donna Reed. . . . But Donna Reed is renewed in the consciousness every year. . . . She gets a rebirth every Christmas with *It's A Wonderful Life*." Tracy stops to motion around the lobby. "This is a remarkable story, but our challenge is we need to get people here. Because every year that passes we're farther away from *The Donna Reed Show*, and we're farther away from the movies."

In a sense the Donna Reed Foundation's challenge is the Heartland's challenge—how to get movers and shakers on the coasts to pay attention to a region that is home to many of the states where the largest percentage of the population is over the age of eighty-five (Iowa, the Dakotas, and Nebraska routinely rank in the top ten), and that itself runs the risk of seeming to the rest of a mobile nation a flickering, black-and-white image of a bygone era. Tracy maintains that the people who do come to this far-off midwestern burg of about 8,000 to pay homage to the most iconic rural daughter in Hollywood often leave with their perceptions changed. "People have a stereotypical idea that Donna was a stay-at-home mom who walked around in pearls, but that was the TV show. The real Donna Reed was the producer of that television show. She was one of the first working moms. She and Lucille Ball were the first two women to produce their own television show. . . . She was a pioneer in things we take for granted today. She was a working mom before working moms were the norm." One gets the sense this is a selling point Tracy has made countless times before, though his recitation for me is no less emphatic. "When people come here and they start to realize the depth of the woman beyond the screen depth, the person she was, I think that's when it relates back to the community," he continues. "Because whether you're a working mom working across the street at the insurance building or over at the courthouse or whether you're a working mom who went to work every morning to produce a television show then went home to her kids, that's a value. That's a *midwestern* value."

I nod my understanding, but I can't help but feel, after Tracy's monologue supplanted Jerry's more somber musings, that the points being underscored for my benefit are in part those required of an adept publicity director of a foundation in need of gifts to "keep the dream alive," as the center's motto goes. Interestingly missing from today's talking points is an equal underscoring of Reed's rural youth, or the fact that she was a farmer's daughter and such a natural caretaker that her own family teased her for her mothering instincts. To market Reed as what she most naturally was—a Midwest country girl—when coupled with her later made-for-TV domesticities, might risk doubly condemning her among a new generation of in-town dwellers. Likewise, the fact that Reed married three times does not find its way into the talking points of the star's life, nor does her status as a peace activist and co-chair of Another Mother for Peace during the Vietnam War. More foundational than any of these roles, though, was Reed's forgotten familial calling card as a Midwest farm girl, and it's this young woman, Donna Belle Mullenger, whom I've driven hundreds of miles to exhume—the one who existed before adoring fans and public relations gurus began to shape her into anything and everything they needed her to be.

So after our talk ends, I follow Jerry and Pam down into the basement of the old Ritz Theater, past a brick boiler room that looks like a handyman's unfinished basement workshop, to a cramped, fluorescent-lit room—what the staff here dramatically calls "the archive."

———————•◦•———————

Donna Reed's bona fides as a prairie girl are many. Biographer Jay Fultz paints the young Donna Belle Mullenger as something of a Molly Pitcher, helping haul water from the Mullenger farm to Nishnabotna Number 3, the country schoolhouse Donna and her siblings attended. "No one was more deeply and permanently marked by the Great Depression than the farm girl who became Donna Reed," Fultz observes. In interviews with *Guidepost* maga- zine in the early 1960s, Reed herself recalled "wind that swept the dry topsoil into great, dark, choking dust storms," and the haunting sound of livestock "crying for water." Still, even as the Dust Bowl and Great Depression took hold, Donna Belle persisted in the usual activities expected of a Heartland country girl, making her own uniform for the Nimble Fingers 4-H Club and winning a blue ribbon at the state fair for her rolls.

The letters Donna Belle wrote her pen pal, Violet, in 1934 and 1935 are, in one sense, the letters of any young girl of the era, concerning themselves primarily with family, friends, animals, trips, and fashion. And yet there is something decidedly rural, even for the early thirties, in her epistles. By today's standards the letters are wholesome to the point of caricature for a high school stu- dent. Even compared to the letters my grandmother Julia wrote and received in the same era, Reed's missives are distinguished by innocence and optimism, devoid almost entirely of slang or catch- phrases or anything that might qualify as pop culture, beyond the occasional mention of a film she had seen at the Ritz where, half a dozen years later, her own pictures would run. In the letters, one hears the solitude of a girl growing up on a little house on the prairie, and imagines her curling up in a window seat or sitting at the kitchen table after dinner to begin a letter to Violet, her friend from Pittsburgh, Pennsylvania, whom she had never met and whose reply she would await for weeks, if not months. In a letter to Vi written earlier in the summer of the same year, Donna relays her country life with a documentarian's eye for everyday detail. "Sparrows are great pests here, although they do not damage crops. Cherries are ripe, also blackberries, gooseberries, and raspberries. I just love fruit. I think I could live on it. There are a few vegetables I don't like. Peas, for example." Still, the missives she penned are not without some worldliness; by 1935 Donna had begun boarding with Grandma Mullenger on Prospect Street in a simple bungalow beneath Denison's water tower. Buses didn't make the four-mile trek south of town in the winter and the roads between the Mullengers' 120 acres and the new school being built on Broadway proved impassable much of the season.

The move to town marked a shift in Donna from a prairie girl sometimes described as "mousy" to someone who, noted for her brains as well as her beauty, was beginning to be shaped by such notice. Letters written after Donna Belle relocated to town show her wrestling, belatedly by today's standards, with issues of identity and conformity—norms of behavior and dress, in what others were reading and thinking, in what they saw in her. "What magazines do you take?" the fourteen-year-old Donna Belle asked her pen pal. "We take the *American, Liberty, Country Home, Open Road For Boys, Pathfinder, Wallaces' Farmer, Poultry Tribune,* and *Hollywood* besides receiving *McCall's, Farmer's Wife,* and *Saturday Evening Post* from friends and relatives." Donna closed her letter with drawings of two beautifully rendered dresses she had designed. "No. 1," she wrote, "is trimmed with white buttons. The plaits run from the shoulders to bottom of the skirt (dark blue). No. 2 is brown trimmed in white. The peplum is white with brown at the bottom of it. The collar is white and rolling."

In her first years of high school the rather plain, makeup-free Donna Mullenger soon found herself, as with so many farmers' daughters, on the wrong end of condescension and snobbery directed at her by peers who little understood her background. According to Fultz, Donna's rough treatment amounted to "a personal crisis. The first to challenge her sense of self-worth." For a year or so she withdrew from her same-sex peers "almost to the point of invisibility." Small-town midwestern life, however, inevitably drew her out, challenging her ability to defend and define herself and her beliefs. She entered a number of speech contests, including one at the Methodist Church, where she successfully advocated the cause of sobriety—her parents forbade alcohol, coffee, tea, and even aspirin in the home—and another in which biographer Fultz reports she placed for a fine recitation of a piece called "Mothers of Men." While Donna's first boyfriend, Tom Hutcheson, would later recall her as his "timid little Irish farm girl," Donna Belle wasn't too timid to begin making inroads in local beauty contests; in 1937, she achieved runner-up status in the Miss Denison contest. One year later, Donna Belle Mullenger was crowned the Queen of May in a graduating class of eighty-five so poor it had to forego the nicety of a high school yearbook.

After Donna's graduation, her Aunt Mildred offered her niece a place to stay in Los Angeles, and Donna, determined to get an education, enrolled in radio and secretarial courses at Los Angeles City College. There, Donna Mullenger was once again elected Campus Queen; it was an era when, Fultz tells us, "feminine beauty reigned" in southern California newspapers that celebrated the Orange Queen, the Sun Goddess, and the Princess of Grapes, among others. At the right place at the right time to snap a glamour shot of the City College queen was a photographer from the *Los Angeles Times*, and on December 2, 1940, the snapshot of Queen Donna Belle Mullenger ran on the front page, leaving studio executives racing to their phones.

Paramount and Columbia wanted to screen test Donna almost immediately, though the biggest fish in the Hollywood pond, Metro-Goldwyn-Mayer, ultimately won the sweepstakes. And that, in a nutshell, is how Donna Mullenger, daughter of the prairie and plains, became Academy Award–winning Hollywood icon Donna Reed. Her new last name was chosen for her by the studio executives at MGM after they tried on Donna Drake (already taken), Donna Denison (the fictional surname created from her real-life hometown strained the bounds of credulity), and the (unimaginatively Anglo) Donna Adams, which lasted for all of one film.

It was indeed a wonderful life, and yet there's one persistent problem with all this fantasy farm girling: the majority of Hollywood's most iconic Middle American "milkmaids" are themselves part myth—fictional characters like Elly May and Daisy Duke whose assonant and alliterative names give away their made-for-television origins. Others, including TV's version of Laura Ingalls Wilder, are not so much myth as mythos—reality-based types that lend themselves well to Hollywood reinterpretation. Even Donna Reed—fair, sweet, comely, may-she-rest-in-peace Donna Reed—is a fiction, if for no other reason than her MGM-coined surname, which distanced her from her rural-girl past and from the alternate future that might have come to Donna Belle Mullenger.

As early as the Jazz Age, a pattern began to take hold in the Middle West whereby the region's rural daughters found themselves "tracked" in a system that prefigured the pattern of youth out-migration later known as the brain drain. If the rural ingénue was especially beautiful or talented, she was drawn into the millrace of the city, where, like her patron saint Donna Reed, she was quickly brought up to speed in the requisite fashion, makeup, and social graces needed to please the eyes and ears of wealthy corporate executives and the young lions who served as their disciples. Most of these young women found it necessary not only to radically change their zip code but to jettison earlier, more homely identities as country girls. For Donna Belle Mullenger, the requisite remaking meant changing her family's name to something that rolled more sweetly off the tongue, though a sweeter, more mellifluous name than Donna Belle Mullenger is hard to imagine. When Donna Belle learned of her new Hollywood identity by reading of it in an industry publication in 1941, she instantly disliked it, though she waited until 1976 to confess that she found it "cold" and "forbidding." "I hear 'Donna Reed,'" she once said, "and I think of a tall, cool, austere blonde who is not me." The myth made of Donna Reed extended to her mode of arrival in

Hollywood, according to biographer Fultz. Legend had it that she had driven a broken-down lemon of a car to southern California with just sixty dollars in her pocket. MGM took the tall tale one step further in its mouthpiece *The Lion's Roar*, wherein it claimed her jalopy sputtered all the way to Tinsel Town, only to have the radiator boil over as she reached the city limits. In fact, Donna Belle Mullenger had taken the train, as would any sensible young woman of modest means traveling alone.

One wonders how the proud citizens of Denison reacted to headlines announcing the first name change—"Donna Mullenger Becomes Donna Adams, Screen Star"—in the May Day edition of the *Denison Review* in 1941. Would they have been proud that one of their own had transcended her humble, farm-Irish roots? Would they have been confused as to why Donna Adams was any better than Donna Mullenger, or would they have simply regarded it as a necessary sacrifice for stardom, possibly even a feather in their community's cap—that a giant like MGM would even take the time to give a mousy Midwest farm girl a new name? The answer begs a broader and still timely question: How do residents of rural hamlets in America's midsection feel when they read that one of their own has made it big in some far-off city, and were they complicit in sending the message that success equaled leaving, especially for their brightest and most beautiful young women? Or is it better in the long run to think of the daughters and sons who leave rural Middle America towns as ambassadors of the region's best traits, translators of them to a larger public who may never come to know its people, in the way that during World War II, Donna Reed proved so evocative of the girl next door that soldiers called her the Bombardier Queen, Goldbrick Queen, and Sweetheart of the Motor Corps? If she had the power to inspire widely, and if her star shone brightly, why not let it shine for all?

"You know how archives work, right?" Pam asks as we pause in a small anteroom housing out-of-season Donna Reed artifacts from the rotating collection on display in the undersized museum. In fact, there's little to distinguish the Temple of Donna Reed whose door Pam has graciously opened for me from an ordinary basement storage room beyond the mothballed displays, a dry-erase board with "It's a Wonderful Life" scrawled in faded red marker, and two books tossed alongside the working mess, the first the biography by Fultz, and the second *Donna Reed: A Bio-Bibliography*, which Jerry and Pam refer to as "The Bible." Everywhere around me are the accoutrements of the Heartland's most recognized, real-life farm daughter, a goddess who, Pam and Jerry confide, also happened to be an unbelievable pack rat.

"You see what I mean?" Pam asks, feigning exasperation as she holds up a crumbling ribbon from what looks to have been a corsage. "She saved everything." In front of us, resting uncatalogued on gray steel shelves, are Donna's brown, patent leather brogues, size seven, perhaps the same ones that biographer Fultz quotes her onetime MGM drama coach, Lillian Burns Sidney, recalling as emblematic of the fresh-from-the-farm Donna Reed: "She was brought in and she wore a little tan skirt and a white blouse and had a tie on and white socks and brownish brogues and of course all you could see were those beautiful eyes and that face that was shy and tense," Sidney remembered.

"They're so small," I whistle, pointing at the shoes, and recalling how, even at 5'9", I'd towered above the life-sized cut-out of Reed that greets visitors on the main floor gift shop.

"She was *tiny*," Pam agrees, holding up one of the actress's dainty blue dress coats as further evidence. On the shelves lay a random sampling of the books Reed owned, some with expected titles like *My Mother/My Self*, and *The Academy Awards: A Pictorial History*. Others, like *Getting Along in Russia* and *High-Performance Driving*, are head-scratchers. Across a small aisle in an archive not much bigger than your average farm kitchen rests a stack of original movie posters with Reed's name splashed all over them. On top is a billboard for *The Get-Away*, a film that Reed once assessed in an especially honest note back home as "a fair B," but which the folks in Denison thought was more than gee-whiz when, in the summer of 1941, they crowded the Ritz Theater to see it. The poster's tagline read "Keep Your Eyes on the Beautiful Brunette!" You get the feeling no one in Denison had to be told twice.

Pam and Jerry and I return to the archive's anteroom for a closer examination of some of the hundreds of studio photos snapped of Donna when she was first put under contract by MGM. Seeking to brand and amplify her image, studio photographers posed Donna in a series of what they hoped would be read as "down-home" shots—gathering eggs, planting fields, and hitching up horses— except that in the photos the rising star wears the kind of short shorts that she would never have donned to do her chores back home in the Midwest.

Next come the family photos in a volume that Reed, an enthusiastic scrapbooker, put together herself. In one green leather-bound volume labeled "Fashions, Tours, and Trips," the photos show a handsome farm family at every stage of their life, the eye forever drawn to the eldest, Donna, before passing to her beautiful sister, Lavone, to her strapping brothers, Keith and William Jr., to her fine-boned, serious, and sensitive mother, Hazel, and finally to the more expressive, dark Irish of her ebullient father, Bill. Individual black-and-white photos of Donna on the farm testify to an ever-changing teen visage. In some, glimpses of a future of evening gowns and red carpets are evident even in her simple farm dresses. In others, she appears plump and girlish, her famous good looks not yet quickened.

As we sort through the snapshots, Pam stops to point out that the chunky high heels Reed wore to compensate for her slight stature are "right back in style." Meanwhile, Jerry photocopies World War II articles from Denison headlined "Donna Reed Here; to Sell Bonds at Fair." The hometown newspaper continued, "With the 1942 Crawford County 4-H Fair already looming as the biggest in history a big added lift was given its patriotic theme with the arrival home Monday night of Donna Reed, Metro-Goldwyn-Mayer film star and daughter of Mr. and Mrs. William Mullenger, who live four miles south of Denison." The editors added, "Donna will reign as queen of the parade here tomorrow, and will ride in a specially constructed war bond float. Immediately after the parade she will autograph war bonds and stamps purchased from her at the stamp booth set up for the Fair. . . . A special souvenir program containing Donna's life and pictures will be issued and sold by the Boy Scouts during the fair. With Donna home for the first time since she was signed to a long-term contract by MGM last year, the biggest crowd since Clarence Chamberlin's historic homecoming is expected in Denison." Clarence Chamberlin had been another of the remarkable "human resource crop" produced by undersized Denison—the first man to pilot a transatlantic passenger flight. He had returned to his hometown on August 24 of 1930 to celebrate the newly declared Chamberlin Day and the renaming of the municipal airport in his honor. Like Reed, he had returned to thousands of hometown faithful lining his path, and brass bands and bugle corps trumpeting his arrival.

While Reed's achievements were decidedly more terrestrial than Chamberlin's, they were no less a badge of honor for Denison, and the hometown newspaper made sure everyone knew it. Accompanying the article announcing the parade in her honor ran a studio picture of a curvaceous Reed caught in the middle of a giant fishnet. She's clad in a one-piece swimsuit, her legs tucked to the side in mermaid position. "A fisherman's daydream," the editors captioned the shot. Beside the display headline ran the latest update on the native daughter's return to her far-flung hometown: "Metropolitan papers, and both the United Press and Associated Press feature the news this morning." The newspaper promised a wartime parade to beat the band—with the Highway Patrol leading the way, and the more than one hundred workers of the town's big employer, the Armour and Company egg-drying plant, marching along behind. For the community's farm daughters and sons, the banner week would include 4-H exhibits housed at the Eclipse

Lumber Co., a 4-H dance featuring Pete Kuhl and his orchestra, and as a "special added attraction," Lacey North, a farmer from nearby Vail, would put his ponies "through an intricate route on the stage each afternoon, and promises to jump a flaming barrier during the evening show both nights." But the main attraction remained the former Donna Belle Mullenger, who rode at the head of the parade with the Highway Patrol, followed closely by reporters and photographers from across the nation.

———≫•≪———

Once we're through poring over the archives, Pam and Jerry are eager to show me more. Pam fires up her Lincoln, agreeing to drive me past Reed's grandmother's old home on Prospect Street, where Denison's favorite daughter boarded in high school to save the long, snowy trip to town from the farm. Together the three of us travel past the newish water tower with "It's a Wonderful Life" painted in can't-miss script, past the high school and gymnasium where Reed danced her high school dances and about which she wrote giddily in a letter to her pen pal Vi in 1935, "We're getting a new school! . . . They have the drawings of it everywhere. It surely is a beauty." We head south next, turning sharply downhill past the 3,800 square feet of the former Conner's Corner Bed and Breakfast—a flawless brick Victorian whose sale will bring less than $200,000—to Highway 30 in the valley over the Nishnabotna River, where we follow Donna Reed Road, a curvy gravel route running the ridge to the site of the old Mullenger farmstead. Though none of the farm's original buildings still stand, the grove of trees and stream-fed pasture remain, the sun setting behind high hills bathed in amber sundown.

We pull in the decommissioned drive and stop in front of where the Mullengers' corn crib would have been, pausing a moment to comment on how closely the land before us follows the "crude map of where I live" a teenage Donna Belle had once drawn for pen pal Violet. The milking barn is gone, so too the cattle shed and the tiny schoolhouse catty-corner across the road, but Coon Creek still flows behind the "garden" and "small pasture" the young girl had illustrated for her faraway pal. "The map of my home is very crude," an apologetic Donna Belle wrote in July of 1935, "but it gives an idea of how it is. From the mailbox to the bridge in the road is about a mile."

Heading back into town, Pam drops Jerry and me off again at the Performing Arts Center before heading home to her husband. Jerry and I stand back to admire the building for a moment. There's more work to be done here, my host admits, much more, but it's nicely tuck-pointed, the marquee and entrance as grand as they were back when Donna Belle Mullenger gazed in awe at the movie palace.

Keeping the dream alive. As I leave the handsome farm town still striving to recapture its former glory, I rehearse the motto like a mantra, until, Zen-like, it opens a door to other, deeper questions. What exactly is the dream that needs preserving here? Reed's? The rural boy meets girl? Our own? And when we wish upon Donna Reed's famous star, are we wishing that some talent scout might discover us, despite odds as steep as Donna Belle's native hills, where we live in our rural routes and small towns? And are we also keening for a time when the small towns of our hinterlands possessed the power to sow the seeds of such unlikely stardom as hers?

In one very real, very important sense, the dream the Donna Reed Foundation hopes to keep alive is the dream of stardom harbored by Middle American daughters and sons living in far-flung, fated places like this one. To make that vision possible, each year the Foundation grants scholarships to college-bound kids who want to pursue a career in the performing arts. And yet even a cursory read-through of the reports on recent scholarship recipients shows that of all the would-be Donna Reeds who listed their Middle American hometowns as places like Donnellson, Denison, and Moorland, only one, 1998 recipient Tasha Eldridge of Denison, stayed behind in a small Heartland town like this one. More typical is the case of

New Hampton's Sarah Utterback, who moved to Los Angeles in 2004 to pursue her dream of acting and managed to land a minor role in *Gray's Anatomy* as Nurse Olivia. Of the past female recipients listed on the Donna Reed Foundation's website, roughly half now make their home in California.

In one sense Donna Reed's dream is still very much alive. And yet for the daughters of rural America, the dream seems now, more than ever, to require leave-taking. It will ask of them painful change and personal remaking—if not the literal changing of their name, then the irrevocable rearranging of their geographic stars, a scattering of the natal and native constellations under which they have navigated their lives thus far. Society and stardom both demand the talented tenth transcend the homey, homely world of their birth.

⟵•◦•⟶

Nearly three hundred road-miles from Denison, I pull into the tiny town (population 135) of Burr Oak, Iowa, just south of the Minnesota border in Winneshiek County, for the second layover on my prairie sweetheart tour, rolling to a stop in front of the childhood home of America's most literary prairie girl, Laura Ingalls Wilder. In every way Wilder's influence and popularity has grown since she penned *Little House in the Big Woods* in 1932, so much so that the National Endowment for the Humanities named *Little House* as one of the top fifteen books to teach children about courage and the U.S. Postal Service issued a commemorative stamp. Online, Laura Ingalls Wilder is a bona fide phenomenon, including a Laura Ingalls Wilder Association, a LauraPalooza annual conference, a full-color biannual newsletter, and, at one time, a Little House Nitpickers Guild fanzine devoted to flagging inconsistencies in storylines between the books and the television series. Laura is big business too, with approximately 60 million books sold worldwide.

While Wilder scholars like Anita Clair Fellman and Diane Lanctot see the cultural impact of the books as "increasingly complex and volatile," such academic conceits are not on the minds of the Laura worshippers clambering out of their minivans and SUVs alongside me today, a day of beatific summer skies a periwinkle shade of blue and the boughs of Laura's old apple tree heavy with early fruit blushing russet. A car full of curious onlookers rolls up the otherwise-deserted street every fifteen to twenty minutes on this, one of the busiest vacation weeks of the summer.

Today I am the only man disembarking from vehicles piloted by the moms and daughters and grandmothers making pilgrimage to pay tribute to the last real-life literary prairie girl in America. After the long drive from the neighboring states that Wilder herself notched in her trek across the prairie—Wisconsin, Minnesota, South Dakota, Missouri, and Kansas—the pilgrims before me are saddle-weary, staggering around the foundations of the old Masters Hotel where Laura's family once stayed. But they are also as giddy as if this were the White House, taking turns at the helm of the covered wagon parked out back of the historic hotel. This is an intensely feminine immersion experience, and though I am clearly in the gender minority here, there's something about the unabashedly deep well of appreciation for Laura that I recognize, and like very much, at first blush. "They [female readers] are often compelled to try to read themselves into texts," writes Wilder scholar Anita Clair Fellman, "in which they are either absent or demeaned." It's a provocative statement, one capable of being felt but not substantiated as we acolytes duck in and out of the Masters Hotel that three local teachers, a native Burr Oaker, and the Pennies for Laura fund-raising drive helped restore to its spartan glory in the mid-1970s. Judging by their license plates, most of today's visitors have come to trace the missing link in the travels that took the Ingalls family from Pepin, Wisconsin, to Walnut Grove, Minnesota, to Independence, Kansas, to De Smet, South Dakota, and to Mansfield, Missouri.

⟹⟹•◆•⟸⟸

The premiere of the *Little House on the Prairie* television series in September of 1974 proved auspicious for all the Laura Ingalls Wilder sites around the region, and especially for Burr Oak, where Laura's legacy had fallen into a too-literal disrepair. Almost overnight, the *Little House* TV family offered disco-era youth the balm and succor of a prairie daughter in prime time. Despite sentiments like those of *Chicago Tribune* TV critic Gary Deeb, who called the series debut a "meatless sausage of cloying sweetness, padded dialogue, and soap-opera background music all brought together by a lisping little girl narrator," Middle Americans loved it when Melissa Gilbert said things like, "Home is the nicest word there is." A few short years later, the National PTA issued its report card and *Little House on the Prairie* was selected the top program. In Iowa, ground zero for the family farm, the *Waterloo Courier* surveyed their readership and declared *Little House* the "runaway winner" for northeastern Iowa's favorite TV show, with another farm drama, *The Waltons*, coming in a distant second and Lawrence Welk a whisker out of third, with 70 percent of the respondents being women. The results caused the paper's TV editor, Jack Bender, to declare that Heartlanders "apparently liked their television viewing clean."

In another 1975 feature, the *Courier* reported that "thousands of people from across the nation" had begun making tours to the historical sites described in the Little House books, including treks to tiny Burr Oak, Iowa, where the family lived in years that, the *Courier's* Kent Baker reported, "did not seem to have been particularly happy for the Ingalls." Still, with the television show in full swing, a grassroots movement grew to restore the old Masters Hotel in Burr Oak where Pa and his family once lived and worked. Once Laura's story hit the television airwaves, children across the country rushed to check out the copies of the original series that had otherwise been gathering dust before the TV debut. Indeed, the *Courier* quoted Cedar Falls, Iowa, librarians as saying that the twelve copies of each book in the series purchased to keep pace with the demand were now "seldom on the shelves."

Nationally, the show's release coincided perfectly with the back-to-the-land movement. In 1975 Roy Reed of the *New York Times* reported a bombshell: Census Bureau surveys in the first few years of the 1970s had shown nonmetropolitan areas growing faster than metropolitan ones. "This is the first time that has happened in the 20th century and perhaps the first time in the history of the Republic," Reed wrote, adding that the trends could not be wholly explained by suburbanization. A report issued by the Census Bureau in late 1974 showed that as many as 1.8 million had left the cities in the first few years of the 1970s, with some of the more popular resettlement areas corresponding, perhaps coincidentally, with the real-life haunts of the Ingalls family: the Ozark Plateau, Minnesota, and Wisconsin. Calvin L. Beale, a demographer in the Economic Research Service of the Department of Agriculture, proclaimed, "the vast rural-to-urban migration of people that was the common pattern of United States population movement in the decades after World War II has been halted and, on balance, reversed."

While the popularity of *Little House* may have been just one factor in the movement back to the land, plenty of circumstantial evidence existed for the show's far-reaching influence in popular culture. Writing for the *Chicago Tribune*, Mary Daniels reported that the show's clout had actually helped produce something called "log cabin fever." She quoted industry sources citing twenty to thirty thousand log cabins then going up annually, a fourfold increase over the per-year numbers since the show became a popular hit in 1975. "No, you haven't overdosed on television, if one day you see a place resembling the *Little House on the Prairie*," Daniels quipped in her feature, conjuring a pastoral ideal of "calico curtains at the windows, smoke curling lazily from the chimney—nestled snug as a hen on a nest in your own subdivision or exurb." The show's popularity had even compelled the fusty Antiques section of the *Tribune* to give Ingalls some ink, providing eager readers with a nutshell version of the family's trek across the Great Plains. In her article's opening paragraphs, reporter Anita Gold referenced the "overwhelming mail" Chicago's newspaper of record had received

from readers requesting more information about the real-life pioneering family, before closing with the latest news—a forthcoming
postage stamp to be issued in Laura's memory.

And it wasn't just log cabins that were going up in record numbers in the 1970s, but teepees, which had received a boost not just
from shows like *Little House*, but from the whole array of magazines
answering, and sometimes creating, the demands of back-to-the-
landers. The most popular of these was *Mother Earth News*, launched
in 1970 by John Shuttleworth in an inaugural issue that contained
complete plans for building a teepee—"not because we thought
anybody would do it," Shuttleworth later told Joseph Morgenstern
of the *New York Times* in late 1974, "but because we thought it
would be a good thing if they did."

Two generations after boomers built yurts and teepees and
cabins in an attempt to re-sink their rural roots, gen X daughters
have made Laura, and all things prairie girl, popular once again
with their own sons and daughters. For those who grew up reading the Little House books and watching the TV series in the '70s,
Laura lived on in perpetuity, just as Lawrence Welk had for their
parents. My friend Becky, who eagerly tuned Laura in each week
on KWWL in Waterloo, Iowa, would choose to become a teacher
because of the show. My farm-reared colleague Sarah, meanwhile,
would find herself so inspired by the love of the books that she
would go on to pursue a master's in library science and a role as a
Laura Ingalls Wilder scholar, blogger, and occasional impersonator
at public libraries throughout the Heartland.

⟫⸱◈⸱⟪

It seems logical that America's most iconic prairie daughter would
have lived in its most iconic agricultural state, and yet years went
by before the Ingalls family's sojourn in Burr Oak became a well-
known fact. Laura Ingalls Wilder had initially written of her year in
this tiny Iowa hamlet in her *Pioneer Girl*, but her publishers rejected

that early draft until she reworked the same material, minus the Iowa scenes, into *Little House in the Big Woods.*

The Ingalls family had decided to give Iowa a try after catastrophes ranging from grasshopper plagues and the death of Laura's infant brother Freddie, landing in the Burr Oak House, a hotel on Main Street with a barn and a spring. After moving out of the bustling, noisy hotel to some rented acres of their own, nine-year-old Laura came to experience the grounded life of a young midwesterner, learning her three Rs at the brick schoolhouse and leading her cow back and forth to the pasture each morning and evening. It took L. Dale Ahern, editor of the *Decorah Public Opinion,* William Anderson writes in *The Iowa Story: Laura Ingalls Wilder's Life in Burr Oak, Iowa,* to ascertain for the larger public details of the Ingalls' stay in the Hawkeye State. In a letter dated May 28, 1947, the editor wrote to Wilder, "Since your daughter informs me that you have 'very clear memories of the place and the people' who have lived around Burr Oak at the time you were there, I should like very much to have you write me briefly of your recollections." Wilder's response arrived less than three weeks later, and ran in full in the pages of the *Public Opinion.* Among other memories, Laura writes most eloquently of her single season spent in the stately woods that lent the town its name:

> In the spring we moved to a little brick house at the edge of town. It was a happy summer. I loved to go after the cows in the pasture by the creek where the rushes and the blue flags flew and the grass was so fresh and smelled so sweet. . . . Often on Sunday afternoon my friend, Alice Ward, and I would walk out on the other side of town, past the Sims' rose-covered cottage to the graveyard. We would wander in the shade of the great trees, reading the inscriptions on the tombstones. The grass was green and short and flowers were everywhere. It was a beautiful, peaceful place.

Now, nearly one hundred and fifty years later, I sally down Main Street on my way to the Laura Ingalls Wilder Visitor's Center and gift shop located in the former Burr Oak Savings Bank. Burr Oak itself is still beautiful—in the ghostly, lyrical way of so many once-bustling frontier towns that declined along with the farm populations they once proudly served. Built in 1910 and famously robbed in April 1931 of the then-prodigious sum of one thousand dollars, the bank itself stands as a metaphor for the kind of cyclical rise and fall that has likewise characterized Wilder's legacy here. It was used as a barber shop from the 1930s to the 1950s and a U.S. Post Office from the 1950s to the 1970s, then for many years after that as a derelict building with boarded-up windows used mostly for storage. The red-brick building received a badly needed restoration in 2004. Inside the repurposed structure awaits everything Laura—Laura dolls, Laura bracelets, Laura spoons, Laura lockets, and Laura tomes by the dozens recounting the life of America's most beloved Plains girl. The Visitor's Center guestbook represents nearly every state in the Lower 48, along with a dozen countries worldwide ranging from Europe to the Far East to Australia and the Philippines. Proud pilgrims can pin their hometown on a map of the United States, and while the majority still come from the Upper Midwest, the bright, primary-colored pins take in small towns and major cities from coastal Maine to northern California.

Sales here are brisk, as are questions: Where was Laura born? Are there any other Laura sites nearby? How long did she stay in Burr Oak and what did she do here? The agrarian Midwest has always been Laura-crazy, as Laura Ingalls Wilder biographer William Anderson points out, citing the volume of letters Wilder once received from Iowa schoolteachers and their students. One such educator, Alfarata Allen Walsh, wrote from my home county seat of Tipton in January of 1935, commenting, "My pupils are interested in you personally. They ask dozens of questions—who you live with, what you look like—and so many more. Would it be asking too much of you to answer some of these questions, and maybe a snapshot?" Anderson cites one particularly prolific dialogue Wilder struck up with a Glidden, Iowa, schoolteacher named Ida Carson, whom she came to regard as a friend as much as a fan. In one letter from 1946, Wilder recalls several recent trips made back to De Smet, South Dakota, where, she notes, she came away "still unsatisfied." Her old stomping grounds, she claimed, had so changed from "the old, free days that we seem not able to find there what we are looking for. Perhaps it is our lost youth we were seeking in the place where it used to be."

As I watch eager visitors slide Laura memorabilia by the handful across the counter for purchase, it occurs to me that those of us here to recapture the life of the long-gone prairie girl may be looking in vain, seeking, as Wilder herself suggested, a chimera of our personal youth, if not the young adulthood of an entire region. I opt not to linger in the gift shop, where I feel a bit like the token male at a quilting convention. I purchase a slim book before returning briefly to the grounds of the old Masters Hotel with its general store–style porch and leaded glass, sagging eaves, and dusty daylilies. Out back, I pause in front of Silver Creek flowing clear and swift with unusually heavy July rains. It's not hard to imagine how a girl in a gingham dress could come here to remark on the cold stream filled with speckled trout or dip her feet up to the ankles on a hot summer day, pining for future adventures and the strong-shouldered suitor who would one day take the yoke of the Conestoga wagon and lead her confidently away from this to some other eden.

But what's not clear is what else a new generation of Laura Ingalls Wilder fans are hoping to find here—a reminder that the country life Laura lived is still possible for their daughters, or their daughters' daughters? And yet how many would willingly choose the edifying hardships of a rural life for their digital-age children and, more to the point, how many would be willing to put a down payment on such a life? And if not a literal template for righteous living in a rural place, could it be today's visitors are seeking some rekindling of the Ingalls Wilder's iconic country values—patriotism, libertarianism, freedom to roam? But if so, why have they chosen

the century-and-a-half-old girlhood days of a prairie girl to carry
the weight of that ideological hope?

All of us here today would agree there is something very alluring indeed about the life of Laura Ingalls Wilder, something that
transcends reductive notions of geography, gender, and socioeco-
nomic class. And yet to read the journals of Laura's childhood trek
across these parts—"For seven years there had been too little rain.
The prairies were dust. Day after day, summer after summer, the
scorching winds blew the dust and the sun was brassy in a yellow
sky. Crop after crop failed"—is to wonder whether it's the depri-
vation itself, and the sacrifice and life-and-death meaningfulness of
the rural life—that draws us still.

Pulling out of Burr Oak and heading to my next Laura Ingalls
Wilder stop in Walnut Grove, Minnesota, I feel reassured that I am
not crazy to be still in love with the sort of self-reliance, resource-
fulness, loyalty, and resilience learned in the Midwest's corn towns,
cornfields, and conservation acres. And I am more convinced than
ever that such virtues might still be found in exactly the kind of
American young men and women who may soon again choose to
make their homes in outposts like this.

———»•◦•‹‹———

"People were coming here and going to the [Laura Ingalls Wilder]
dugout site north of town. And the family, the Gordons, that owned
the land came to town and said, 'Hey, we're getting too many people at our farm.' She [Mrs. Gordon] was baking sugar cookies for
visitors, and they're walking into her farmhouse at all hours of the
day. They said to us, 'We need some help! We need something for
these people.' *The Little House on the Prairie* TV show started in the
fall of 1974, and the museum opened a month or two after that first
meeting was held."

I am visiting with Amy Ankrum, longtime director of the Laura
Ingalls Wilder Museum in Walnut Grove, Minnesota (population

just under 900), where a youthful Laura and her family relocated in 1874 when Laura was barely seven years old. Ankrum is describing for me the almost unbelievable stroke of good fortune by which the museum she has directed since 1999 came to be one of the most iconic and most visited of the Laura sites around the country. As I settle in opposite her in a backroom office, I remark on the prairie-styled clothing in piles everywhere around us. She tells me that five grandmas in the area make all the museum's bonnets and dust-caps and dresses and apron sets. The same gift shop that reminds its youthful clientele, "Now you can dress just like the Ingalls girls when you are playing pioneer," sells more than seven hundred bonnets a year, making each of the granny seamstresses a couple thousand dollars. The Laura played by Melissa Gilbert on the hit TV series is a significant driver of the local economy here. "We'll be the first to say that the TV show put us on the map," Ankrum confesses. "We could have been little Burr Oak or Spring Valley. But because TV decides to plop her in Walnut Grove we're bigger than some other sites. If they'd have said, 'You know, Burr Oak, Iowa, is the Little House on the Prairie,' we'd be this little two-room facility like they are."

Unlike Burr Oak, the Laura Ingalls Wilder Museum in Walnut Grove is a shrine as much, or more, to the television show that won the hearts of girls and their parents than it is to the real-life Laura Ingalls whose family homesteaded here briefly on a flood-prone stretch of land along the banks of Plum Creek. So all-pervasive and saturating is the TV vision and revision of Laura that visitors arrive here every year who can't figure out why there aren't mountains like there were in the TV show (filmed mostly in Simi Valley, California, and Tucson, Arizona), why there are fields of corn instead of wheat, and why this little village exists at all, considering that the town of Walnut Grove was blown up by dynamite in the two-hour series finale that aired in 1984. Some visitors are shocked to learn that Laura Ingalls was a flesh-and-blood girl and not simply a sweet, strong-willed, and occasionally fiery fictional girl-protagonist on television.

It's the Hollywood Laura—the myth of Laura—that made this museum and its campus of prairie schooners and mothballed train depots viable in the first place. The museum itself is chock-full of memorabilia left by stars from the show on visits to the annual Laura Ingalls Wilder Pageant, which is attended by thousands each night for the pageant's six-night run in mid-July. Awaiting me in the general store–style building are scale models of the homes the Ingalls family lived in on the television show, alongside accessories such as Pioneer Barbie.

Ankrum grew up in Walnut Grove, 150 miles southwest of Minneapolis–St. Paul, at exactly the historical moment when the town became ground zero for all things Laura. Born in 1970, she was approaching kindergarten age when the hit television series began dominating the airwaves and, like so many girls of her era, her formative years corresponded exactly with the girlhood and young adulthood of the prairie sweetheart growing up before them on screen. "My town's on TV. . . . That's so cool!" Ankrum remembers thinking, while thrilling to the pride she felt later when, as a teenager, out-of-state visitors would stop to ask her questions about her and Laura's home community, and about the show that put it on the map. In fact, nearly all of Ankrum's most important life moments have been circumscribed by the Laura phenomenon, including her wedding day in 1992, which conflicted with the appearance of former *Little House* child star Alison Arngrim. "I was not happy. Trust me, I yelled at my husband several times," Ankrum recalls, laughing good-naturedly at the memory of having to choose between her two greatest loves. "We had a horse and buggy [for the wedding], and we drove by the park Alison was at and she waved. . . . Yeah, it was *very* disappointing for me not to get to see her." Seven years later in 1999, it was Laura again whose enduring providence produced Ankrum's dream job—the directorship at the little museum that was growing proportionally to Laura's growing legend. The gig allowed Ankrum and her growing family to move back to her old stomping grounds. For that, and for so many other goodnesses in her Laura-blessed life, Amy Ankrum is eternally grateful.

The TV image of Laura helped fuel a renaissance not just in Ankrum's life, but for the entire real-life town of Walnut Grove. The town's population hovered at around six hundred inhabitants for most of Ankrum's young adulthood, but now approaches nine hundred, thanks in large part to an infusion of Hmong immigrants who migrated to tiny Walnut Grove on the strength of its connection to the Laura Ingalls Wilder ethos. "It was *because* of *Little House*," Ankrum explains. "The adults were trying to get their kids out of the gangs in the Twin Cities . . . and a [Hmong] girl kept watching *Little House*, and told her dad, 'Let's go live in Walnut Grove.'" And they did.

Already a small Laotian community had achieved a foothold in nearby Tracy, some eight miles west down the road from Walnut Grove, but this immigrant influx proved unprecedented in the modern era of the town's history. Ankrum attributes a population increase of roughly two hundred residents entirely to the Hmong, pointing out that their presence here resulted in growing school enrollments and added jobs in education, construction, and social services. Home values, she estimates, have shot up $20,000 at least. The town's latest émigrés, in addition to being attracted here by Laura, are a lot like Laura herself, Ankrum maintains, as they face an exciting and sometimes daunting life in a new land in a new language. "It's that pioneering/pilgrimage thing again . . . only one hundred and fifty years after Laura and our ancestors did it," she tells me.

And it's not just Laotians that Walnut Grove's prairie sweetheart is bringing to this far-flung rural community, but Laura-obsessed young girls and their families. Ankrum shares the story of one preteen who fell so much in love with the *Little House* books that her father built her a pioneer cabin in the backyard of their suburban Twin Cities home. Not long after, father and daughter temporarily relocated to Walnut Grove so the daughter could perform the starring role of Laura in the annual pageant, a "family-oriented outdoor drama" that reenacts to sell-out crowds the Ingalls' arrival in 1874. The appeal is not just to millennial children, but to their gen X and gen Y parents as well. "It [the audience] is all of us who as little girls wanted to live like that," Ankrum opines, recalling the

powerful rural yearnings Laura evoked in her as a child. "I wanted a
horse. I lived in town so there was no horse at my house. I couldn't
understand why my grandparents couldn't have a horse for me on
the farm. . . . It [*Little House*] was that sweet simple life. You got to
play; you got to go fishing; you got to play in the creek."

The museum, and indeed the town, celebrate a willingness not
just to restore and re-conjure a wished-for or imagined past, but
to role-play that past in ways not typically encouraged in stoical,
no-nonsense agricultural towns like this one. Three generations of
Laura acolytes routinely show up at the museum together wearing period-appropriate dress. Sometimes the third generation—
the granddaughter—comes wearing the Laura dress and bonnet
the grandmother sewed for the mother in the 1970s and that was
passed on to the next generation. Ankrum's grandmother made a
bonnet for her too when she was a Laura-crazy preteen. "People
my age grew up watching it. . . . They're the ones now buying the
DVDs so their kids can grow up with it. It was a good wholesome family show. . . . Now it gives us forty-something-year-olds a
chance to go back in time."

My tour of prairie sweethearts and their childhood haunts and
homes is destined to end here, on the banks of Plum Creek north
of town, where the Ingalls built their dugout. But the reverberations
of what I've found on my latter-day pilgrimage still intrigue me as I
say thanks and good-bye to Ankrum, and walk out past walls lined
with brightly colored quilts and ageless dolls into a still-sultry late
afternoon. I'm thinking of the ways these long-gone prairie girls—
Reed and Wilder—still inspire, and the way Hollywood amplifies
their life and legend can be a lesson to us post-moderns.

Those of us—and there are millions—who fell in love with
the screen versions of Donna Reed and Laura Ingalls Wilder come
to places like these to fall in love again, for better and for worse.
Places like Walnut Grove, Burr Oak, and Denison offer themselves
up to house our spirit-crushes, letting these pilgrimage sites and
others like them serve as repositories of cultural memory. The long-
abiding crushes nurtured here not only take us back in time, but

arrest us in time, which explains why, for instance, some Laura fans arriving in town, Ankrum told me, are surprised by the presence of electricity and indoor plumbing—things TV's Walnut Grove conspicuously lacked. Time in places like Walnut Grove and Denison and Burr Oak is agreeably frozen for our collective benefit and to our collective detriment—frozen so that we can be young again in a condition of imagined pioneer purity only hindsight and Hollywood can reliably manufacture.

As I clamber into my modern, four-cylinder prairie schooner for the long overland trek back home, I'm thinking of how what we celebrate when we visit such far-flung childhood homes is not just a life lived on the land, and hard work, and families sticking together despite impossible odds—all those quintessential Heartland values—but the innocence and importance of girlhood itself, of being young at heartland in a landscape that frees, feeds, and ultimately sustains hungry imaginations.

Youth Votes

As irony would have it, I am zooming across northwestern Canada when I'm struck by EHD (electoral homesickness disorder). It's less than forty-eight hours until the Fourth of July, and I'm feeling a bit blue so far from the green tractors and purple politics of the mostly red, white, and blue region into which I was blissfully born and corn-fed.

Like most in my generation, I was born into political treachery, arriving in the world just six months before the headlines in our local *Press-Citizen* decried the politically illicit tapes of Richard Nixon, around whom, in April of 1974, a debate raged concerning whether the Watergate transcripts would include the president's many profanities or would instead deploy the euphemism "expletive deleted." When eventually the sanitized versions made the rounds, even the *Chicago Tribune*, whose editorials had once supported Nixon, was left to conclude, "He is humorless to the point of being inhumane. He is devious. He is vacillating. He is profane."

But life, thanks be to the gods, allows even the painfully backslid or chronically negligent a chance at redemption. Thus do I find myself in the middle of a making-up-for-lost-time venture of my own, a once-in-a-lifetime trip to the various natural wonders I had heretofore managed to skip. Already in this, my excellent adventure, I've oohed and ahhed at Old Faithful and breathlessly crested the Going-to-the-Sun Road in Glacier National Park. I've ogled the snowcapped peak of Rainier, swooned over the pristine glacial lakes of Banff National Park, and cooed at the brilliant blue of Puget Sound, all while wondering how I had managed to omit such inspirational places as these from my list of places I would one day like to visit. And now here I am, spirited on my way to Vancouver via another national marvel, the Trans-Canada Highway, and somehow all I can think of is my peculiarly political home state.

Back home in the Great Plains it's hot enough to wilt corn, but in Kamloops, where I exit Highway 1 in an electoral dither, it's perfect room-temperature, British Columbia summer weather. I ease into a roadside parking spot, cut the engine, take a deep pull on my bottomless cup of gas-station brew, and check the news on the homepage of my local TV station, where the day's headline reads, "Bachmann Touts Iowa Roots at Iowa Tour Kick-Off." It's datelined Iowa City, that college town on the edge of the prairie where I stole my first kiss, and where this very day newly declared candidate Michele Bachmann is breakfasting at the Bluebird Diner. "I think Iowa's very important," the home girl says. "We want to do very well here. . . . It's so wonderful to be back."

Bachmann's sentimental dish puts me squarely on the horns of an existential dilemma. I've driven two thousand miles from my unusually rooted life to, as the quintessentially midwestern saying goes, "expand my horizons." Belatedly, I am determined to experience a UNESCO World Heritage Site, the stunning Rocky Mountain peaks and glacial fields of Banff National Park, while for the first time, and in the back of my mind, seriously considering the idea of moving to the Canadian prairies as a personal protest vote against the status quo of American politics. I had inherited this escapist fantasy from my father, a successful Middle American grain farmer who forty-plus years earlier had sworn to my mother and his parents that he would rather renounce his citizenship and live as an exile in the frozen north than fight Nixon's Vietnam War. For my father it had been an especially stark choice, a lose-lose decision. Had he been drafted in 1968 or 1969, we would almost certainly have lost the product of six generations of toil, our century-old working farm. Had he dodged the draft, there would have been precious little he could have done in our socially conservative homeland to save face.

His father—my grandfather—had volunteered himself for service in World War II only to be rejected by the double whammy of a rare blood type and the national-priority status of his chosen trade: farmer. Now, more than four decades after the draft board miraculously passed over my father and the farm, I find myself drawing perilously close to indulging his escapist tendency, locating all political and civic good in the capacious Elsewhere north of the border, while meanwhile, back in the fatherland, a true national treasure, Middle America's living laboratory of in-person politics, the famed Iowa caucuses, have kicked off without me.

After a half-hour roadside existential crisis, I swallow hard, breathe deep, and point my high-mileage vehicle away from Vancouver and back south and east, toward the promise of some life-giving political engagement and the prospect of a fresh start in my life as a citizen. What better season for a second chance with my estranged Uncle Sam? What better time, I reasoned, for some Ma, apple pie, and a political dalliance with a real-life daughter of the Great Plains: Michele Bachmann?

———⟫•◦•⟪———

Behind me rumbles a herd of John Deere 6430s with 115 horses under their hoods pulling Windstream trailers with candy-striped awnings whose sole job it is to keep the blazing sun off the midwestern body politic. Atop gussied-up pull-behind trailers ride dozens of smiling, corn-fed Middle Americans like me, pleased as punch to witness the homegrown spectacle. No light rail for us, no prettified trolley or space-age Segway scooter, just an inglorious, all-wheel-drive people-mover pulling the equivalent of several offensive lines' worth of homegrown ruminates bent on participatory politics. Indeed, the Iowa State Fair is the debutante ball and crown jewel of any serious presidential bid, a cotillion attended by a million-plus in which the nation's unlikely arbiters of presidential ambitions get their first real look at the prospects on the hoof and in the flesh.

The state fair to which I've been delivered after an hours-long Interstate 80 Autobahn is Middle America's Mardi Gras and monster truck rally rolled into one, involving as it does a ritualizing and deifying of noisy, earthy appetites widely regarded as verboten the rest of the agrarian calendar year. For two straight weeks each and every August, the objects of our don't-ask-don't-tell desires are not the curvy pole dancers and bottomless margaritas of The Big Easy, but the fifty food-items-on-a-stick and hard-core politics of what might appreciatively be called instead The Big Feedbag. Here fair organizers annually turn gross excess into exquisite art form, debasing and at the same time elevating any and every foodstuff imaginable to portable edibles. This year's five unlikely food items bound for popsicle stickdom include peanut butter and jelly sandwich, chocolate-covered fried ice cream, chocolate-covered deep-fried cheesecake, something called griddle stick (turkey sausage wrapped in a pancake), and butter-on-a-stick. They have joined old reliables such as deep-fried Twinkies and the all-but-unimaginable salad-on-a-stick.

Comparisons between the *Des Moines Register*'s Soapbox, where yesterday the nation's GOP hopefuls kicked off two straight days of political salesmanship and retail politics, and where livestock competitions are pretty much unavoidable. To begin with, the inimitable soapbox is staged at something closer to a manger than a venue tailor-made for inside-the-Beltway political stagecraft. Square bales of hay, not folding chairs, orbit a three-foot-high platform atop which this or that candidate addresses the issues of the day, while we, the discerning electorate, weigh their pedigree and personal temperament. If the powers that be would let us put our hand on Romney's rump, or squeeze Bachmann's tenderloins as a measure of presidential fitness, we surely would.

Today the broken-record weather for which Heartland summer fairs are famous continues unabated: it's a windless 85 degrees with enough wet-mitten humidity to make even the most strait-laced midwesterner's hair curl. A full slate of powder-fresh candidates, by contrast, hide out under the banner shade provided by vinyl signage displaying quaintly agrarian scenes of barns and farms and fields of flowing grain of the kind typically reserved for bank calendars and twenty-five-cent postcards. Meanwhile we in the political peanut gallery shade our eyes against what can only be described as a merciless sun. The candidates come before us, one by one, and we squint at them, these caesars and sitting ducks.

The soapbox is supposed to be a no-nonsense, gloves-off exercise in Middle American retail politics, but for us it's also a chance to be swept off our feet, to forget our innate electoral cynicism and indulge in a late-summer political fling, an infatuation with the political potential of a more perfect union. It's a chance for flesh-pressings, rubbings of shoulders, and exchanges of political capital that, outside of New Hampshire, only happen here on our populist prairies. And without a doubt, the belle of today's ball is Michele Bachmann, whom the organizers of the soapbox have very cleverly saved until the end of the day, as if the Mitt Romneys and Newt Gingriches of the world were mere opening acts.

⸺➤◆◀⸺

Generationally speaking, I'm about the last person you'd expect to devote a week of his life to following Michele Bachmann and the other candidates from soapbox to straw poll. After all, the pundit class has long claimed my generation, generation X, was born under a bad sign. And as work took me around the Midwest in my mid- to late-twenties, the shoe seemed to fit. In 2000 my first gig as a political reporter coincided with the *Bush v. Gore* battle royal back home in Cedar County, Iowa, when the national media swooped down to commandeer our modest newsrag's offices after a dead tie between Bush and Gore in our county made national news. Commuting to a new job across the Mississippi River in Illinois in 2003 did little to get the monkey off my back, corresponding, as it did, with a twenty-two-count indictment of the state's thirty-ninth governor, George Ryan.

My experience seemed to confirm an entire post-Watergate generation's hypothesis. In the words of the immortal Bob Dylan, everything was broken. Who could blame us for being skeptical to the point of political disengagement? And yet, throughout the late 1990s and early 2000s, plenty did. In a now-infamous headline, the *Washington Post* went so far as to call my cohort "crybabies." The *Atlantic Monthly*, in an equally famous cover story, observed, "The 1990s opened with a frenzy of negative stereotyping of the roughly 50 million Americans born 1965 to 1978; they were slackers, cynics, whiners, drifters, malcontents." As recently as 1972, the *Atlantic* claimed, nearly 50 percent of those aged eighteen to twenty-four voted; by 1996, only 32 percent of us even bothered, further fueling the sour-grapes claim that members of my age group were more likely to have a "negative attitude toward America" and to place "little importance on citizenship and national identity." We were America's first tech generation, detractors said, and if we'd spent our formative years watching *Dukes of Hazzard* and playing Donkey Kong until we drooled, small wonder we couldn't be bothered to get involved in the less-than-glamorous world of so-called retail politics—the stump speeches, soapboxes, town halls, meet-and-greets, coffee klatches, and candidate all-you-can-eat fund-raiser suppers and barbecues that were our parents' and grandparents' electoral bread and butter. In fact, when surveyed in the early 2000s, over 60 percent of generation slacker agreed with the statement, "Politicians and political leaders have failed my generation"—surely a self-fulfilling prophecy, if ever there was one.

And yet for all the sweetness of my generation's belated about-face, many pressing questions remained regarding our political and civic modus operandi. "A generation of leaders," avowed Lakshmi Chaudhry in an article for *The Nation*, "is at the right age and moment, with the skills and knowledge required to change the political landscape, plus the gift of historical hindsight. It's an important moment, but its outcome is uncertain." Between the lines Chaudhry's analysis hinted at what I myself had come to believe. Maybe, just maybe, the reason only one in five of my gloriously underrated generation reported trusting their national government is that we'd never really sought grassroots agency in the political process—the give-and-take of the Heartland-style ground campaign—the flesh-pressings, the feet-to-the-fire questioning, the look-them-in-the-eye candidate appraisals. Like our grandfathers' natty houndstooth cap or our mothers' pearlescent Jackie O. dress, our civic inheritance had been there waiting for us all along, asking only that we stop and try it on.

In retrospect, learning the lost art of the ballot in the American Midwest should have been a no-brainer all along. My native Hawkeye State, in addition to being America's first presidential proving ground for two generations running, perennially ranks in the top ten in citizenship. In fact, all the congressionally funded stats substantiate the deeply held American belief in the Midwest as a kind of strategic reserve for civility and political engagement. Iowa, Kansas, Minnesota, Nebraska, and South Dakota dominate the top five spots in rates of volunteerism, while humble Minnesota, South Dakota, and North Dakota occupy the top three spots nationally in voter turnout.

A reputation for niceness has historically made early-deciding states like mine congenial places for campaign trial balloons and the sometimes green politicians who float them. Here an unusually nurturing citizenry is willing to listen to you, feed you, and even bandage your bruised egos if you'll let them. The old-fashioned soapbox turns out to offer a nearly ideal venue in which to blow off some electoral steam; its roots are planted firmly in the class warfare of Victorian-era Britain, where agitators and reformers, gathering in London's Hyde Park and seeking a platform for an impromptu speech, would leap atop the wooden crates used for shipping soap. The years after World War I, steeped in vocal socialist uprisings, constituted a golden age of soapbox oratory. But for all the potential civic feel-goods produced by such up-with-the-people street meetings, the powers that be regarded them warily as incitements to radicalism, crime, and mob rule. In the early 1900s, soapboxers drew crowds sufficient to impede public right-of-ways, and heck-

lers and boobirds, when inevitably they roosted, made the rhetor-
ical occasions ripe for fisticuffs. Little wonder that the soapbox,
despite a minor resurgence in the civil rights era in hotbeds like
Berkeley and New York City, has been on a decades-long hiatus, at
least in the Midwest, during the markedly peaceful coming-of-age
of generation X.

And yet yesterday, right here in front of the very bale where
today I've staked my soapbox claim, Mitt Romney, whose designs
on the Oval Office Iowans derailed in 2008, appeared before us
beautifully coiffed and navy poloed, expecting to deliver his usual
stump. There we were, beneath periwinkle skies, listening to Mitt's
yada yada yada, our stomachs rumbling for a lunch as yet two hours
away, when an older man sporting a sun hat and liver-spotted skin
started giving Mitt the high-decibel what-for, barking at the former Massachusetts governor that he'd better protect Social Security and Medicare or else. A perfectly un-Lutheran shouting match
had ensued that eventually found a small but mighty Asian woman
wearing a bright bluc "Believe in America" shirt jabbing an angry
finger in the face of the screaming sun-hatted man until the former
governor himself attempted to quiet the fracas by uttering the by-
now campaign cliché, "Give the man a chance to speak." By the
time the dust settled, the usually slick Mitt had been baited into
a national catchphrase—"Corporations, my friends, are people"—
destined to appear on T-shirts across the land, the national news
media had scurried off, sated, to file their stories, and the instigators
of the whole shouting match, an organization called Iowa Citizens
for Community Improvement, got the kind of microphone time
they wouldn't otherwise have been able to buy for love or membership dollars. David Goodner, the group's grand pooh-bah, had
hung around long enough to tell folks he was "pissed off" at the
erosion of entitlements and to assure a titillated press corps that he
and his agitated brethren had merely been exercising their First
Amendment rights.

For his part the principal heckler, who turned out to be a
retired Catholic priest, had with his tantrum ensured his own fifteen

minutes of fame, which he'd used to remind an obliging press that
the stridency of his tone had been nothing, really, in comparison
with the nation's ongoing assault on entitlements. Meanwhile, the
John and Jane Does in the crowd who hadn't come to the soapbox
flying any particular political banner, the dinosaurs of a day when
individuals rather than interest groups ruled the Plains, gawked at
the angry priest and the retinue of Sony digital irises poised to cap-
ture his every snarl and muscle twitch. Mr. and Mrs. Doe walked
away from the fray, shaking their heads the way weary old-timers
do when the world turns, considering how a thing as precious as
civility somehow, somewhere, got thrown under the campaign bus.

Today, the second and final day of the soapbox, we are promised
an afternoon of not less than five high-profile soapboxers crammed
into a three-hour, after-lunch smorgasbord. The old-fashioned
modus operandi here is a cinch to understand: anyone with a legit
campaign for the presidency, and a token Democrat VIP or two
hell-bent on rebuttal, can take to the stage for twenty minutes to
become public straw man, scarecrow, and Oz all in one. It's just one
of the feast of political riches the denizens of America's first presidential proving ground enjoy in our fiefdom of old-school politics,
a Norman Rockwell twilight zone where things like soapboxes and
stump speeches and chautauquas and straw polls seem to live on
with family farms, Cracker Jack boxes, and Lawrence Welk reruns
on public television.

I sidle up to the hay bales in time for the climax of the speech
given by today's darkest of dark-horse presidential candidates, Jared
Blankenship, a tall-drink rancher and presidential wannabe from
north Texas who looks a bit like Clark Gable or a rail-thin bullwhip
of a young Southern preacher, the latter of which turns out also to
be true. While yesterday at this very same soapbox, Romney had
generated crowds by the hundreds and enough "corporations are
people" sound bites to choke the fair's main attraction, the eight-
foot-long, 600-pound Butter Cow, Blankenship is working hard
today just to wake the thirty or so onlookers from our lunchtime
coma. The usually noisy soapbox has gone quiet in the vacuum left

by a national media that's mostly AWOL in search of a deep-fried déjeuner before the afternoon's heavy hitters take the stage: Democratic National Committee chair Debbie Wasserman Schultz and Congresswoman Michele Bachmann.

"What odds would Vegas have given them?" Blankenship, a former high school teacher and part-time preacher, bully-pulpits before us, speaking of the incendiary rebels who long ago founded our star-crossed republic. "A bunch of traitors, a bunch of heretics, a bunch of zealots and nuts. I'm not worried about long shots. I'm interested in principle and the freedoms that we hold so dear. Ladies and gentleman, I appreciate the opportunity to be with you. I ask for you to . . . vote as a write-in candidate for Jared Blankenship. To stand up for those of us that believe that anybody can run for president. Anybody can succeed in America."

The night before, while planning my soapbox viewing, I'd googled Blankenship, whose name, I'll admit, didn't ring any bells. On paper he seems like he'd be a Middle American darling. He's coached high school basketball, football, tennis, and baseball in a one-horse town on the Texas plains, married his college sweetheart, stepped away from the classroom to take the reins of the family farm, and proceeded to build a familial agrarian enterprise into an eight-thousand-acre dukedom. His hobbies consist of coaching youth sports and showing animals. He hails from a town named for a respectable breed of cattle, Hereford, and presides over the Deaf Smith County Farm Bureau.

I seek out Blankenship in the shade of the *Des Moines Register* building and bend his ear at the conclusion of his twenty minutes of fame. You can do this in the parallel universe of the retail politics season—simply walk up to a presidential contender and start jawing with him or her about this or that. I ask Blankenship what he'd do for Middle American farmers, a question over which candidates here were once routinely grilled, but which, in rapidly urbanizing farm country, can seem as much an anachronism as the old-style candidate standing before me now. In the trademark up-close-and-personal of the ground campaign, I'm close enough now to see the follicles in Blankenship's well-groomed moustache, and to nod energetically at everything he says in the idiot way you do when you can barely hear someone and feel compelled to overcompensate with overzealous head-bobbing. Truth be told, I'm pleased to have corralled in this, my first truly iconic stop on the midwestern retail politics circuit, a candidate for the nation's highest office for a one-on-one on a subject few presidential candidates dare discuss these days: the *culture* in agriculture.

Blankenship confesses he's sick and dog-tired of ethanol's preferential status and government crop insurance and the hand of Uncle Sam in everything he tries to stick in the ground or pull from it. He wants to let the market work as an alternative to what he calls "the burdensome hand of government" and the cheap-food policies that typically spell death to the American farmer. "We've gotten further and further removed from the farm, from agriculture," he tells me. "The public sees large equipment that's worth high-dollar on the farm, and think we're living high. It's not that way at all." Blankenship is living proof of the difficult politics of farming—at least partially explaining why the last presidential candidate with any real practical experience on the land, peanut farmer Jimmy Carter, was all but run out of his thermostatically controlled Oval Office by the time most gen Xers reached the first grade.

Blankenship can read the writing on the wall. He is, after all, asking for our vote for what amounts to a career change from food-producer to chief executive. In that sense he wants what the rest of urban America seems to want—a steady paycheck and some choice office space close to where the real deals go down. Even with the equity head start of his inherited acres, Blankenship concedes, it's his wife's in-town jobs that keep the family farm afloat in lean years like this one.

In the Texas Panhandle, as in the Midwest, the young and the educated have been fleeing the farm for the city for at least a decade, the candidate tells me. Blankenship is a few years older than I am, but at just a whisker past forty, he's still young at heartland. "You can count them [the stayers] on one hand in my community. They've all gone somewhere else. That's the decline of agriculture. That's a result, in many ways, of this mind-set that farmers can't make much money. This is a national security issue. We don't like being dependent on foreign oil. Imagine the day when we're dependent on foreign food, and it's not that far away. Agriculture in many ways is the last bastion of production in the United States of America."

I ask the candidate whether he's getting some traction here in the Heartland, and his answer is appropriately circumspect for a man new to the ground-campaign wars. "I don't know what the results will be. . . . We are not a conventional campaign by any stretch," he says, his campaign poker face breaking for the first time into a good-natured grin. "We've embraced that concept and it's fun. . . . We'll get ten people here, thirty here, twenty there. Our form of campaign right now is hard to quantify exactly. The main story is every vote that we get is a vote of commitment, a belief in what we stand for."

"There aren't many states out there where you can do what you're doing," I remind him. "Maybe Iowa . . . New Hampshire."

"That's the thing," he agrees, enthusiastically piggybacking. "This methodology . . . this model had never been played out, never been floated out there in this capacity. So this is testing all the variables and whether decisions hold here in Iowa, and finances hold here. . . . As a part-time preacher, I'm comfortable with that."

Beside us the hay bales have begun to fill again for the soapbox's next victim, Fred Karger. I tell Blankenship, sincerely, that I'll consider casting my vote for him. I am searching for the polite words or gestures that will make my leave-taking politic, the way it's necessary to beg a thousand pardons before leaving the family Christmas party early. I'm a voter after all, I remind myself, and thus I am excused in advance for the necessary fickleness of my affections. Retail politics calls on me, as it does every serious ballot-caster, to embrace our inner window-shopper, a difficult task for the characteristically loyal midwesterner. I'm merely trying Blankenship on for size and owe him no apology for first testing the rest of the afternoon's glass slippers to see if any of them fits.

Next up on the soapbox is another dark-horse candidate for prez, Fred Karger. I didn't even realize Karger was running until just yesterday, and judging from a handful of empty spots atop the usually competitive hay bales orbiting the soapbox, I'm not alone. Karger has been in the race since March—longer than anyone else, as it turns out. But today the buttoned-down, bespectacled Republican doesn't look quite so presidential as he does on the campaign buttons sported by a handful of his backers. Dressed in khakis and a pin-striped office shirt rolled up at the sleeves, Karger looks more like he's hosting a corporate luau than soliciting votes for commander-in-chief.

"I'm from next door in Illinois," he tells us, grinning amiably from behind a pair of self-tinting lenses. "I moved to California at twenty-three when I graduated college, and I didn't look back. I was an actor for about three years. Some of you who are baby boomers may remember I did some television commercials. I was on the Edge shaving cream commercial, the credit card guy. I was on a lot of shows like *McMillan & Wife*. I even did a *Welcome Back, Kotter* spinoff." Late middle-age husbands and wives search their memory banks and come up empty, while Karger charges on, undaunted. "Then I followed my dream and my passion—politics. I started like many of you here at about six years old in suburban Chicago in a town called Glencoe. I would go to the train station with my father who was our Republican precinct chairman. He had my brother and me pass out campaign flyers for Dwight Eisenhower to commuters, and I liked it. Who's going to turn down a six-year-old kid when a campaign flyer is handed to him? So I got a great reaction. I love politics. . . . I'm now what you call a political junkie. I moved to California; I loved it out there. Those of you who have been to California, particularly southern California, Laguna Beach . . . it's a magnificent place. I found a very comfortable home there, and I've been very happy working in politics. I worked for nine presidents. I worked on nine presidential campaigns. . . . I worked for Ronald Reagan in 1980 and 1984. We had a lot to do with his reelection campaign, in carrying forty-nine states. . . . I got to shake his hand within five minutes of his being sworn in as president of the United States. . . . Then I went off and did a campaign for George H. W. Bush."

Karger is heavy on the exposition, still he's trying to establish what campaign operatives call his "narrative"—the carefully crafted story that will help us differentiate him from the other former actors from California (and I can think of a handful) whose dream it is, or was, to occupy the White House as their latest and greatest studio. However, so far and judging by the glazed looks on the faces around me, Karger is, as the politicos say, failing to connect. "Actually, we brought forth the name Willie Horton that some of you may know. . . . This was in 1988. We've done a lot of work with crime victims. We help them tell their story. I think that was a very important part of the campaign, so we could have another great Republican president, George H. W. Bush. And it's the kind of thing I did behind the scenes for many, many years."

"Very dirty rotten campaign ads," some boobird calls out no more than a few paces from the soapbox itself.

"We didn't run the ad you're thinking of. There were two different campaigns," replies the candidate, fumbling.

"Bull," goes the guy in the crowd.

"There was an ad with the crime victims, and it was a very emotional, and these were people whose lives were personally affected. Donna Cuomo lost her sixteen-year-old brother and the couple who was raped. The man was stabbed twenty-two times while his wife was tortured. We helped them tell their story, and I'm proud of that. It's very indicative of Michael Dukakis's record, and the public needed to know that."

Taking all the liberties afforded him by the soapbox, the boobird crows in reply, "The law he got out on was passed by the governor *before* Dukakis."

"Let me finish. I'll get to that. Dukakis was the one who signed his furlough papers. It's indicative. He was a very far left candidate out of touch with the public, and we were helping to tell that story."

I'm itchy and hot and fully prepared to ditch Karger's Reagan-era reminiscences in favor of a cold lemon ice when, out of the blue, he segues into another life venture of his. "I came out of the closet. I became a gay advocate for gay civil rights in this country. I've always been gay. I kept it a deep dark secret. Because I was ashamed. I thought I was going to harm my career working in Republican politics. I thought it would jeopardize the relationship with my family, and I was from a very close loving family, and I wasn't sure how that would go over. I decided to step up to the plate to use a lot of the experience I had learned in twenty-seven years as a political consultant to help my community, and I became active in what was the Proposition 8 campaign that you're familiar with, I'm sure. It was the California version of what you saw in other states. In California our supreme court did what your supreme court did here. . . . They took a bill up and allowed gay marriage in California. Well, five months later it was yanked. It is a little hard for me to come from California, supposedly an enlightened state, to Iowa. I'm a little sheepish, but I want to commend Iowans on the courage and exactly the right thing in allowing couples who are loving to marry."

Another round of asymmetrical applause happens as we are reminded by this emissary from a foreign land of a season of heady idealism back in 2009 in which gay marriage was legalized. And we're reminded too of the fall-out when, not so many years later, voters recalled three state supreme court justices for upholding the same law. And now here's Karger informing us that he's a bit sheepish to praise us publicly for our original political rightness. It's an awkward moment of political theater, to be sure, and in its wake I'm feverishly searching my phone to see if this Republican dispatched to the Heartland from the Golden State is really legit or just some stand-up comedian doing a GOP parody. Sure enough, the "About Fred" section of his website trumpets, "Karger is the first openly gay presidential candidate from a major political party in American history." On the candidate's website, in fact, I can put my dollars where Fred's mouth is by purchasing a range of feel-good merchandise ranging from the iconoclast's autobiography, aptly titled *Fred Who?*, to something called a Fred Who? Equity Pin, to a Fred Who? T-shirt and various other sundries including Fred Frisbees and Fred notepads. It's a brander's paradise. In my political slumber of the last decade and a half, I'm beginning to learn, America's electoral MO has turned from winning votes and to winning hearts and minds, to winning ears and eyeballs, to winning the right to sell us Chinese-made XXL T-shirts. The presidency, after all, is the nation's biggest marketing platform.

On the makeshift stage clutching one of those Frisbees, Karger is now doing his best to reassure his conservative base. "I'm not out to beat up the corporations. I like corporations too, but corporations have responsibilities, and if corporations are contributing to the political process, they have the responsibility to abide by the law. I mean we need to create jobs, and it is the private sector that is going to create the jobs and save this country." Here he stops to acknowledge a question from a woman in the crowd. She's representing a clean-air citizens group. The interest groups arrive here by the busload every morning, and most of them eventually come to roost at the soapbox. Karger's time, however, is up, and he will have to save the softball, interest-group pandering for another time, as from behind the bully pulpit oozes a deluge of Dems, creeping into our ring of fodder like a slow moving, highly partisan flood. They've come in advance of the main attraction, DNC Chair Debbie Wasserman Schultz, who apparently, after the fashion of the contrarian-loving soapbox, signed on to serve as an antidote to an afternoon of overabundant Republicanism.

Wasserman Schultz is a liberal's liberal whose landmark legislation during her time in the statehouse was the Florida Residential Swimming Pool Safety Act. Suffice it to say she's a fund-raising dynamo, though, a definite up-and-comer, and pretty jazzed to be at the state fair using the GOP field for target practice. "The reason I'm here is the same reason Democrats are working in the trenches every single day," Wasserman Schultz calls out to our homespun assembly, her native Long Island accent still audible beneath the fiery rhetoric, "is to make sure, like President Obama has said, that Americans need to understand that we are at a crossroads. We are at a crossroads in America where we have a very stark contrast, a very clear choice that we can make. We can next November make a decision to go in the direction that the nine Republican candidates pledged a rigid adherence to, that the Tea Party wants to drag us in . . . making sure that we protect corporate America, that we protect the most fortunate Americans." Boos resound for the Tea Party from the Wasserman Schultz partisan faithful, and the congresswoman pushes forward, buoyed. "In their response to a proposal to have a ten to one cuts-to-revenue ratio, they all raised their right hand and said, 'No revenue, no balance, no compromise.'"

More jeers and hisses for the Republican candidates' recent across-the-board pledge not to raise taxes.

"I'm here to tell you that I think that's unacceptable. The other choice that Americans have is to continue in the direction that President Obama and his leadership have taken us. . . . Let me take you back to the time when we were bleeding 750,000 jobs a month. And that's thanks to the failed policies of the past, which all Republican presidential candidates are embracing once again. Fast forward two and a half years later, and we are seventeen months straight into private-sector job growth."

Applause and a pregnant pause as Wasserman Schultz sums up Obama's state-specific bona fides: 2,200 jobs created in the first six months of the year, 6 percent unemployment, 34,000 new jobs as a result of Obama's Recovery Act. "That's real leadership," she adds. "What we need to do in addition to create jobs and get our economy turned around is come together. Now I know it's going to sound a little funny from the chair of the Democratic National Committee to say that we need to come together and compromise, but that is what Americans are looking to us to do. . . . We need a little unity in America right now, and that's what Democrats have been committed to under President Obama's leadership. . . . We ended with a debt-ceiling deal that, as President Obama said . . ."

"It was bad, bad, bad!" a man in the crowd blurts out. He's beet-red beneath a DayGlo orange baseball cap, whether from unbridled anger or sunburn, it's hard to tell. Wasserman Schultz looks momentarily stunned, like a heavyweight champ who just got tagged in the chin by a scrappy lightweight.

"It wasn't perfect," she concedes.

The naysayer in the crowd is only just warming up. "It was *bad*! Horrible!"

"It wasn't the deal that he would have written if left to his own devices, but you know what . . ."

"Obama signed it!"

"You know what, I'm a mom . . ." She's actually doing it—playing the mom card with a guy who's nearly old enough to be her father.

"You stand up to him! Don't cave in to him!" the guy woofs at her.

". . . as a mom of young kids, one of the things that I always talk to my kids about is, you know, I know you want it 100 percent your way, but the reality is that's not what life's about. And we're not going to come together and solve our nation's problems if one party rigidly insists on it being 100 percent their way all time, crosses their arms, stamps their feet, and refuses to compromise and work together."

The guy's still yelling his head off, and the hysterical applause conjured by anxious Dems to drown out his protest nearly deafens the rest of us. Wasserman Schultz shrills over the din. "At the end of the day, my message to Americans . . . my message to all of you here at this fair, is that we have an opportunity to come together. We need to reject the politics of the past. We need to reject the notion . . . that corporations are people."

The anti-GOP boobirds have roosted again, this time lustily, and the Dem's favorite soapboxer is surfing their emo-angst. "Is ExxonMobil a person?" she asks.

"No!" the mob yells.

"General Electric . . . Do they have human-like qualities?"

Her tireless backers oblige one more time. "No!"

"No, they don't, and it's absolutely imperative that Americans understand that in order to make sure that we can get a handle on our economy, make sure we can quicken the pace of recovery as President Obama is so committed to doing, that we go back to Washington and make the kind of investments in infrastructure that President Obama will be championing."

Wasserman Schultz rattles off her Democratic wish list of upgrades—roads, electrical grid, health care, Medicare—still the red-faced guy in the crowd isn't buying it. "But the debt ceiling deal puts that on the chopping block, baby!" he catcalls. "Stop caving in to Wall Street!" And when, finally, the DNC chair realizes she cannot shout this particular detractor down, she sees fit to dismiss him as "an example of the division in this country," and the pro-Dem crowd obligingly whips up their just-in-time, white noise–generating tsunami, chanting, "Debbie! Debbie! Debbie!"

And again the lobster-burned agitator raises his hackles. "The debt ceiling deal puts that on the chopping block! Stop caving!"

Now it's melee. It's the House of Commons. Someone in the crowd yells at the guy, "Shut up! Go back to your own people! You're not needed here! Sit down!"

"You shut up."

"Sit down."

"Stop caving in to Wall Street!" the guy screams one last time to anyone who will listen.

And from our conflict-averse, Middle-American vantage, the whole thing looks like it's come to the edge of real fisticuffs when the Wasserman Schultz bots begin chanting "O-bam-a, O-bam-a" and the goddess of the DNC thrusts her speech into hyper-warp speed, sensing armageddon, and the whole thing ends in a cacophony of cheers and jeers from all sides. "Democrats . . . will work together every single day from now until Election Day to get this economy turned around. We'll do it with your help. On to victory!" Half the crowd of Dems shouts "Debbie, Debbie"; the other half "Yes we can!" until the two canned excitations have a midair collision and become "Deb we can!" and an elderly man falls over a hay bale, and when we, as good citizens, attempt to help him, he shrugs us off, saying, "I'm okay, I'm okay," and what we have here, ladies and gentleman, is proof positive that a soapbox can be a very dangerous thing indeed.

As Wasserman Schultz escapes with a wave in the direction of the tenderloins and elephant ears, I find myself drawn into a pas de deux with the vocal agitator in the fluorescent orange cap and yellow tee. Not more than twenty seconds pass before our conversation is interrupted by an intrepid reporter drawn by the heady perfume of a potential story about an angry outlier. The speed of the journalists' descent startles me. As the Wasserman Schultzes of the world make fewer and fewer truly public appearances, and as the country swings back to the throw-the-bastards-out sentiment of the late '60s and early '70s, this afternoon's designated shouter is destined to get at least as many column inches as the party chair herself, at least if the scribbler sidling up to us now has anything to say about it.

"What's your name, sir?" she asks the red-faced heckler, butting into the perfectly civil conversation I had been having with him.

"My name is Hugh Espey."

"Your age, sir?"

"That's a good question." He laughs a bit too loudly. "I'm fifty-seven."

"What county do you live in, sir?"

"I live here in Des Moines," he says, not missing a beat. "My point to her is that this stuff about *compromise, compromise, compromise* is a bunch of crap. We need to *lead*. Obama and the Democratic leadership time after time over the past three and a half years have caved in to Wall Street greed and the big banks, and it's time for them to stand up to them and to the Republican leaders and say, 'Look, enough's enough. We're gonna make sure Wall Street and the big banks pay their fair share of taxes, and we're going to take Medicare, Social Security, and Medicaid off the chopping block."

"And sir—"

"If they're gonna lead, lead! Make government work for people. We want government of, by, and for the people. What they're doing every time is caving in to Wall Street and the big banks. We're sick and tired of it."

"And you voted for?" So efficient is this reporter she's giving every appearance of listening while she's actually moving through the usual list of diagnostics with clinical speed while Hugh, whom she has presumably already identified as a nutcase, prattles on.

"I voted for Obama, and I'll tell you what, lots of folks voted for Obama, and they're not going to vote for him again because he's too weak."

"Let me get a picture of you, sir."

"We're sick and tired of it. It's time to make Wall Street pay. The economy is in shambles. The budget is in a deficit because of the economy. The economy went south. It's time. Let's go after the corporations. They need to pay, and we need to stand up for everyday people. There, how's that?" Espey puts the rhetoric on pause to smile beatifically as the scribbler snaps the headshot.

"Take your hat off," a guy with a vaguely Germanic accent barks at Espey. He's apparently convinced this subversive is trying to evade public recognition beneath the broad bill of his ball cap.

"We're sick and tired of being sick and tired. If you're gonna lead, lead! Tough talk, weak action," Espey responds.

The Citizen Jane next to us, who's just wrapped up giving an interview of her own, can't resist weighing in. "So you said you weren't going to vote for Obama. Who are you going to vote for?"

"I said it's to be determined. He better spine up! There's a lot of other folks . . . that voted for him that are telling me he better spine up. We're sick and tired of caving in to the corporations and Wall Street. And all these cuts, these cuts that just happened. There was no tax increases. That's what we need—tax increases on the super wealthy, big corporations, and the Wall Street banks. That's what we need."

"They've got to save that money so they can give themselves a raise," Citizen Jane says, apparently trying to one-up Espey's cynicism.

"Debbie Wasserman voted for the debt ceiling. She voted for it," the man of the hour reiterates.

Another reporter joins our impromptu scrum. It's Luigi from Ustream. "Is it okay if I speak to you from here?" he asks, hay bales coming between him and where Espey and I are standing. "Are you a registered Republican? Or are you a disenfranchised Democrat?"

"I'm a registered Democrat," Espey confesses, as if Luigi and I and everyone else hadn't figured that out by now. "I voted for Obama, and it's up in the air now. I know a lot of other people who voted for Obama, and now they're wondering . . . Where's the hope? *It's nope!*"

"One last question, sir. We're talking about cutting programs that people actually pay into; pensions, Medicare, social security, and they're unwilling to raise taxes on individuals over $99,000 per year and corporations. Why do you think that is?"

"We've got a political system now where money matters more than people, in terms of big contributions, and what we need is a system where people matter more than money. We don't have that. So they listen to their big-dollar donors, whether it's Republicans or Democrats. We're tired of Wall Street greed ruining our lives. It's time for Obama and the democratic leadership and the Republican leadership to stand up for everyday people, to put people before profits and communities before corporations. That's what it's all about."

And with that Hugh Espey is done—fully vented, thrice interviewed. It's exhausting being the voice of reason. While we wait for Newt Gingrich to assume the soapbox position, I work my smartphone on a hunch that this Hugh Espey, whoever he is, is a bit too willing and able to filibuster through a dozen carefully rehearsed

talking points to be the hapless, modestly unhinged Everyman of
a tourist in the mismatched hat, shorts, and T-shirt today's covey of
reporters have mistaken him for. So I do what any curious digital-
age citizen would do: I google him. The first hit turns out to be
MichaelMoore.com, where Espey earns props as a featured blogger.
It's the same guy, definitely—different ball cap, wider grin, same
irascible politics. "Hugh Espey is the Executive Director of Iowa
Citizens for Community Improvement," the profile reads. "He has
worked with the organization for the past 30 years. He was awarded
the prestigious Leadership for a Changing World Award ($115,000)
by the Ford Foundation and Advocacy Institute in 2004 for tack-
ling some of the nation's most difficult social problems. In 2009,
under his leadership, Iowa CCI was chosen as the 'Most Valuable
Grassroots Advocacy Group' in the U.S. by *The Nation*."

Honestly, the bombshell leaves me feeling duped. We'd assumed
we'd encountered a specimen of the fierce, pitchfork-wielding rustic thought extinct, a man out of his element, a man without the
slightest bit of fashion sense, a humble, salt-of-the-earth *Mr. Smith
Goes to Washington* type uncompensated for his advocacies and
seized suddenly by the rare and fleeting courage to confront the
nation's leading Democrat.

"Welcome to the new world of grassroots midwestern politics,"
the Internet dish seems to say, "where things are never quite as they
seem."

———⇒●⇐———

After nearly eight hours of standing, cattle-like, in the hot sun listening to the hot air issuing from a surfeit of otherwise promising
presidential candidates, after a half day spent jockeying for a view,
and otherwise trying to remain as civil as a group of "Don't Tread
on Me" people can be when packed in to such close confines, we
learn the disappointing news that Michele Bachmann is running
late. And there are rumors—juicy rumors—that she has deliber-

ately delayed her arrival to allow time for the Sarah Palin crowd to dissipate and to avoid, as word on the midway has it, a conservative "catfight." It's true; non-candidate Palin had earlier this very afternoon breezed in sporting a decidedly plunging V-neck tee, stopping in front of the booth with the blowup SpongeBobs and Dora the Explorers to mix and mingle with her supporters. Ever since, afloat in the languid August air, have been giddy recitations of Palin encounters like the one being recounted beside me now, which begins, "So she was over at the lemonade stand" and ends, "So I said, 'Hello, Sarah,' and she said, 'Hello,' right back!"

All of which excitations leave the soapbox folks in a bit of a bind. No one's been as late this week as Bachmann is now, and the congresswoman from Minnesota is batting cleanup for the day. Twice already the dignitaries at the *Des Moines Register* have grabbed the mic to inform us that Representative Bachmann is stuck in traffic, and to beg our indulgence.

Some things are difficult to do at a Middle American state fair— eat vegan, for instance—but killing time is not one of them. Thus the Bachmann delay provides a perfect excuse to go in search of the world's biggest boar—not Romney, but the ironically named Tiny, a 1,196-pound Hampshire owned by Blake Everman of Postville, Iowa, that yesterday beat out Fatty, the pig exhibited by Ben and Neal Wikner of Farmersburg, for the state title. There's time also to shoot the bull with a couple of FFA girls who stand to inherit more land than dark-horse Texas farmer-cum-presidential candidate Jared Blankenship. There's time enough even to sit in the "world's best massage chair" whose disclaimer advises "must be 21 to sit in chair," before circling back again to the soapbox to check out the cherry-red Chevy Bel Air in the classic car show on the grand concourse while waiting more interminable moments for Bachmann's much-ballyhooed arrival. We the faithful are on the verge of pulling up stakes when, at long last, the campaign bus pulls past the Land O'Lakes dairy truck whose side panel reads "Delivering the goodness" to disgorge the authentic conservative herself, clad in something perilously close to a little black dress. The crowds part as the five-foot-tall dynamo makes her way to the stage with the aid of a police escort to whip us all into a frenzy we hope will be proportional to our wait.

The candidate is a bundle of energy late in the day. "Hi everyone, from one Iowan to another. . . . This is where Barack Obama got his start, and this is where he's going to come to his end! Did you get the change and the hope you believed in?"

"Noooooo," the crowd goes.

"Time for a *real change*. We're going to repeal Obamacare. . . . As nominee of the Republican party, I will not rest until I elect thirteen more titanium-spined senators"—she stops and spins, midspeech, to do that provocative thing where she points to the vertebrae that provide uncompromising support for her conservative bona fides—"and we're finally going to repeal Obamacare, Dodd-Frank, turn the economy around, create jobs. And it won't take more than three months to get the whole shootin' match up to speed. . . . We're gonna do it. . . . Tomorrow is the day we make the down payment on taking the country back! I'm coming out to shake your hand and see you now. God bless you, everyone."

The entire speech lasts three minutes. And just as soon as the applause dies down, the complaining starts. "C'mon . . . say something! I've been here forever," some big moose hollers, followed by a high-schooler in designer glasses and a trendy Western shirt who leaps atop a hay bale, points his finger in Marcus Bachmann's face, and screams, "According to Marcus, I'm a barbarian. Ready to pray away the gay, right, Marcus? You treat me like a second-class citizen!"

Marcus and Michele Bachmann, obliging long lines of autograph-seekers and celebrity hounds, ignore the jeers with all the grace of a would-be First Couple, until the kid starts chanting "Shame on You! Shame on You!" The AYM (angry young man) is literally two feet away from the candidate, punching the charged air between them with his fist, his passionate personal protest counterpointed by the usual saccharine platitudes that float on the deep-fried-scented breeze—"Oooh, it's so good to see you" and "Michele, can I have my picture with you?"—and that serve as a backdrop to the serious dressing down the candidate is getting. "I'm a second-class citizen according to you, Michele," AYM screams. "What about life, liberty, and the pursuit of happiness for every American?"

"You're going to wreck the country and ruin my retirement," someone calls after Bachmann as she clambers down from the speaking platform with difficulty. "That was a two-minute speech," cries the moose, then, turning his venom on the screaming teen: "You can't pray the gay out of *that guy*."

I am one of the groupies crowding Bachmann's difficult exit, possessed, for the first time in my rural life as an assiduous avoider of both crowds and autograph-hound hero-worshippers, to reach out and touch someone. Already the guy ahead of me in the impromptu receiving line we've formed is yelling, "I touched her fingertips!" And now I too can claim my first flesh-pressing by the belle of the presidential ball at the height of her powers, and it's intoxicating. I have been touched by greatness, I convince myself, like Clinton shaking JFK's hand in 1963, planting some invisible seed. Some presidential ectoplasm or cooties of greatness have been conferred unto me, I'm tempted to believe, and unto the whole tenderloin-on-a-stick Middle West affair in which we've all just played a small but indispensable part.

As Michele's bus parts the crowds on its way out, the camera jockeys pack up their tripods, and the political junkies begin the long march to the satellite-truck lots, I linger in the state fair sundown, thinking about the political halo surrounding the day's events. The mysterious young protestor in plaid had sent the press corps to frenzied googling, and in less than an hour he'd been unmasked as Gabe Aderhold of upscale, suburban Edina, Minnesota, a still underage, self-declared "civil rights activist" who drove 250 miles from the Twin Cities to confront Marcus Bachmann on the matter of his allegedly anti-gay counseling center in Lake Elmo, Minnesota.

At twilight, when the twenty-one-and-over crowd floods the fairgrounds in search of cheap midway thrills and overpriced beers, at the crepuscular hour when the bass beat begins thumping from the bar tents and ID bracelets come out, I head for the state fair gondola, which, once I am safely buckled in, lifts me into the leafy green canopy from whence the whole of the fair—the Ring of Fire, the Tilt-A-Whirl, the Wacky Worm—unfurls before me, facts properly lit and put in perspective. Strapped into the cars in front of me, long-married husbands and wives stare off into the smear of carnival lights while young lovers hold hands and peck out text messages, and together we become the human equivalent of hanging chads suspended in midair as the gondola makes its programmed stop to afford us a view of our midwestern world as calliope.

I am agog not with hormones but with the heady notion that the candidates for the nation's highest office will come to this far-off prairie to flip burgers and squeeze flesh and talk with people like me seated on ignoble hay bales. And I am unstitched too by what I have witnessed—professional activists and rabble rousers descending on a peaceful agrarian republic with very public axes to grind, while the cameras roll all too obligingly. A national press corps so large at times it choked the concourse until there was scarcely room enough for the average citizen to ask a substantive question of the very men and women whose sorting and ranking we have uniquely been tasked with. But it is precious too, this fecund mix of old-fashioned soapbox and homegrown populist fodder fermenting and fomenting here for at least two generations. And as the first harvest in what figures to be a full-on renaissance of retail politics the likes of which gen X and gen Y have never before witnessed, it serves as deliciously fattening political prologue.

Digital Divides

After years of fitful celibacy on my far-flung farm, I a seventh-generation rural midwesterner, abject failure in love's final exam, frequent poser of the existential questions, "to be or not to be? to flee or not to flee?" have duly resolved to do as the city folks do and "get myself out there." Well-meaning urban friends have told me over and over that I have to "put myself in circulation" if I really want to find someone to share this prairie life with. How would a would-be lover, they ask, ever find you where you live?

The Internet has practically become a love-lifeline, my urban friends convince me, with a missionary zeal in their voices I have not heard in a while. Every year or two they take this tone, always in moments when they sense stoical pride losing its grip on me, my sometimes too-rigid moral code letting go, becoming more fluid—more like their own. "Corrupting" a country cousin has become a good-natured pleasure for them, like waking up a cat sleeping peaceably in the sun or handing the town's resident teetotaler a glass of chardonnay, then standing back with an anthropologist's pith-helmeted detachment to see what happens next.

Over the phone they read me newspaper stories all about the new phenomenon of unmarried "bachelor farmers," as they like to fancy me, finding Internet matches all over the United States. Hundreds of years of economic, social, and demographic isolation could now be cured, like most everything else in our society, with the click of a button. At this point in our urban/rural pas de deux it's expected that I'll hem and haw about whatever it is, but ultimately give in, and they'll hang up the phone feeling smugly satisfied that they've eroded my characteristic agrarian refusal of something that would, in their view, ultimately be "good for me." If it's come to this—my phoning them up in the middle of a perfectly good workday to complain about my lot—my legendary resistance has already begun to crack. From high-speed Internet (accepted), to cable television (rejected), to repeated attempts to get me to move to town (rejected), we have, as the saying goes, "seen this movie before." How could I summon the heart to burst their proselytizing bubble and admit to them that not long ago I'd tried a trial membership at an online dating site specifically for rural folks and come up empty?

Post your profile on one of the big national dating sites, they advise me, and let us know how it goes. Per usual, they seem to have the prescription for what ails their country cousin, and indeed their country cousin always seems to be missing something relative to their own urbane abundance. A hundred years ago, the very zip-code based boons my urban friends now enjoy—coupledom, quiet domesticity, abundant economic and cultural opportunity, jobs provident and prosperous enough to support a family—had been the province of the young in the "settled" countryside, not in the isolating and alienating metropolis. Now, all that's flipped.

One hundred years later the advice my well-intentioned urban friends give me boils down to the Internet panacea and cure-all: Take two doses of Chrome and one of Bing and call us in the morning.

⟹◆⟸

I am duly surprised—a better word is shocked—when, after reluctantly taking my friends' advice, I join a mainstream online dating site and there find pictures of two frankly stunning women who list their homes as two tiny hamlets not far from my own with quaint-sounding agrarian names like Farmersburg, population 302. Both are fair-haired and endowed with movie-star good looks, their taglines designed, it would seem, to appeal to the earnestly sincere in me: "Let's go fly a kite." Something about their listings and their looks, though, seem out of place in my down-to-earth area code—too good to be true. And yet I want to believe, I really do. In an agrarian world, why shouldn't women like these—attractive, family-oriented, honestly plainspoken—choose to root down in prairie towns like mine? Theoretically, at least, it is possible that they are real, despite all demographic evidence to the contrary.

Flush with hopefulness, I decide to message them, as thrilled as if I've just spotted an extinct passenger pigeon in the wild. When one of the blondes from "down the road" writes soliciting my personal e-mail address, I happily oblige. Less than a week later, I receive this e-mail in reply:

Hello!

I am very glad and very excited to see your letter again. Zachary, I never had acquaintances through the Internet. I think, that It is very interesting, when two persons have an acquaintance by an I-network,

I not It is assured, that I have put the photo correctly. I very badly know How to use the computer and therefore I hope, that is correct Has put my photo. I wish to know about you directly more, But if you have any photos, please send to me Them.

I wish to tell to you about me directly. My name is Ksenia, i am 29 yeard old, I live in city Sidelnikovo. I work The seller-adviser in trading department. I very much love children. This most Valuable, that is in our life. How you consider? You agree with me?

I live innot the big city where approximately 20 thousand persons live, I realy from Russia, and I regret, that my profile on a site of acquaintances is told, that I from your country. It was my silly error, I at all do not

know as, Thus it has appeared, but if it is possible, we
could have The further conversation while. I think, that
the distance relation will not be Problem for you? I
would like to hope for it. I am assured, that The distance
for us will not be a problem.

As I had a bad mood that day, and I have smiled
Only because of when my girlfriend has photographed
me, has told To me "Cheers!" To me it became ridiculous
after that words, but most of all As this which it has told,
seemed to me ridiculously. I hope, that You can see my
photo, I also will be glad to see yours Photo. Zachary, I
search man which wishes to live for love, for Families.
I believe, that those who searches for it find treasure. I
want, That it was strong, careful and attentive. I wish to
feel, that Strong shoulder I can lean. I wish to feel me as
real The woman about it and to be convinced, that it can
protect me. I search The person who will consider me
as the usual woman as its wife Children. I man should
respect the woman, care of it and understand, that It has
been created specially for it :). I prefer to see man without
Very bad habits healthy, optimistic, loyal, Sociable, fair,
clever and intellectual. I search for the special person in
this beautiful life! I do not want that man, was Especial
but if man me will understand and love for me, it will be
The most special. I will be glad to answer your questions,
please Write to me about yourself more if you are interested in the further dialogue With me. I with impatience
will wait for your letter,

Sincerely yours new girlfriend Ksenia.

Part of me is indignant, embarrassed that from the seed of my
sincere need for companionship has grown abject gullibility. The
wounded, duped vigilante in me wants to expose these dating double agents, draw them out . . . maybe lead them on for a while

before blowing the whistle on their deceit. But it's not in me, not in this already cold season. Who's to say that any of us wouldn't undertake the same sleight of hand if we desperately wanted out of some city, with its long lines and drawn faces, with its political instability and corruption, with its steady rain and wind in our face. My other, truer voice cautions me against judging, reminds me that we, the romantically disadvantaged and passed-over, are all in the same uncertain boat together, our silly words like oars rowing us toward a love whose exact geographic coordinates we cannot seem to locate.

⟫◆⟪

Eros, the little prick, grants me reprieve. After my initial foray into the world of big-time online dating, I have sold my soul to the site once again in exchange for the one thing overwintering in the graying countryside has made me most desirous of—not fresh citrus or fresh coffee, but fresh hope.

This isn't my first rodeo where rural dating is concerned. I already know, for instance, that rules of the dating game differ dramatically for a remote soul like me. If I hope to attract a mate to my far-flung acres in the ides of this unforgiving season, there are several faux pas unique to my demographic that I must avoid:

> I cannot mention my distance from a major college or university town.

> I cannot respond to an urbanite's criticism of the Heartland's small towns and rural places with reciprocal critism of the metropolis.

> I cannot let the urbane window-shoppers, who are accustomed to well-stocked markets, get a hint of my existential loneliness or urgency, for fear they will take their business elsewhere. Abject lonesomeness, after all, strikes one as perilously close to neediness,

and neediness, in turn, might suggest a lone-wolf
type unhappy with the isolation of rural life.

For ruralites like me, the old cliché has never been
truer: beggars can't be choosers. I cannot afford a
laundry list of deal-breakers the way I might if I
were living in the well-trafficked center of the hive.

Call it self-sabotage, but I don't invest much in my online dating profile or in the obligatory photo—taken in front of the barn,
with me looking hollow-eyed and vaguely sinister—or in the text
of my all-important definitional statement itself, which reads,

I'm thoughtful, concerned, compassionate, passionate,
active, and reflective. Most of all I seek someone who is
comfortable with themselves, seeks the pleasures of presence rather than absence, prefers real face-to-face communion to e-mail and texting and cell phoning, and who's
creative by nature. . . . I love the countryside, and am sym-
pathetic to forgotten or overlooked or underappreciated
places.

I'd count myself lucky to find a true companion for
adventures great and small.

While I'm serious about finding a soul mate who
would one day like to begin a family, I'm happy to meet
many types of people and always grateful for good and
lasting friendships however they arrive. Whether friendship
or relationship, seems to me the same principles apply . . .
willingness to spend time together, meeting "half way"
geographically and metaphysically, and achieving joyful
reciprocity and mutuality.

Next, I am prompted by the site to describe a possible first date,
and here I decide it is better to be abstract rather than risk alienating my hoped-for constituency by listing an activity that I would
actually prefer to do but might be perceived as either (a) passé,

(b) cliché, or (c) hopelessly old-fashioned. Of the more conventional dating activities—movies, coffee, even bowling—the nearest options are nearly twenty miles away, a long drive in wintry conditions. Assuming a would-be dater would be responding from the nearest "city" with a population of 7,500 or greater, a central meeting place would be at least an hour's drive for her. If the first meeting went well, I could hardly suggest a second date at my place. I cannot have someone risk life and limb on the gravel roads and snowdrifted country lane, driving to a home so remote I cannot see even the rooftops of the farms neighboring mine.

I end up describing my "ideal date" thusly: "some combination of moving and rumination, action and contemplation, outside and inside, making light and making serious." Still I am unhappy with my profile when it's finished. It strikes me as cowardly and half-assed, lukewarm, redolent of the lonesomeness that has cornered me, unwilling, where I live. A keen reader would surely pick up on such barely latent grief, and yet I find I have no desire to hide it, no inclination to "dress up the pig," as my father would say.

I search my local zip code and, predictably, find nothing. I expand the search radius to fifty miles to find one young woman of interest—a willowy soul who describes herself as intelligent and creative (certainly better than the feature on the site that allows members to choose their butt or their chest as their best, most redeeming feature) and who looks in some pictures like a platinum-haired female version of Buddy Holly and in others, sans spectacles, like the beanpole in your high school class who grew into a beauty. She is pictured standing beside the rustic sign for Big Sur, on California's Highway 1, presumably on one of those once-in-a-lifetime, bucket-list vacations sometimes indulged in by we midwesterners. I e-mail her and, several weeks later, as my membership is about to expire, I receive a canned reply—one of the quickie options the platform provides for you when you're too overbooked and overscheduled to write personally. Her message reads, "I will respond if you e-mail again."

I am giddy even for this crumb, replying enthusiastically and hopefully, checking in once every several hours in spite of barnyard chores that need to be done, to see if my digital Cinderella has replied. Finally, as the clock ticks down on my paid-for membership and, with it, the chances of hearing from her again, hope gets the better of me and I re-up for another month, anticipating a reply that sadly never arrives.

Another prospect does, though—let's call her Doreen—a girl who captures my interest; she lists in her profile a love of old black-and-white movies, '80s music, art, and writing. She wants someone who's a foodie, who can order wine with expertise and panache, who "must love dogs." I *do* love dogs, but not in the warm-fuzzy way I imagine she requires. I've inherited my father's and my grandfather's distaste for lap dogs and show dogs and pedigreed pooches kept in undersized apartments and fed diets more healthfully persnickety than the nutrition afforded many rural children. Like most of my rural brethren, my heart belongs to working dogs, to sheepherders and cattle-wranglers, to dogs weathered to stand up to trying conditions, and to dogs with a heart for chasing the cars that kick up plumes of gravel dust on my rural route rather than the kind that doesn't even get up from his cushion long enough to bark at the mailman.

I'm not sure Doreen and I are hearing the same tune, but I'm convinced my melody at least partially resonates with hers. The trouble is, my earlier failures have required me to dramatically widen the radius of my love-search, and Doreen, I learn, lives in the far northwest suburbs of Chicago, though her profile doesn't say where exactly. Beggars can't be choosers, I remind myself, sitting down at my desk as outside the snow flies and the wind howls to compose a note that reads in part,

> I think I've just about everything to offer that you list on
> your profile. But I'm not a citified person. Do I order red
> wine self-consciously? Yes, and I always will. Do I have
> a wine nose? Absolutely not. I refuse one. Do I know
> viticulture, Old World wine cultures, the literature of
> wine, the romance of it? Yes. Do I cringe when a waiter

opens a new bottle and pours some to taste while looming over me? Yes, it makes my farm boy's blood curdle . . .
such needless airs, such ridiculous formality. I hate people
pumping my gas for me.

If I were a dog . . . well, I wouldn't be a dog. But I
would be canine. I'd want to be a fox . . . fleet of foot,
home-minded (den-minded), learned, soulful, vigilant,
caring, alert, comical (not always intentionally), spirited,
hard-pressed, and magic. I wouldn't be a lap dog, and
I wouldn't be a . . . dog that lays around all the time. I
wouldn't be domesticated at all. . . . I admire wild things.

I've prattled on. I know this makes no sense. I know
it's weird, and hugely off-putting, and I hope I haven't
completely worried you or turned you away while
knowing that if I have, it's okay too.

I'm full of the guarded optimism of New Year's. When Doreen
replies, a correspondence begins—one of those e-mail back-and-
forths that feels like a lifeline when temps in Sioux City and North
Platte hit nineteen below and the local weatherman closes his seg-
ment with somber reminders to his viewers to pack their "winter
survival kits" in their trunks. Meanwhile, we ruralites have had our
old pair of lined coveralls, a stocking cap, and a backup pair of boots
and wool socks in our cars since December's first snowfall.

The New Year has come and gone now, but I'm still the
same old me—doctrinaire, overly disciplined, a fuddy-duddy
with a passion for rural America. Still Doreen's and my back-
and-forth pushes toward an inevitable meeting. We talk once on
the phone—I am sick with a winter cold and so congested I
sound like Kermit the Frog. The results are mixed. I don't feel
the electricity of an effortless rapport, or the pregnant silence of
two Intendeds who have nothing and everything to say at once.
Her voice is not a voice I recognize—not the one, if indeed I can
trust my love-hunches anymore, the universe tuned my strings to
at birth. Still, I will not allow myself to be as closed-minded as I

have been in the past. Who am I—an increasingly middle-aged
rural quack seemingly gone to the dogs—to say that love must
arrive from a particular zip code? I should be grateful, shouldn't
I, if it zips at all?

During our get-to-know-you call, I learn all sorts of interesting things about Doreen. I learn she spent part of her summers on
her grandparents' farm in Wisconsin, though she is, by her own
admission, a far cry from a country girl. Commuting on an early-
bird train every morning to the Chicago Loop, she lives in a small
condo in the suburbs next to a forest preserve where she can take
her two dogs on pre-dawn walks. For fun, she watches black-and-
white flicks at the Gene Siskel Center, glorying in the old-time
romantic comedies and film noirs. On her way back home on the
Union Pacific North Line each night, she sketches off-the-wall
fashion designs she hopes may one day make her famous. It's not a
life I would choose—she yearns to one day try her luck in the grist-
mill that is L.A. and Hollywood—but hers seem sincere enough as
life plans go. If she's willing to give me a fair shake, especially with
all my advisory comments and obvious anomalies, then I should be
willing to do likewise. So I reply:

> It was very thoughtful of you to send your recommen-
> dation for meeting places. I know how busy you are and
> the fact that you took time out of your morning to send
> those speaks so highly of you. I already regard you as a
> very special person, a peach, as they used to say back in
> better days. I've been meaning to tell you now nice it is
> to hear your intelligence and kindness bubbling up—
> breaking through—even in mundane conversations.
> Thank you for bearing with me. . . . You surely caught me
> at a low, low ebb. But I begin to feel my life-force return-
> ing, despite still being dog-tired and snotty (as in the nose
> kind of snotty, not teenager kind of snotty).
>
> I have arrived at a very strange conclusion, after
> much thought, and wanted to share it with you to see

what you think. And this is only my conclusion; it doesn't have to be yours.

I really did want to drive out and meet you tonight. That's the kind of person I am. I cursed the logistics, and the traffic, and the lateness of the hour when I would arrive and then have to leave and decided for once to be practical. You see, while I like to drive, I hate traffic, and I loathe the suburbs. You mention you dislike driving, that Galena seemed a long way, that Starved Rock State Park seemed out of the question. Truly understandable. And in the past I would have said, "I understand totally," saddled up, and arrived at your castle. I once dated a woman in Chicago—she was like something out of *Great Gatsby* . . . worked in one of the skyscrapers in the Loop for one of the premier Chicago companies. And I was always the one meeting her, by train, by car, by whatever, because she was the one in the center of the hive, behind the wall, in the great Metropolis, and why wouldn't I, she implied, want to be at the center of it all? Where else would I go? And didn't I have more time than she did?

But I disliked this Faustian bargain intensely. . . . 'Middle American' to her was like a fiction—she had never been there, didn't know anything about it, didn't care. She'd effect a mock-hick accent and dismiss it as 'Middle America,' saying everyone was fat, tragically unhip. . . . For her, Chicago was where it was at—or Rome, Venice, Paris. And I swallowed this for a while until I could swallow it no longer.

———————

Chicago, that toddlin' town of the shores of Lake Michigan, has been the Midwest's capital and flame for over a century, the great hope and horror of every rural kid dreaming away his hours of too-literal fieldwork. Hamlin Garland wrote of his approach to the Windy City, where Corn Belt gave way to Rust Belt. "Had it not been for the fear of ridicule," he recalls in *Son of the Middle Border*, "I think I should have turned back at the next stop. The shining lands beyond seemed hardly worth a struggle against the dragon's brood which the dreadful city was a-swarm." Decades earlier, Frenchman Paul Bourget sketched a similar attraction-repulsion in his 1896 travelogue *Outre-Mer: Impressions of America*, writing of the city's "business fervor" and "unbridled violence like that of an uncontrollable element." Bourget observed, "It rushes along these streets as once before the devouring flame of a fire; it quivers; it makes itself visible with an intensity which lends something tragical to this city, and it makes it seem a poem to me."

Chicago, for all its poetic potential, was the darkly romantic city Carl Sandburg (a native of Galesburg, Illinois) famously called out in his 1914 poem of the same name: "They tell me you are wicked and I believe them, for I have seen your painted women under the gas lamps luring farm boys." But it wasn't just farm boys the great immigrant "City of the Big Shoulders" drew in droves at the end of the nineteenth century, but farm girls too, from all over the Midwest. Many came for a glimpse of better futures on display at the Columbian Exposition of 1893—futures of neon lights and Ferris Wheels and Juicy Fruit chewing gum, all new for the World's Fair that year. They imagined how innovations like these would set their rural routines on their ears, how the future would be better than the past, sure as Chicago existed. "There is a Chicago that lives in the minds of young people all through the Middle West," midwestern novelist Floyd Dell would write in December of 1913, "a Chicago that exists by virtue of their aspiration and their need, and that begins to die with their first sight of the town."

The Columbian Exposition of 1893, visited by some 27 million over its remarkable six-month run, marked a great diaspora of the Midwest's young women to the great metropolises along the lakes—Milwaukee, Minneapolis, Detroit, Cleveland, and most of all Chicago, a city already bursting with over a million people by the

1890s. Undergirding the epic in-migration was a palpable sense of possibility and a subtext of romantic desire calling those who felt stunted and censored by what they saw as the inhibiting agrarian mores of their far-flung corn towns and farm hamlets.

Midwest novelist Ruth Suckow captured the zeitgeist of the moment best, writing in an essay that appeared in *American Mercury* in 1926, "The flocks of talented girls graduated every year from [our] colleges must go East if they were to live up to the flowery expectations held for them. Boys and girls no sooner got away to college, perhaps eighty miles from home, than they began to regard the hometown from the standpoint of detached superiority, with a lightly humorous and patronizing touch." Still, the contribution of the Midwest's most talented rural women and men to play queen and drone in the urban hive turned out to be a bittersweet gift, one given not begrudgingly but with a profound sense of loss and sadness that would last a century.

In the modern era, Iowa's courtship of Chicago, in particular, peaked in 2000, when then-governor and future presidential candidate Tom Vilsack, desperate to stanch the flow of the educated young out of his aging state, trekked across the Mississippi River to the great mating pot, where he hosted a reception at the gleaming Hyatt Regency in the South Loop. "Opportunities abound in our state," the governor reminded his skeptical listeners. "The state's outstanding mix of career opportunities and high quality of life make the environment in Iowa ripe for continued growth. With cutting-edge companies creating outstanding career options, there has never been a better time to find rewarding and challenging opportunities in Iowa. We invite you back."

Vilsack's pitch that June night in 2000 amounted to a literal courtship—an attempt to put a stop to a centuries-long seduction of small-town midwesterners as starry-eyed about life in the region's cities as were the youthful midwesterners who stood, gobsmacked, before the electrified neoclassical White City of the 1893 World's Fair, with its many allurements. At its core Vilsack's message boiled down to this: if you love home, come home. It was a simple, perhaps even simple-minded, message, too much so for the sophisticates in the Windy City who had long ago decided to jump sinking ships, and who for a century had been sending back glowing reports of abundant lives to their less fortunate country cousins across the Mississippi River.

———————

Despite my prickly protestations and willfully off-putting stick-in-the-mud mulishness, Doreen calls my curmudgeonly bluff. I say I'm not a city dog, and she says it doesn't matter. I say I'm a farm boy who can't order a "good" merlot without blushing, and she finds a way to defuse that excuse too. I play the I-don't-want-a-long-distance-relationship card, and she trumps that as well, at least being willing to entertain, with obvious anxieties, a halfway meet-up. I'm still hesitant, though, still feeling drawn into a geographic quagmire promising only the most fleeting and unfulfilling of meetings. I've been praying for nearness, yearning for a country girl of farm or ranch or grassland, and now Eros, the imp, has given me something 180 degrees and 180 miles from my wishes. Worse yet, Doreen writes that she suffers terrible anxiety when she leaves the city in her car alone and heads into the wide open spaces. The last time she tried to make the drive back to see the grandparents' old home place in Wisconsin, she suffered a panic attack and ended up having to turn around en route. To me her phobia sounds preposterous, still I know Doreen is far from alone in her fear of the silences and spaces out here on the prairie. It's a certifiable condition—twice as common in women as in men for reasons no one fully understands—this fear of open spaces.

In city-world we are all viewed as potentially damaged, all entitled to accommodations. The question is, where does accommodation cross the line into inanity or impossibility? How does one accommodate a city girl unable to endure the anxiety of driving into the remote countryside hours beyond Chicago's outermost orbit? And how does one accommodate a country boy who feels unsettled and ill at ease in the hemmed-in confines of the city? Doesn't Doreen's and my wished-for liaison amount, as we say out here in the hinterlands, to a dog that just won't hunt?

A compromise seems as if it might be in the offing when I write,

> D—I don't know about you, but I'm a little addled. I feel very pressured to court you in a way you deem acceptable and at your convenience and geography while respecting your fears and phobias. . . . I don't think meeting somewhere in the middle of Illinois next weekend makes much sense: 1) There's nowhere good to meet, and 2) It's winter, ruling out a picnic, a good long hike, kayaking, or canoeing and all those fun summertime things. The only place that's remotely between us and easy to get to, and has some history and some possibility is Galena. . . .
>
> I propose that we meet where you want midweek, on Wednesday, and that we meet where I want on the weekend and then see where things stand. Look, I'm willing to have a second date with you either way, and you're entitled to that much consideration, unless of course you're completely egregious, or disrespectful or utterly horrific, which of course you're not. So I guess I'm proposing a sort of home/away game where home for you is Chicago or . . . , and "home" for me is Galena. Otherwise, we end up meeting in a place neither of us is really interested in.
>
> So what if I agreed to meet you somewhere downtown near Union Station for dinner or coffee or drinks or whatever Wednesday around 6:00. And in return I would ask you to give me the benefit of the doubt and meet me in Galena on the weekend? And then can we just see how we both feel and if we want to continue?

It seems a hopeful and equitable compromise, and we see it through. Doreen makes it to Galena, persevering through an acute anxiety attack en route to arrive at the De Soto House Hotel, the very place from whose soaring balconies home-boy Ulysses S. Grant and Illinois favorite son, Abraham Lincoln, once campaigned. We meet on a foggy February morning when the high hills of Jo Daviess County, Illinois, are positively socked in. We wander the streets, dipping in and out of kitschy shops, grabbing a warm drink at the venerable hotel, and playing a couple of improvised games by the fire. Our favorite is a game we call Doors. The rules are simple: draw a distinctive door and see if the other person can guess whose door it is, or who would be most likely to walk through it. It's a difficult game—the kind whose answers even long-marrieds would struggle to divine. In the final round before Doreen must part, I correctly guess, after many attempts, a series of doors custom-designed for the Three Little Bears. As we bundle up for our respective drives home, I can't help but wonder . . . If somehow she could conjure a door perfect for me, or indeed for us, would I have the self-awareness and the courage to walk through?

Our subsequent "away game" in Chicago is rained on, but not rained out. Too timid to drive all the way downtown, I park the car in the suburbs and ride the Metra in, showing up at Union Station road-weary and red-eyed—like some strung-out over-the-road trucker too long in the saddle. Doreen, bedecked in an old-timey, velvety, knee-length coat, meets me in the marbled Grand Hall at Union Station and leads me into an icily insistent rain. She slips her arm in mine as we walk down Adams Street scooting in under my umbrella, and suddenly I feel like Gene Kelly. We puddle-jump all the way to Greektown, where the pungent aroma of frying cheese overpowers the damp, and settle in for a quiet Greek dinner, if that itself is not an oxymoron. Outside it's cats and dogs.

Doreen proves funny and charming and soulful and comes bearing her sketchbook full of what must be some of the more fantastic personages ever etched with graphite—men with British Restoration–era caps and canes that look like Oscar Wilde might have wielded them well; men who are half tree and half human; women with treachery in their eyes. It's a fantastic menagerie. The restaurant on this rainy, midwinter, midweek night is scarcely half full, and the waiter, a Greek, fawns over us. I know that my date desires formality in the worst way, and while I consider myself a gentleman, I remain a rough-around-the-edges farm kid who's not about to put on airs for anybody. When it is time to go, I am too self-conscious to help her on with her coat, and self-conscious again when, back outside, she intertwines her elbow in mine in a gesture that feels to me prematurely intimate. We part without a kiss at Union Station, her train headed to the northwest suburbs, mine headed west to a car that waits in a remote lot for the hours-long ride back to my acres.

The ride back home to the farm is a drowsy one, my mind wandering equally to the possibilities and limitations in a state of post-date Zen I had forgotten in years of geographically enhanced celibacy. I am stuffed full of eggplant parmesan and weirdly hopeful along the Autobahn back to the hinterland, suddenly open to all the weather love might bring.

When I wake the next morning, it is to a reality check that this will not, *cannot* work, that I am only being drawn away again from my core, from what I need to seek unapologetically—a love homegrown. And I am anxious, all of a sudden, at the promise of the relationship I have helped create after two logistically difficult dates and nary a kiss.

The phone, when I turn it on, comes bearing a good morning text from Doreen, whose warm message elicits in me not gratitude but a wild need to end things before they have begun. I head to the computer to compose what seems like one in a series of sad Bartleby the Scrivener I-would-prefer-not-to notes. Again, it's a country mouse/city mouse chord I've struck, and I am sick both of it and of myself.

> Thank you for your lovely text of this morning, which
> felt so good to receive. Hope you had a good night's rest.

I realize after sleeping on it and wrestling with it again this morning that I am dreaming, letting yesterday's magic get the better of me. I got so excited at what I was feeling that I neglected to fully consider the "facts of the case" as they stand, and these are that 1) you live in Chicago and have a two and a half hour door-to-door commute round-trip 2) You don't like to drive.

It occurs to me that our existing life choices mostly predict our future . . . your choices suggest a life close to the cultural opportunities of a big city, to meeting a man similarly inclined towards the benefits of proximity to the hive, to the engine. And you will achieve it, I've no doubt.

Me, on the other hand, I've wedded myself to a woebegone place, kept the hive at a distance, chosen a life betwixt and between . . . I've cast my lot with the Old Building and Loan. . . . My commitment to this place is sometimes inexplicable to me, and often personally challenging if not damaging, but I am steering by my natal charts even if often I am running aground.

What choice do I have other than to meet someone here, or someone within a hair's breadth already of radically changing their life . . . looking only for an invitation before they move, literally and figuratively, to a place like this one. A sprinter poised to sprint. To meet someone for whom change might, or might not, be in the offing a year or two down the road feels like an unwise bet for me, a distant maybe.

I'll admit sometimes I am reckless . . . dreamy, prone to great leaps of faith, and deeply loyal and sentimental. What choice do I really have other than to meet someone of similar innerworkings, someone for whom chucking a city life and raising kids in some place like Galena, Illinois, or Nowhere, USA, would be an adventure worth leaping.

All of what I wrote yesterday, about what I value about you, and what concerns me, remains emphatically

true. Today's note is a commentary on me, not on you,
and it is a commentary on damned circumstance.

Hitting Send, I am wearier of myself than ever, sick of myself
to the core, tired of the same old dilemma and dogma, of the same
seemingly unwieldy and unyielding choices. I feel antagonized,
dogged even by my own nonsensical choices—to hang my hat in
the countryside while persisting in the stubborn belief that still
somehow it should be possible to meet an educated, strong, open-
minded young woman, a love homegrown ready to make a home
in a rural Heartland with which her peers long ago broke up.

A "relationship" ended is never clean, even if barely begun.
In the coming weeks Doreen and I will once again attempt to
meet halfway, but this time her anxiety will get the better of her,
and she will turn back as I am nervously walking out the door
to get in the truck to drive hours to meet her after working all
morning to clear my country lane of snow. For both of us, it is
the proverbial last straw. Our difficult denouement is fraught
with underlying difference. She feels I should be more understanding of her rural anxieties; I feel her last-minute cancelation
reveals her ignorance of the hours it takes for me to get my
snow cleared and the truck ready to drive the many miles of
snow- and ice-covered rural roads to meet her. And after all the
finagling and heart-and-soul-baring e-mails exchanged late into
the night—for all this fuss—we have only twice met in person.
Completely unaware are we of the historical reputations of our
families for virtue or vice, for dogged determination on the one
hand, or dastardly desertion on the other. We have never seen
one another's homes, or heard one another's record collections,
or considered the view from our respective windows. It would
not have been that way if we had grown up within a stone's
throw of one another.

This is exactly what I had been protecting myself against—a
certain uncertain kind of disappointment, a confirmation of an
underlying hypothesis. The emotional investment made in what

turns out to be a romantic pipe dream makes me indiscriminately angry—at myself, at Doreen, at someone or something—like falling victim to one of those Nigerian e-mail frauds you knew damn well weren't true, and yet you fell for anyway.

I am done with e-mail dating, I tell my friends when I call them, and they, as good friends will do, at least give me a little R-E-S-P-E-C-T for trying. It feels good to hear their voices on the other end of the line, but they too are hundreds of miles away in the city. How do I tell them how dejected and lonesome and, yes, even depressed, I feel? This failed and ill-fated dalliance with the Internet has, far from being a panacea, left me feeling more heartsick and bereft of prospects than ever.

This is precisely why, I remind myself, warming up my own bed each night, a graft of a country mouse with a city mouse is so often bound to be rejected, destined not to take. And in the unlikely event it's found, only to be forced, it's prone to result in an inherently unstable hybrid barely able to stand on its own two feet—Dr. Frankenstein's monster stumbling through the hinterlands, moaning for a mate.

And if the present-day statistics documenting a still more dramatic demographic shift away from Middle America's—and indeed the world's—rural places prove true, won't our search for love inexorably send us *not* down a country lane, as we might with our whole heart have wished, but up an interstate to the nearest metropolis—in other words, up a creek? And if looking for love necessarily means looking cityward, what becomes of the hinterland's most celebrated virtue: making miracles with what and whom are near at hand. Finally, if a culture like ours cannot educate and sustain its sons and daughters long enough to ensure their introduction to one another as potential life partners, what chance does that culture ultimately have of survival, of the self-perpetuation that these days seems the sole right of the city?

My great-grandmother got angry with the other rural girls in her letter circle in 1912, begging the question of her city-loving brethren: "Girls, what do you say about this? Or are all you against

Walter Jack and Amber Jack, circa 1917.

farming as the boys? I am a farmer clear through, and I think it is the ideal life to live."

Amber Jane Pickert went out and found herself a man, Walter Thomas Jack, a young schoolteacher, farmer, and budding writer down the road some, who agreed to come hang his hat on the family land Amber's great-grandfather settled in 1855. Walter, adopted as a boy, found a love of home when he found a love homegrown. He put that native understanding and gratitude into words half a lifetime later in 1946. Married for nearly thirty years by then, he wrote, "For every person there is a spot, a place they pledge themselves to return some day, because they were happy and contented there. It, no doubt, is the old home, the haunts of their childhood. These places are of the Earth—only things of the Earth have that magnetic power . . ."

If the place of our childhood possesses a mysterious, magnetic power, do the people who grew up there possess the same attraction by association? And what of the many born of the Heartland's farm towns and woebegone whistle-stops who feel repulsion rather than attraction to their home place, feeling the pull instead to some place else, some place undeniably more powerful and broad-shouldered, a toddlin' town of steel girders and steely gazes, rebuilt from ashes—a place clearly and inevitably "going places." What we feel, or don't feel, for our hometowns and home places is no more or less than a romance, and the ways we love it or don't—the permutations of love—conform to the archetypes of the lover. As the old tune goes, there must be fifty ways to leave your lover. The ways, codified in song, recall that the crisis of the brain drain is at root a roman-tic crisis of the jilted lover—the one seduced, educated, or simply called away to more "charming" prospects different than those they woke up to this morning, or a thousand other mornings, in the old bed, in the old place. The youthful out-migrator breaking bonds, or faith, with the old home place is the very one the song exhorts, the one who gets a new plan, slips on the bus (no need to discuss much)—just drops off the key, and sets themselves free.

Tell me, where are the songs of those who stay?

Escape
Velocities

Part II

Jack and Jill

"A trip to Expo '67 with a friend in his 'Vette was an interesting experience in this senior boy's life," read Sandy Donohoe's February 1968 "Senior Interview" with her classmate Michael Jack, the Midwest farmer's son who would become my father. For thanks, my dad credits in his interview "his parents for all the help and guidance they've given him, and Gail W. who is a wonderful and understanding person."

The mysterious Gail W. was my father's sweetheart from Rural Route 2, Mount Vernon, the farmer's daughter (my future mother) my father had met at the local A&W drive-through where, my mom recalls, his first words to her were "Careful not to scratch the car."

Parked in the drive on the farm, the Corvette that took my dad all the way to Canada and back.

The '67 Expo was the Category One World's Fair held that year in Montreal to celebrate Canada's centennial, and my father had shocked the senior class by loading up with a buddy and driving the Corvette the one thousand miles and twenty hours required to get from the self-proclaimed Pork Center of the World, Mechanicsville, Iowa, to the

136

capital of Quebec, stopping—or not stopping as the case might have been—to send Gail W. and his family postcards along the way. The first arrived bearing a George Washington five-cent stamp, post-

marked July 24, 1967, from Rolling Prairie, Indiana. The front showed a cartoonish map of the then eleven-year-old highway across which was splashed "Indiana Toll Road," and on back my father had written a single-word message: "Hi!" The boilerplate caption above his cheeky inscription read, "This beautiful super road provides services for the motorist and his car every few miles." Speed-minded motorists throughout the Heartland had cheered the arrival of the major east-west artery in 1956, dubbing it "Main Street of

My father, circa the late 1960s, posing in front of his first love: wheels.

the Midwest." The Indiana Toll Road Commission seconded the motion, producing in 1962 an eight-section foldout brochure thick enough to qualify as a paperback. The booklet's title, "You're Never Alone on the Indiana Toll Road," was accompanied by an equally promising subtitle-cum-slogan: "Safe, Swift, Scenic . . . an adventure in pleasant motoring."

The Corvette my father piloted across the U.S.-Canadian border to the Expo that summer of 1967 was the same star convertible on whose backseat my mom had perched, waving Jackie O.–style, as my dad cruised her down First Street in the Miss Mount Vernon parade her junior year. The punny banner hung over the side of the

My mother (on the far left) in the 1967 Homecoming Court, Mount Vernon, Iowa.

'Vette read "Jack 'n' Jill." My mom might well have been a candidate for the Iowa's Favorite Farmer's Daughter contest instead of just Miss Mount Vernon. She was possessed of almond eyes, wide yet discerning, a fashionable sweep of chestnut-colored hair falling somewhere shy of shoulder-length, and a flawless complexion. Like many country girls of her era, she did not do backbreaking "outdoor" chores alongside her father on the farm, but instead threw her energies into community and school events, where she was elected to the homecoming court and cheered for the Mount Vernon Mustangs during football season.

Black-and-white glossies of the 1968 homecoming court show Mom cradling a bouquet of flowers twice as wide as she was—the only candidate for queen not wearing black heels and the only one to pose gloveless. My mom wore a green velvet dress and yellow patent leather shoes with a transparent heel; she'd had them for years, waiting for the right occasion. To her left stands another farm-girl classmate, Carol, who looks as if she could be my mom's bob-haired twin. In the middle of the shot stands Jane—shorter, likeable even at a glance, not as conventionally attractive as the other girls perhaps, yet pretty in a knee-length skirt with wrap-around lace. To the far right stands lovely Anne DuVal, the sole blonde on the court, teacher's pet, member of the Home Economics Club, a comely town girl a head taller than all the others—the one any objective observer might have predicted would win, and did. My mom finished runner-up.

Behind the would-be queens stand five side-parted candidates for king in ties and boutonnières, one looking wayward, one with eyes closed, one with horn-rimmed glasses thick as Henry Kissinger's; just one, the second from the right, qualified as a farmer's son. My mom was one of two farmer's daughters among the court of five young queens-in-waiting that year, a harbinger of a more profound shift away from the farm to come. The country girls at Mount Vernon High, Mom tells me, might have been a little more independent, a little more quiet, maybe not as social. Sometimes they made their own clothes. She suspects they could probably entertain themselves better, and that they didn't have quite the same level of expectations as some of her friends in town.

For my mom the bubbly extroversion required of a cheerleader wasn't always a natural fit. "I was kind of shy, so it was a stretch for me in a lot of ways," she admits. A speedy runner, she would much rather have run track, but she and the other young women in our Middle American farm community would have to be content with G.R.A.—Girls Recreational Association—and the dance classes offered at city hall. A few years earlier my mom had won the title Best All-Around Dancer, helping fuel her interest in dance and advance her self-belief. Cheerleading practice, she recollects, offered a "welcome escape" for a country girl without her own car. After practice, she parlayed the extra hours she had to wait for her mom to pick her up into an after-school job at the local care center where she would be retrieved around suppertime.

Just before turning sixteen, my mom secured a job as a waitress at the same place where her two older sisters had worked, the

A&W drive-through. "It was *the spot* to work," Mom tells me. "It was a good place to meet people like your dad. I had a sense then he was a little different. He was the only guy who wouldn't let me attach the tray to his car . . . big red flag." She laughs at the memory, and I press her for more. Was it the fact that my father was a farmer's son, and thus able to play country Jack to her Jill, that drew her to him? She shakes her head no. "He was just different," she reiterates. "He didn't need to be a jock. He didn't care about belonging to a group." Michael Jack had spent as much time out of Mechanicsville High suspended for tardiness or expressing contrary opinions as he had in it. At sixteen his heart beat for speed and the mint-green Chevy convertible he'd purchased upon receiving his license.

Given the era, theirs was a typical farmer's son meets farmer's daughter liaison, his life to date a study in machines, in mobility, in making things happen; hers a study in keeping close to home and deepening and sweetening ties to community. Each of them was a product of older agrarian mores that seemed, at the end of their long run of cultural relevancy and cachet, to be yielding unintended consequences. For example, the very skills inculcated in my father on the farm—superior mechanical aptitude, self-reliance, independence of mind and deed—by the late 1960s marked him, paradoxically, as someone more likely to leave the farm than to claim it. Meanwhile, my mother's culturally validated tendency to choose a "boy" over the opportunity to leave home for a higher education put her squarely in the rural-girl tradition and at the same time, in an era of second-wave feminism, made her susceptible to future regrets and what-ifs concerning roads less traveled. Jack and Jill found themselves suddenly in very liminal space—out of step if they followed the choose-love instincts cultivated in them as young ruralites, and out of place if they turned their back on that love and left home for the greater glories awaiting them in the city.

In her popular book *The Prairie Girl's Guide to Life*, country girl Jennifer Worick, who grew up in the Reagan-era Midwest, includes a chapter on the "Art of Courtship" from the prairie girl's perspective. "I'm a modern girl," Worick begins. "However, when it comes to dating, I'm decidedly old-fashioned." Advising the new generation of prairie girls in the time-honored art, Worick advises, "When you take notice of a young man, make eye contact. Shy glances, looking away, and then looking him in the eye will convey your interest without being too forward." Elsewhere Worick reminds young women that, "While a young man might come on like a house on fire, once he's reeled in, he might take you for granted or lose interest if you display too much interest. You don't want to scare him back to his homestead. Give a man space to come to you, to bring something to the table, to *win* you. Let him be a man, and enjoy being a girl."

Worick walks a fine line in her book, addressing a modern audience of young women—girls only in the colloquial sense—in the vernacular of the past. Her tack involves an often difficult mingling of the old and the new and yet, underpinning it all, lies the notion that some things never change—that a "girl" can exude a classic, pioneering spirit whether she lives in Manhattan, New York, or Manhattan, Kansas. In a sidebar labeled "The Modern Prairie Girl Way," she reminds urban women that "while it may seem near to impossible to meet eligible men in these modern times, think about how challenging it would be for gals on the open range. Pickin's were slim, as there probably weren't a lot of unattached men from which to choose, especially in the surrounding towns. But as prairie girls are wont to do, they made do." Worick exhorts young women to be strategic in their survey of potential loves. "On the subway, sit next to strapping men who are ringless, or at a bustling café, ask a boy if you can share his table."

Worick's worldview begs a larger question: Is it possible to be a prairie girl in spirit without really being one in practice or *in place*, similar to the way that a North Side Chicago hipster with a healthy trust fund and an abundant love of country music might parade

down Halsted Street wearing rhinestones and cowgirl boots without the slightest whiff of self-consciousness? And more than that,
do self-styled, latter-day pioneer girls imagine a wholly different
kind of romance and a different kind of partner than their fore-
mothers yearned for? Concerning courtship, what does a prairie
girl, whether real or simulated, really want, and how intent is she
on finding a mate who is the real thing?

In the country life movement of the early 1900s, that very question became a matter of national policy, as experts and technocrats
attempted to engineer a better country life to slow the migration
of the region's young to the cities. A slew of books accompanied
the movement, some offering academic treatments of the rural
out-migration problem while others approached it in the manner of chummy, just-between-you-and-me advice columns. Iowa's
"Uncle" Henry Wallace tackled courtship and other pressing matters facing prairie girls and boys in his 1897 *Letters to the Farm Boy*,
issued by MacMillan in a remarkable five editions between 1900
and 1918. Wallace, a former Presbyterian minister turned farmer
and editor of the iconic *Wallaces' Farmer* in Des Moines, earned the
colloquial title of uncle by virtue of his homespun, avuncular style,
as evidenced by his entrée into the difficult subject of finding the
right girl: "I sometimes think that it is essential to the right development of a boy that he should have, first, a dog; second a chum;
and third and last, his best gal." Elsewhere, in a letter titled "The
Farm Boy and His Start in Life," Uncle Henry, never one to mince
words, cautions,

> You will not get the right kind of a start by going in debt
> for a courting buggy, to spend your evenings in going to
> dances, circuses, etc., with some good-looking girl, who, if
> she would speak out, does not value you above one of her
> hairpins, who eats your caramels and ice cream, thinking,
> if she thinks about you at all, that you are a silly goose for
> wasting your substance in that kind of entertainment. She
> more than half suspects that the buggy is not paid for, she

knows you are wearing more stylish clothes than you can afford, and she secretly makes up her mind that while she will have all the fun she can with you, she will say "Yes" to an entirely different sort of fellow.

At other times Uncle Henry Wallace, grandfather to the future vice president and Progressive candidate for president Henry A. Wallace, recalls for his grandchildren the courtship strategies of his own young adulthood on the farm, forwarding them by way of recommendation:

> In the days of my youth the young man did not buy a shiny red buggy, and go in debt for it when he was courting. Instead, he managed, if possible, to get a good-looking horse, saddle, and bridle. If we younger boys saw any of the older boys taken with a sudden love of horseflesh and the trappings thereof, and saw one of them, in the cool of the summer evening or in the storms of winter . . . going to a certain house along about eight or nine o'clock, we knew there was something going on. If the horse was tied to the hitching post, we knew there was nothing serious yet, but if the young man put his horse in the barn and took off the saddle, then it was evident that he had become a "steady," and something pleasant was imminent. If there was a quilting bee, and certain mysterious nods and winks among the girls, then we were quite sure of it.

Author and humorist Homer Croy, who came of age in Maryville, Missouri, in the early 1900s, wrote of the intricacies of courtship between young men and women in his popular 1947 memoir *Country Cured*. Croy, whose farm memoirs sold in the hundreds of thousands and were issued in Armed Services editions beloved by homesick American GIs missing the Midwest, refers to the process as both art and science in his essay "Our Hat-Tipping Problem." Croy and his adolescent farm buddies hotly debated the question of whether interest should be shown a girl by a tip of the cap or not, as hat-tipping was then considered risqué, cutting-edge stuff. When Croy and his friend Harland see the prettiest girl in town, librarian Grace Langan, walking toward them, it's time for action rather than doctrine.

> How pretty she looked . . . how fashionable, [Croy recalls]. Inferiority laid hold of me and a sudden desire not to be seen gripped me. I wanted to edge over to the store window and pretend I had suddenly discovered something over-whelmingly interesting. . . . A craven thought came to me; maybe I could discover that one of my shoes had become unlaced and make a dive at it. She came closer, she saw us, and then—oh, then—she smiled and spoke. For one terri-fied moment I stared at her, paralyzed; then my hand shot up and I snatched my hat off and murmured "Howdy-do."

In Croy's day the star attraction for farm boys continued to be city girls, those specimens of beauty and refinement and exot-icism. Courtship in the countryside, among farm daughters and sons, was more measured—work, play, and incipient romance min-gling seamlessly at agrarian social institutions like the husking bee. Illinois filmmaker and farmer's son Herb Nadelhoffer recalls the "mating" opportunities of the husking bee in his 2010 documen-tary *Farmers, Corn, Cows & Hazy Memories*:

> Soon the huge harvest, silver-golden moon rose slowly in the eastern sky and flooded the scene with soft moon-light. The bonfire was roaring. The steaks were cooked by different men showing their caveman, bonfire prowess. Everyone dug into the food. After a while Warren Wells, a well-liked friend and prankster, jumped up and hollered out, "Husking Bee, Husking Bee. Grab a sack!" Everybody clapped, grabbed a gunnysack and rushed off into the nearby cornfield. Soon, shouting and laughter came drift-ing out. Everyone seemed excited, with even more shout-ing and laughter. Little did I know that an ear of Indian

corn was a ticket to have a free and unencumbered kiss with a person of their choosing. Not much of a reward, I thought at my young age.

Likewise, in an essay written for *Collier's*, Croy recalls the juicy details of the once-a-year husking bee in his home state of Missouri:

> Old Mr. Taylor, who lived on Clear Creek, had a large family of girls, and it didn't take him any time to get his fodder shucked out. Along in the fall he would spread his fodder on the hall floor of the barn and have a shucking bee. Every time you found a red ear you had to kiss your partner, and I certainly loved to shuck corn. It is my favorite recreation. The work never galls on me. I'm not much on standing corn, but when it comes to fodder I dearly love to strip the ear bare of its ensheltering, fibrous coat.

As quaint as Croy and Nadelhoffer make husking bees and corn-picking contests seem, the bees, with the dances and picnics and bonfires that often accompanied them, remained arguably the primary seasonal event at which rural young men and women met and mingled late into the 1940s. As late as 1948, my grandfather Edward Lee Jack had taken second in the National Plowing Contest as a crowd of 40,000—as many as today might attend a home game in the heart of Big Ten football country—looked on, rapt. Forty-mile-per-hour winds whipped up that day as Indianola's Robert Bowery bested Edward Lee Jack in a nail-biter where Bowery turned up thirty-two acres of earth and buried 90,000 hateful corn borers in a half hour, according to the *Cedar Rapids Gazette*. Reporter John Reynolds, incredulous before the magnitude of the event, set the scene as a novelist might, writing, "By noon the state highway patrol estimated that more than 8,000 cars had streamed through over the dust-clouded neighborhood roads and into the parking areas provided for them. From then until the sun began to slant sharply, the thousands milled over the ground followed the plowing contestants . . . and bought the biggest part of 30,000 sandwiches, 1,800 dozen ice-cream bars, thousands of bottles of pop, and hundreds of cups of coffee."

When the dust settled, my grandfather was awarded his second-place trophy by that year's Plowing Queen, Carolyn Wiese of nearby Bennett, Iowa, who had been presented her crown by Iowa's junior U.S. Senator Bourke B. Hickenlooper, begetting the unforgettable headline "Hick Crowns Queen." It had been a clean sweep for the Hawkeye State—first and second in clean-plowing and first in beauty in the form of the young Ms. Weise. A United Press news story from that very same year reported the excitement generated by another romantic competition happening at the national farm and garden show in Chicago. "Thousands of city folk crowded into the huge livestock show to watch the best products of the nation's fields judged," the dispatch read in a coy reference to the Prettiest Farmer's Daughter contest mounted that year. Competitions like these made explicit what those in farm country had long known: a crop is a crop is a crop, whether a corn-raised girl, boy, or ham hock.

By 1961 my grandfather had been married for just over two decades, but the romance of the Heartland corn-picking con-

test remained, as did its associations with the agrarian virtues of strength, stamina, and endurance. "Iowa not only grows tall corn, but also grows the men who know how to pick it. That's the indication from the results of the National Corn-Picking Contest held recently at Worthing-

Edward Jack, state champion corn-picker, 1961.

National Corn-picking
Contest, Worthington,
Minnesota, 1961.

ton, Minnesota," the *Akron Register-Tribune* reported that fall. My
grandfather had made it to nationals again after winning the 1961
state corn-picking championship competition sponsored by WMT
Radio, though lady luck ran out on him in Worthington. "Ed Jack,
Mechanicsville, placed seventh in the picker-sheller competition,"
the front-page article in the *Register-Tribune* read. "His machine
had developed an undetectable shelled corn leak shortly after
starting his contest run, which cost him points for shelled corn left
in the field." The day had been a resounding success in every other
way, however, with attendance topping 50,000, and the wheels
of many other courtships well-greased along the way. R. Sargent
Shriver, director of the newly formed Peace Corps, made a strategic appearance to court young farm sons and daughters into the
growing ranks of the peace army John Kennedy had created with
an executive order earlier in the spring of that year.

Despite the unexpected mechanical failure of his beloved Oli-
ver corn-picker, my grandfather was all smiles after the competition. Pictures show him grinning gamely, a ribbon pinned to his
pinstripe coveralls, his squeamish right-hand man and understudy,
my eleven-year-old father, and his best gal, my grandmother, both
standing at his side.

—»•«—

In 1950 my father came roaring into the world. He would later claim that he had flown in as a starchild, an interstellar traveler crash-landing on the endless American prairie, a boy Superman.

Records on Planet Earth, however, say he was born into the world on the July day in 1950 when Ted Williams broke his elbow in the all-star game in Chicago. Like so many baby boomers, my father was unplanned, an accident, a gift from God, the last of four children, the fated and feted late-arriving boy-child. After being blessed with three consecutive girls, my grandfather thrilled at the idea of a son, a lifelong helpmate and one-day inheritor of a family farm that had, by 1950, already been running nearly a century.

Michael, the archangel, the slayer of the serpent, the defeater of Satan, prince among men. By the summer of 1950 my grand-parents' union had abided just a few months shy of a decade. Theirs was not an easy marital knot to untangle; by instinct, they disagreed about most everything, including what names their children ought to have. On the naming front, they fought and ultimately won a difficult truce—my grandmother would choose the children's first names and my grandfather would choose the middles. The even-tual appellations came out sounding like what they in fact were: a mash-up of two remarkably different people. In my father's case my grandmother chose the mellifluous Michael, and my grandfather the almost inexplicable Allen, a middle name my father considered kryptonite from his first day on Planet Earth.

Fate decreed that my father would be born not in Chicago, St. Paul, or Omaha but in Mechanicsville, Iowa, a farm town and self-professed Pork Center of the World. The local sawbones, Dr. Littig, delivered him back in the days when small-town doctors sought the grace of bringing blithe souls into the world while the cows lowed in the fields and family members were dispatched to fetch cold compresses. Mechanicsville was not Palm Beach or Virginia Beach or any kind of beach for that matter, but a rail stop for hundreds of thousands of hogs destined for slaughter in the Chicago stockyards. Despite his landlocked hometown, my father was born into travel every bit as much as if he had been born in Istanbul or Gibraltar or the Panama Canal. The northern reaches of our family land bordered on U.S. Highway 30, a leg in the legendary Lincoln Highway, the first transcontinental route across the United States. Just a few years after my father's birth, Eisenhower's National System of Interstate and Defense Highways would come along, but before that, his hometown was one of hundreds located on the one major east-west artery on the entire continent. He might as well have arrived on wheels, honking and flashing his high beams.

My grandmother, bless her, possessed a talent for many things— art, ceramics, cooking, sewing, and all intuitive matters of the spirit—but she was decidedly awful at recordkeeping. The pages of my father's baby book are to this day mostly void of entries, whole months passing without remark at the family's new miracle. There must have been something especially auspicious to her then, when in May 1951, a day after my father took his first steps, she recorded that he said "bye-bye" to her and waved. At ten months my father was already on wheels.

My dad in 1951; still in diapers, but on the move.

In 1955 he had only just begun to read, yet his favorite story, the one he would learn to read from, was a parable about an owl who flew too far and too fast away from his parents. The reading was followed in his school workbook by a small test that my grandparents would save for the next fifty years despite their son's subpar performance on it. Whether the baby owl had a moral obligation to return to the nest was an existential question their son was not yet old enough to answer. If one had the power to fly, why on earth would one ever submit to having one's wings clipped? More to the point, why would an owl-father who was himself a flyer by nature, if not in practice, ever ask his owl-son to remain near the nest?

By the time he turned fourteen in 1964, my father's need for speed, for movement, had grown to encompass flying. At an age when many of his peers spent their days agonizing over what to wear to school and who was their favorite Beatle, my father was flying Aeronca and Taylorcraft single-engine prop planes high above our fields. Twelve months in, his nascent enthusiasm for aviation caused his father to begin taking the same lessons. The dream of the fourteen-year-old boy and his forty-seven-year-old father coalesced in the air: hard-won perspective, mobility, and the freedoms that lay beyond mere duty.

When his high school newspaper caught up with my seventeen-year-old father in the spring of 1968, farming was the last thing on his mind. "Mike's favorite pastime is flying their airplane, the Taylorcraft," dished budding journalist Sandy Donohoe. With my grandfather's help, he had built a hangar and widened a watercourse between two cornfields into a grass runway running north and south. "He has a student pilot license and is working on his private license. Mike hopes to attain advanced ratings and secure a job flying in the future. . . . We at Lincoln would like to wish Mike the best of luck in the future," the paper said in something like a send-off.

My father might have wished he could return the magnanimous sentiments where his alma mater was concerned. High school had felt more like a prison camp or detention center to him. Though he had participated in newspaper and yearbook, he had spent as little time within the confining walls of Lincoln-Stanwood High School as possible, his farm-bred sense of self-reliance and independence of mind already conflicting directly with the authority-minded, buzz-cut conformity demanded by an agrarian high school in the 1960s. "P.S. That is, if the Service doesn't get me first," my father had added at the conclusion of his senior profile, knowing full well that in 1968, an eighteen-year-old young man without a college deferment and with hundreds of hours in the air would be on a direct collision course with Uncle Sam's draft.

⟹••⟸

My parents wed in 1968, just nine days after my father's eighteenth birthday and less than a month after they had finished their senior years. "The bride, given in marriage by her father," the *Cedar Rapids Gazette* article covering the nuptials read, "chose for her wedding a white gown of rose point lace styled in an A-line with an emporia waist, round collar and short sleeves and wore a floor-length veil of silk illusion gathered to a white bow head piece adorned with roses. She carried an arrangement of white roses and babies breath."

There's something bittersweet in reading the yellowed newsprint that captures my mother at a defining moment, the pinnacle of her young life and the height of her powers. She was a Midwest farmer's daughter, naive by comparison with her town peers, taking a mighty chance on the love of a nearby farmer's son. Much like my grandparents' union, my parents' marriage promised to yoke two successful farming families. The agrarian order of things, it seemed, had been preserved. My mom, the *Gazette* article reported, was employed at American College Testing Program, better known by test-loathing high school kids everywhere simply by its acronym, ACT, but it did not mention that her job was purely clerical, fill-in work—nothing permanent or sustaining. "As a farmer's daughter, it was not really important to my folks that their daughters go for a college education," she tells me. "They thought that we would be taken care of, or that we would get married and have kids. Higher education wasn't really encouraged; in fact it was a little discouraged. I knew pretty much from the tenth grade on that I was on my own to figure it out. And then I pretty much felt like I had a choice of getting married or going to college, so I chose getting married and always regretted it." Back then, she reminds, it wasn't unusual to get married at eighteen in the small-town Midwest. All of her best friends were married by twenty.

In the summer of 1968 my parents moved away from their families' farms for the first time ever and into a small mobile home my father's parents had helped the newlyweds purchase on the outskirts of Iowa City. It was a challenging moment for a farmer's son and farmer's daughter in their first year of marriage. The threat of the Selective Service and the specter of global communism hung over my father, while the growing women's liberation movement simultaneously concerned and compelled my mother.

In his class with Professor Pope, my father deconstructed the law-and-order presidential campaign of Alabama's former governor George Wallace, opening his paper with a paraphrase of *Time* magazine's 1968 article "Fear Campaign." "Law and order," he wrote, "is a pervasive and obsessive issue in view of the rising crime rate, ghetto unrest, disrupted universities, and violent demonstrations." Elsewhere, my father, who opposed the war in Vietnam, wrote in his "Analysis of the Relationship between Man and Society in Marx, Mill, and Freud, and Dostoevsky." "I view Marx's communism as very degrading of human nature. In Marx's 'classless society,' I feel man would be reduced to an un-thinking machine without any drive to improve and differentiate himself and, thusly, he would soon lose his identity among the masses. This, I believe, is the true tragedy of communism." At other times Dad found his own plight as a farmer's son reflected in his study of Western civilizations, where his hand-scrawled paper on feudalism no doubt echoed the plight of his fellow young farmers nearly an hour away in Cedar County, where my father worked, unpaid, for his father during the plowing and harvesting season:"Fief—a fief is an element of feudalism; a fief, or a grant of land, was given to a vassal by his lord in return for the vassal's loyalty and military service." Next Dad contemplated the French peasantry in an essay for Professor Schneebeck, and here again his writings reflected on the agrarian culture he came from, a culture that, a mere generation earlier, had produced the Cow Wars, the first agrarian rebellion since Shays' Rebellion in the Revolutionary War. "The peasantry," he wrote of the reign of King Louis, "had many social and economic grievances at this time. The peasants were utterly in famine from the high prices, lack of employment, and high taxes that were imposed upon them. Under the manorial system the peasants were obliged to pay their lord many duties and taxes. Thus, the peasants resented the nobility."

My father's worst grade in his abbreviated two-year stint at the University of Iowa came on a paper about women and marriage, the institution he himself had newly entered, and it came in a class that had been his strength back in high school: literature. In his paper for Professor Searle on Chaucer's "The Merchant's Tale" my dad wrote, "Before considering the tale itself, I must confess being somewhat predisposed concerning Chaucer's views on marriage by my reading of some of the other *Canterbury Tales*. In two I have read ('The Nun's Priest's Tale' and 'The Wife of Bath's Tale'), Chaucer incessantly reiterates his obvious contempt of women and marriage. It is also my understanding that, historically, Chaucer's love life was quite unpleasant and this undoubtedly led him to treat women and marriage in such a harsh manner." Professor Searle, whose exceedingly high standards my dad would recall with fondness years later, sparred with him in the margins of his papers, writing, "this is of questionable relevance, though interesting. Chaucer was not all that much miserable."

Dad concluded his paper with a brand of moral certainty that would be one of his lifelong calling cards, writing,

> In my analysis of this tale the main thematic conclusion seems clear; Chaucer executes a point-blank blast at the deceitfulness of women and their role in marriage. Chaucer also presents other subtle entities concerning women and marriage which may be implied if not directly ascertained: one should be cautious in choosing one's mate; physical infatuation is not a basis for true love; great divergence of age is a detrimental factor in marriage. . . . In

other words Chaucer leaves the tale open to a variety of interpretations which are dependent on the personal inclinations of the reader. However one may infer, translate, or construe this tale, Chaucer's poignant and bitter views on women and marriage leave no margin for interpretation.

Beyond his high-spirited debate with young Professor Searle, the farmer's son and aspiring pilot in my father had begun to win out, and increasingly, he and my mom found themselves separated, both by their off-campus status and their shared rural roots, from the more pronounced, more grandstanding radicalism of their unmarried peers in the dorms. And though academe's grander, more abstract truths tempted them both, my father in particular grew frustrated with their lack of real-world application, and the practical pleasures of piloting began to call him anew.

While my dad searched the want ads for jobs in aviation, my mom had quit her job grading exams for ACT ("I always hated desk work") and had likewise let go a job at Sweeting's flower shop due to the overt sexism of her boss. On a whim she walked into Enzler's gift shop one day pretty much without prospects. She was offered a job the very next day.

That my father would drop out of the University of Iowa to help his father farm and to pursue a career in aviation; that my mother would soon be pregnant with her own farmer's daughter; that my parents would go on to struggle mightily in their marriage; all these remained as yet unseen in the winter of 1970 when my father walked to the dean's office to officially withdraw from the university. "For their wedding trip to the Wisconsin Dells the bride wore a navy and white striped mini dress," my parents' *Gazette* wedding announcement had read, and for a blessed moment in the life of a small farm town the details of their own auspicious union—who served the tiered cake and who carried daisies—mattered as much as communism and feudalism and race riots. Somehow, in spite of all these, Jack had found Jill, as Shakespeare himself reminded his audience in *A Midsummer Night's Dream*, and naught had gone ill.

By 1974, when my father left his new job as the manager of the Iowa Falls municipal airport to help my grandfather farm, he voted with his feet at precisely the hour of greatest need for a midsized family farm like ours in a profession the Associated Press called in 1971 "one of the biggest gambles on earth." He hadn't wanted to return to the family acres, but a host of compelling arguments for doing so had presented themselves. Already he had run afoul of his hard-driven boss at the airport and his infant son was seriously ill with a not-yet-diagnosed malady. But the true tipping point proved to be the news from home that his sister Barbara had been pressed into "active duty" in the barnyard by my grandfather, so desperate was he for help.

Some forty years later, I ask my mom if any of her boomer friends have remained married to working farmers. After lengthy consideration, she shakes her head. Some of her town girlfriends had married hobby farmers later in life, but that was about it. I ask why she alone was the first among her four sisters to marry a farmer's son, but she sees no special cosmic logic to it, no underlying element of fate. "It was a roll of the dice," she tells me. "I hate to say this, but things were more simple back then. . . . I don't remember thinking about who I was going to marry, or how many kids I was going to have. . . . Back then you're going for good-looking, smart, best car. . . . If I was a deep-thinker I probably wouldn't have gone for that because at that time I didn't like being on the farm."

I'm tempted to chalk my mom's feelings about the farm up to that centuries-old narrative—girls and young women feeling confined in the hinterlands and yearning to break away into the fashionable and fun life of the city. But I know too that something different—something troubling if the *sustainable* in sustainable farming was ever to continue—was just then taking root.

⟫●⟪

By the late 1970s, even the family unity created by the Wind in the Walnuts rural arts fair we'd hosted had likewise given way to sexual division. My mother had initiated the first of several separations from my father, taking us to one of her own father's family farms a half dozen miles from home. My aunt Susan, the only one of the daughters to have moved more than a half dozen miles from the farm after marriage, had divorced her husband, bringing her three children back to the farm that had been the site of our arts fair; my aunt Patricia would divorce her husband and reclaim her country home in the years to come.

The agricultural crisis of the 1980s found my sister and me splitting time between the temporary home my mom had made for us in rural Johnson County, nearer Iowa City, and the family farm in Cedar County. But even in our new temporary home, the breakup and breakdown of the farm life seemed to follow us. In 1985 our *Time* magazine arrived a day before Christmas bearing the latest grisly news from the farm crisis. This time the violence had struck close to home—ten miles down the road from where my mom had moved my sister and me—at a branch of the bank whose principal offices were just a few miles away from our temporary quarters. Fifteen hundred mourners turned out for the memorial service for the banker whose life had been taken by a disgruntled and desperate family farmer, Dale Burr. I remember flipping through the pages of *Time* that Christmas wondering grimly if Iowa had made national news, only to find my worst suspicions confirmed. The article, "He Couldn't Manage Any More," took for its title that matter-of-fact observation of Burr, whose family had worked the land for three generations, gone flat broke, and ended up owing more than a half a million dollars in debt on his 560 acres in Lone Tree, Iowa, about a dozen miles south of where Mom had enrolled us in elementary school. The article continued, "That pride, perhaps mingled with psychopathy, boiled over in Burr last week when he went on a calculated shooting spree, killing his wife, a bank president, and fellow farmer before taking his own life. The grotesque tragedy reflected the agony of America's beleaguered farm belt, where in the past three years, thousands of spreads have been foreclosed and dozens of banks have shut down in the worst economic crisis since the Depression."

The president of our state's banking association, Neil Milner, pointed out that Burr had been "far from destitute" and that the equity in the farm alone would have easily paid off his debts. As always, the members of the perpetrator's rural community, when asked, expressed shocked disbelief. "Nobody thought Dale would do things like that," a neighbor farmer of Burr's told *Time.* "His life was his wife and that farm of his." Shootings like the one in Hills had also happened in Minnesota and Nebraska, causing even established farmers like my dad to question the sanctity and security of their chosen profession.

For a third-grade penmanship exercise, I was asked to write about a happy moment in my life. "One day I was with my dad in the country," began the piece I dutifully titled "A Happy Day." "We were driving down the road to visit somebody and we saw five eagles flying above the trees. They were gliding very slowly. But pretty soon they were out of sight. After that, I felt happy." Still, by the late 1980s, it seemed there wasn't much to be happy about where my father, and the farm he superintended, were concerned. Shortly thereafter came the announcement he would semiretire. We would keep our land, but the real work of planting and harvesting would fall to neighbors, with my dad managing the farm and providing an operational assist when needed.

The first of what would be two auctions of our farm, held more than twenty years apart, was scheduled for March 3, 1987, one day before my mother's thirty-seventh birthday. The very same auction year in which my dad downsized our operation by two-thirds, my class was assigned a prompt from our language arts teacher: "Imagine you have received the name of a pen pal in another country. Write a letter to your pen pal, introducing yourself and describing your family, and your community." Ink pen in hand, I began:

> *Hello my name is Zachary Michael Jack. I am on the short side with dark brown eyes and light brown hair. As you may or may not have heard, Iowa farmers are going through some very hard times. My dad is a*

farmer, so I understand some of these problems, and I would like to explain these problems. In general it is becoming very unprofitable to farm. The farmers have grown too much crop and the government hasn't been able to sell very much. Therefore the prices have gone way down and many farmers cannot turn enough profit to pay back their bank loans so the bank must take their farms away from them. Nothing worthwhile is being done by the government to save these farmers. The Midwest has often been called the nation's heartland and just as in the body if your heart stops pumping your whole body dies. I love the farm and the farm life, and I think it would be a great loss if the farmers could no longer farm the land that has been farmed before them.

On a happier note, I hope to receive another letter from you soon.

<hr/>

"It has rightly been said that we 'grow on the back of giants.' The men and women who chose our land to people were pioneers, giant types," read an epigraph in our town's centennial history. Included in a list of "pioneer families" were my grandmother's people, the Puffers, and a complicated, almost biblical family tree whose last paragraph ended in me: "Julia was married to Ed Jack, parents of: Patricia, married to Charles Coon, parents of Arminda, Timothy and Jason; Susan married to Robert Sullivan, parents of Rodney, Sara, and Andrew; Barbara; Michael, married to Gail W., parents of Tasha and Zachary."

Other dusty tomes on the shelves of our local library traced the pioneer lineage back still further, to my great-great-great-grandfather Everette and his brother Ray, of whom biographer C. Ray Aurner wrote in 1910, "The grandfather Charles Puffer was

On the back of giants, pioneers Everette and Grace Puffer, 1905.

one of the first settlers of . . . [the] county coming to the Middle West from New Hampshire. From pioneer times therefore the Puffer family has been identified with the growth and progress of this section of the state." At the feet of Ray's brother, Everette, the book also laid laurels:

> Farming constitutes the foundation of success in all life and he who carefully and conscientiously tills the soil contributes to the world's progress. On a farm on section 26 Pioneer township lives Everette Puffer who tills the fields and feeds his stock upon a tract of land of one hundred and twenty-five acres while altogether he operates two hundred acres. His homestead was also his birthplace his natal day being April 24, 1879. The paternal grandfather was one of the first settlers of Cedar County and amid pioneer surroundings the father was reared sharing in the hardships and privations that always constitute an element in frontier life. After attaining man's estate he chose as a companion and helpmate for life's journey Miss Arminda Boyles who was born in Pennsylvania and gave him her hand in marriage in 1873. They began their domestic life upon a farm and to the usual duties of the agriculturist Mr. Puffer continued to devote his time and energies until his death which occurred about 1894. His wife still survives him and is now living in Mechanicsville. Their family numbered three children: Ray a farmer of Pioneer township who is mentioned on another page of this volume, Mabel the wife of Claude Harper of Saint John Washington, and Everette, who is the youngest of the family.

Love and its cousins Longing and Desire grew our family tree, but our place, the place in which we had rooted ourselves—the place with which we had entered an enduring bond and contract—had also helped make our happy prospects. How different are they, really, soils and seedbeds, sewing and reaping, marital knots, sacred vows, long rows to hoe, seeds to be planted and nurtured, and sometimes, when things go bad, root-kill, failure to thrive? And where would any of my family be, I wonder, had the union of Everette and Arminda not endured and borne fruit? The biographer continues, "At the time of his marriage Mr. Puffer took up his abode on the farm where he has since lived his attention being largely given to the raising and feeding of sheep and hogs his specialty being Shropshire sheep and Chester White hogs selling three carloads of each annually. He cares for his stock after the most modern methods and therefore sends them to market in good condition and receives therefore a high price." It helped that Everette had set up shop in a railroad town that would become known as the Pork Center of the World, but without husbandry of all kinds, the business of farming, which was synonymous with the business of marriage, would surely have been bankrupt.

Though my own parents would come back together again on the farm in the years to come, their separation, coupled with the wake-up call of the farm crisis, had shaken us all into a sense of profound vulnerability. We had come this close to losing it all—farm, family, legacy, identity—and in the years that followed I would feel my role as heir-apparent becoming increasingly ceremonial. While as a farmer's son, I felt deeply loved and empowered, I doubted that I was the standard-bearer my father needed me to be, at the very same time that he had preempted any real choice I might have had to follow him into the profession by selling off all but a few of the heaviest pieces of our equipment. He thought he was doing me a favor, lending me the kind of wings he'd desperately wanted when, years earlier, he'd left home to run the airport, only to be drawn back less than a year later by the gravity of a father and a needy farm. For a brief, dizzying moment he had achieved what astronauts call escape velocity.

And just as swiftly as the auction came and went, my father and I were free, tethered together in our collective untethering, feeling an exhilaration that felt like love: its rush, its vertigo, and its free fall.

—————»•«—————

In 1995 I took a chance on an elective class taught under the auspices of the anthropology department at my state's land-grant agricultural college. The class concerned the ancient Greek mystery
cults, and our bespectacled, smart-as-a-whip professor had done
fieldwork at many of the ancient sites, and thus I hung on her
every word. I scribbled note after note, highlighted her more salient
points in green, and especially those related to the oracles. "Divination was widely resorted to by individuals and by states in Ancient
Greece," one note read. Below it I had taken more copious notes
about the methods thereof—divination by lots, interpretation of
signs such as Roman auspices, and finally, the most prestigious of
all, I noted, "oral divinations" heard at the source. My notes make
mention of divine vapors exhaled through the rock at the temple at Delphi set atop the *omphalos*, the navel-stone, the center of
the world—the way Mechanicsville, Iowa, was the *umbilicus* of my
Heartland universe. The spirit of a place was its *genius loci*.

Turning the page I'd crowded my slate with further remarks
grouped under the heading "Private Roman religion at the lararium." The lararium, I noted, was the part of the house where offer-
ings and sacrifices were made beneath representations of the family
and its descendants, a shrine within the house where the family
guardians, the Lares, were worshipped and the family relics kept.
"The Lares," I highlighted back in 1995, "almost always come in
pairs as two young men, wearing country clothes, and carrying
drinking horns. The Lares flank the genius of the paterfamilias," the
clan's principle of generation.

In my notebook *genius* is defined as "the guardian spirit of a
man, a family, or a state. In some instances, a place, a city, or an institution had its genius." The *genius* was not easily portable or inter-
changeable. The Lares, those two country boys, lived in a house, at
a place, and along with the Iuno, or Juno—the attendant genius of
the women of the house—owed their power and their currency

to a particular plot of earth. The man's *genius* or the woman's *juno* could endure away from home, but only when the *genius* of the place and its people matched their own could the man or woman fully realize their personal power.

The guardian spirit of a man, a family, or place. It was the *genius* of the place I grappled with most when I considered my and my family's romance, its nearly fatal attraction, to our corner of the good earth. The *genius* was unique to a place, to a region, to the man and the woman, Jack and Jill, begotten of its soils. The *genius* had the power, if you let it, to show you the house where love truly lived.

Young and the Restless

Years ago I drew circles in an oversized Rand McNally atlas my best friend, Jarod, absentmindedly left behind in one of our many adolescent road campaigns together. There had been our aborted attempt to hop a freight train on the tracks south of our junior high school; the college road trip to visit our mutual friend, Jonathan, in Hope, Michigan, during which we unsuccessfully posed as two authors writing a book about the best milkshake in America, hoping, of course, to score gratis vanilla malts en route. In the years since those youthful flights of fancy the orphaned atlas has become the Velveteen Rabbit of road maps. Loved too well and too often, its loose pages now slip from its cover like oysters from the half shell.

The aspirational oblongs and escapist vectors I sketched in my own atlas did not encompass Florida, as my father's and grandfather's did, but instead marked a parabolic path from the Missouri Ozarks to southern Illinois's Shawnee National Forest, and across the muddy Mississippi to western Kentucky. Anywhere in this unbroken circle I hoped to gain purchase in a culture metaphysically and topographically different from the flatter lands I called home. The elliptical orbits I'd sketched represented my own awkward gestures at grace, at inscribing the vectors from which new lives sometimes take unexpected flight. Native midwesterner Vance Randolph once wrote of the Ozark region in which he transplanted himself, "resistance to change has always been the chief regional characteristic of the Ozark people," who, he claimed, were the "most deliberately unprogressive people in the United States."

At the time I was eager to be among people who clung even more fiercely to their ways than I did to my own.

Perhaps the circle's greatest allure, in the end, is that it inscribes no rigid logic. I was looking for a spot within a day's drive of my home place where one might experience something like wilderness and where one might enjoy a more mild winter clime. It ought, I reasoned, to be accessible by major road, but not too accessible, folkways forever falling before interstate highways. And it must be eminently affordable, a place where a small home and a handful of acres could be acquired for the price of a middle-of-the-road sedan. All these factors, and others, pointed me in the direction of Vance Randolph's Ozarks.

It may have been this same instinct, a kneejerk reflex away from the entrapment of a heritage farm that had been my family's blessing and cross to bear since 1855, that had likewise caused my grandfather to snowbird his brood down to Florida each winter beginning in 1955. And it must have been some particularly virulent strain of that same yeoman's wanderlust that had caused him once to buy a quarter-acre lot from a pitchman at a weekend convention, sight unseen, in what he thought was Florida, and where he was assured a first-class resort community would take root alongside a piney manmade lake. My grandfather visited the property only once, finding it not, as he had been led to believe, in the Sunshine State, but a few miles across the border in Alabama. Already the street signs had been choked by kudzu in a development that had never quite gotten off the ground.

The anticipatory circles I drew across southern Missouri in my own Rand McNally atlas, then, had in a way been genetically prefigured. Such a sentence no doubt sounds positively medieval— whimsical in the extreme, this alchemical notion that a grandson could inherit his grandfather's wanderlust in the same way he might inherit his passions or addictions. Or maybe the grandchildren are merely socialized into such intergenerational affinities— fated to love what their forebears loved, destined to dust off their maps leading to places named Success and Happiness. In any case I had been taught early on that the measure of a man's success could be taken, in part, by progress toward two unattainable standards: weed-free farm fields and a week or two away from the tyranny of a midwestern winter. The man who could achieve both in a single lifetime would be a Merlin of the Midlands, his road map and atlas as integral to his magic as his hoe and plowshare.

⸺•◦•⸻

My grandfather's maps and the sojourns they described didn't begin with Florida, but in the more familiar "foreign" lands nearer our native Corn Belt: Missouri, Arkansas, and Louisiana. In 1939 he agreed to serve as chief chauffeur and travel companion for his own aging mother and father on their first trip to the Deep South, via Missouri, where a branch of my grandmother's people had pioneered in tiny Show-Me State hamlets like Mercer, Lucerne, and Cleopatra in the early 1870s. Still, the farthest south any of our kin had ventured into Missouri terra incognita had been Excelsior Springs. On this trip, however, my grandfather and his parents pushed deeper into the hills, visiting Lake Tanecomo in the Lake of the Ozarks, and staying briefly at the legendary Musser's Ozark Resort south of the Bagnell Dam north of Eldon. The popular resort featured a dance pavilion, tennis courts, a golf course, and an enormous luxury swimming pool, but my grandfather lacked his best gal alongside to enjoy them with. "Am missing you every minute," he wrote Julia Mae Puffer, the woman who would become his wife one year later, on a postcard sent from Springfield. "The Ozarks are beautiful."

Still, the road that had promised my grandfather romance had instead brought him loneliness. Late on a Sunday night in November of 1939, just a few short days after Thanksgiving, he had written my grandmother to tell her he would go mad if he didn't see her soon. "I am not having the fun on a trip like this that I should have, all because you are not here. I would much rather be with you

MUSSER'S OZARK RESORT
9 MILES NORTH OF BAGNELL DAM
3 MILES SOUTH OF ELDON MO.
HIGHWAYS 52 AND 54

LAKE TANEYCOMO
IN THE OZARKS

right now than travel around the world. What good does it do a person to travel if he is unhappy?"

From these nearer-by lily pads came the leap further westward to California in late 1936—his first cross-country trip. To be a young midwesterner in the 1930s meant being on the move, and in packing their suitcases the young at heartland undertook a delicate balancing act. Offered up to the wider harvest—the reaping—of ambitious young people reared in a region founded on Yankee values of education and civic-mindedness, midwestern youth had become a sought-after nursery species as their entire agrarian region served as seedbed for the boomtowns of the West. When a Heartland parent dropped off their nursery stock at the local train station, there loomed the omnipresent threat that their youthful emissary would become a permanent transplant in the elsewhere to which they were headed, just as the song lyrics warned would happen if ever the earnestly farm-reared saw the lights of "Gay Paree."

By the time my grandfather turned teenager in 1930, nearly 40 percent of Iowa-born people lived outside their home state's borders, with similar rates of absenteeism prevailing in many states in the nation's Heartland. The dramatic exodus of the region's young compelled Wisconsin writer Glenway Wescott to conclude that the Midwest boiled down to "a state of mind of people born where they do not want to live." The Middle American members of the Lost Generation—most famously Wescott, Sherwood Anderson, Ernest Hemingway, F. Scott Fitzgerald, and Gertrude Stein—weren't the only young minds putting Wescott's quip into practice. By the Great Depression many of the region's young had pulled up stakes for the West. In Los Angeles in 1930 youthful émigrés from Illinois, Iowa, Missouri, and Ohio numbered in excess of 200,000—nearly one-fifth of the city's population. A generation later, historian Jon Gjerde writes in *The American Midwest*, out-migration from the Heartland to the West continued, with a 1960 survey showing most newcomers to the City of Angels had been born in Minnesota, Iowa, Missouri, North Dakota, South Dakota, Nebraska, and Kansas.

Parents to a twenty-year-old farmer's son, as my grandfather was in 1937, would want their son to spread his wings—but not so much, or so fast, as would take him away from hearth and farm permanently. And yet to deny him the right to try, especially after years of delayed gratification, would seem harsh and overcontrolling—out of step with modernity not to mention the Jones's boy or girl down the road, who had already disembarked to see such far-off places and who had, in many cases, already found lucrative work or military station in some distant boomtown. In effect, Heartland farm parents of the 1920s and 1930s wanted postcards from their leave-taking young men and women, pretty pictures of the breath-taking sights along the route, so long as the road led their wayfaring children back home again. Wish-you-were-heres must originate with them—the family left behind on the home acres keeping the light on and the chickens fed—not from the prodigal on the road. "I hope you got my letter I wrote before telling you to send . . . a postcard view of different places, just a remembrance is all, and they will be glad to get them," my great-grandmother reminded her son on his first big trip out West. The prodigal children of the Middle West were to be allowed the sowing of few wild oats, the seeing of the sights, a temporary bunking down with an old high school chum who'd since moved away perhaps, but not much else. After all, the continuance of the farm life depended on their return from the bright lights of this or that American Paris.

My grandfather had played the part of eager cartographer since his boyhood days in the one-room schoolhouse at the crossroads down the road from the farm, Pioneer Number Five. He had barely learned to tie his shoes, in fact, and already his teacher was assigning him to draw maps of the United States, over and over again, until he had its shape and proportion down. By the time he turned ten in the winter of 1927 he could draw the outlines of his expansive, travel-friendly nation in his sleep, though his maps show a tendency to pinch the East and gift the largesse to the West—an understandable sleight of hand for a boy growing up west of the Mississippi.

A decade later he decided to follow, for real, the exploratory lines of those early dewy-eyed schematics, hitching a ride west with his pal Bert who was traveling to the promised land of California. His first letter home to the farm from California dated Monday, November 30, 1936, read,

> Dear Folks:
> Well, I am finally in Hollywood. Boy, it sure is a big place. We got here about 6 P.M. last night (Sunday night). We left Oklahoma City at 10:00 P.M. Thursday night. Bert's sister's husband's mother came with us from Clinton, Oklahoma, to Banning, California. It sure is warm here. We rode all yesterday afternoon with our sleeves rolled up and the windows rolled down. That doesn't seem possible, does it?

With their new passenger in tow, the boys—or is it more accurate to call twenty-year-olds making a cross-country trek over muddy mountain roads *men*?—drove from Phoenix to Los Angeles in roughly ten hours to reach the Hollywood Mission Garage where their old buddy from high school, Scoop, worked. Scoop, however, was gone for the day. My grandfather picks up the note: "I looked around until 6:45 and who should drive into the garage but Scoop and his mother. They had been out riding all day. They said they were sure glad to see someone from home. She asked over and over what was new at home."

Imagine the relief a Heartlander must have felt in the waning days of 1936 to see a face from her hometown some two thousand miles away—a little farm town on the edge of the prairie that must literally have seemed a distant memory. And now here they were—familiar emissaries from a life Scoop and his mother had left behind, and that my grandfather was now seriously thinking of jettisoning as well. It had been a harrowing journey from the flatter lands back home, through snow so thick in the mountains, my grandfather wrote, "we couldn't even see the radiator cap." A terrifying skid that pushed them against a rock wall (and dented the fender of their car) had been the act of grace that saved them from plunging down the mountainside to certain death.

My grandfather arrived to find Scoop rooming with another of the service station employees in a tiny house with only two beds, meaning my grandfather and his out-migrating old pal from home had to share a bed. "I don't know whether to try to get a job or not," he wrote, already at loose ends. "Might just stick around for a few days and then start for home. Well, I can't think of anything else to say. Unless if you want to write to me you can put this address on it:

> Edward Jack
> 1232 N. Highland Avenue
> Hollywood, CA.

He must have written the address with a twin sense of fear and wonderment, as if he had temporarily stepped out of one skin and into another. Still, I imagine there must have been no small amount of pride in its inscription too—"little ol' me in sunny CA . . . and the folks half a country away huddled around the woodstove at the old home place." Elsewhere, almost as an aside, he writes, "I saw Mary Astor's ex-husband last night. He is a doctor and stopped in at the garage for gasoline"—the brief anecdote no doubt calcu-

lated to impress his mother and younger sister back home, Sissy, for
whom he also included a Star Map of all the famous Hollywood
celebrities that lived near the service station.

The letters from home my grandfather coyly hinted that he
would like to receive arrived in the coming days bearing six-cent
airmail stamps with a picture of a biplane and the caption "airmail
saves time." Somehow his mother must have sensed the leitmotif
of homesickness playing between the lines of her son's first note
home, or perhaps my grandfather had merely summoned those
introductory blue notes for his mother's benefit, to ease her pangs
of separation and loss. To admit to joy, to name it, would have been
to abandon his inherited sense of midwestern fatalism. Better practiced at consolation than at jubilation, my grandmother's conciliatory note in reply shows a woman who must privately have felt
she had won the battle for her son's geographic loyalties, such that
she could afford to be magnanimous where the Golden State was
concerned:

> I believe by the trend of your letters you don't like
> California as well as you thought. I wish you had some
> means of getting out in the country and seeing around,
> a city is just a city wherever it is but the country must
> be pretty there if you just had the chance to see it. . . .
> Ed, if you don't want to stay don't try to get a job—just
> stay long enough to see around and do try to take in
> all you can while you're there, for it's a long ways out
> there and the trip can't be made very often, so make
> good use of your time there if you can. If you need more
> money just telegraph for some—Bird Bennett paid his
> thresh bill so don't be bashful—just say if you need
> more. Don't skimp on yourself in any way. There's no
> need of it this year anyway and you may never get the
> chance to go out there again. Bring Sissy some little
> souvenir from Hollywood, but don't mind the rest of
> us. We don't care for Hollywood as she does. . . . Ed, I

think you better come home by train instead of bus as the highways are not the best this time of year and a train is best all around I think. . . . Monday night we went to see Ramona. It sure was a beautiful picture. It was filmed in California and if the countryside looks like it did in the picture it is worth taking a look at. It's a wonder you boys weren't killed on that mud road. Why in the world did you take such a road as that? You will probably have a hard time getting back with all those clothes to look after. Check your suitcases if you can and find out there which would be the better way to come back—train or bus. I think train would be more comfortable. You can just sleep right in the seats. See about getting a train. . . . Well, Ed, I guess this is all for now. We are all well. Have all the fun you can while you're there.

    Bye-Bye, Mom

A mere few days into my grandfather's trip to Hollywood, my great-grandmother could afford to be generous. On the surface her letter conveys an air of casual acceptance—*see the sights, my boy!*—but a mother's son could read between the lines just fine—*it would positively break your mother's heart if you even thought of staying.* Great-gram's second letter written later that same week carried on the same conversational tone, at least on the surface, and she made sure to pack her letter full of news of young people moving westward, as if reminding herself that her son's leave-taking might not be as anomalous as she had at first feared.

    I saw in the Hawkeye today that Gene Carbee who lives in Pasadena came through Lisbon Wednesday on his way to Detroit to get a new car. I suppose when he hits Lisbon on his way back he'll have passengers, as there's sure somebody that wants to go back to California. . . . I suppose Buz and Don are there

*by now. I also saw in the Hawkeye where Harvey
Ellison's boy had gone to Texas to see her brother Floyd
Heneks. He lives at Plainview . . . you must have
gone through on your way out. Well, is California
like you imagined it to be?*

By contrast, in my grandfather's sister's letters, enthusiasm for California veritably bubbled over. A teenager herself, she could hardly wait to kick the gravel dust from the heels of her Mary Janes and leave her middlewestern rural route for good. "Dear Ed, how's Hollywood?" she began her note of December 3rd, adding "I wish I was there!" Sissy had seen *Ramona* as well, and gushed to her older brother about the all-color picture and its spectacular southern California scenery. Sissy added,

*Well, I hope you see a lot of movie stars. Here
is a list of good places to go to see some—Coconut
Grove, Biltmore Hotel, Kraft Music Hall, and some
of the radio broadcasts. Fred Astaire is on the Packard
Hour every Tuesday night. That is where I would go.
Is Mary Astor's ex-husband nice looking? I have a
few pictures of him. He looks neat. . . . Well, I can't
think of anything else to write, so I'll close. Try and
see movies stars and write and tell me if they look like
their picture.*

By Saturday morning of that same week my great-grandmother was on her third letter to her prodigal son, and by now she had begun to turn the volume down on the breezy enthusiasms of her "we'll-support-whatever-decision-you-make" notes. In the meantime a second letter had arrived from Hollywood bearing news that her son—evidently not so displeased with the prospect of living in California as he had first let on—might have a job opportunity.

*We got your letter just now saying you could get
that boy's job. Now Ed if you <u>want</u> to stay just stay but
<u>if you don't like it well enough</u> to stay just come home
after you have your visit out. I don't suppose those
uniforms cost much, and if you like the job, take it.
But if you <u>don't think you would like it</u> there, or the
job, why, don't take it.*

My great-grandmother, bless her heart, endeavored to stay
open-minded, but the underscored sentiments in her letter reveal
her truest feelings, reinforcing the message almost subliminally—
mother to mama's boy—that he should not like it, or at least not
like it well enough to keep him away long. To a midwestern farmer's wife, Hollywood amounted to the kind of girl you might cut
a rug with at a few dances, but ultimately not the kind you would
take home. Maybe my great-grandmother was right to caution her
one and only son about the deprivations and depravities of the
West. Along and near his route my grandfather passed California
towns with names like Weedpatch, Bitterwater, and Death Valley,
the names themselves cautionary notes inscribed for future generations who might pass by possessed of a similarly unquenchable
thirst. Encoded in the very place names was a warning from earlier
visionaries, voyagers, and vagabonds not to linger long: *Keep going,
son. It's dry here.*

What is a map, in the end, but a record of where we've been,
and what we found there—Bitterwater, California; Barren County,
Kentucky; Success, Missouri; Hope, Arkansas.

Surely though the fountainhead of them all must be a spring
called Wanderlust.

⟫•⟪

Like my grandfather's, my own story of how I came to earn a
foothold in those southern climes far from hearth and Heartland
is mostly, but not entirely, foretold by the marks I made in my road

atlas. I maintain that my magnetic attraction to the Missouri Ozarks isn't revealed in those original exploratory circles I penned in my own Rand McNally road atlas so much as it is in the compulsion by which those circles came to be drawn in the first place.

Flush with the prospect of adventure, I'd suggested to my friend Margaret that we take a trip to explore the Ozarks, where I had touched down just once before, having chosen it from a full palette of more glamorous destinations as the site of a family celebration of my college graduation. More than a decade after that expedition, I found myself thinking with increasing frequency of Thoreau's injunction in his essay "Walking": "In wildness is the preservation of the world." One glance at my road maps of the Midwest demonstrated that if an accessible concentration of Southern wilderness could be found within a comfortable day's drive of my farm home, it would be in the Ozarks.

If Thoreau had come to know Concord in the company of surveyors, I reasoned, why shouldn't I avail myself of the help of a local real estate professional to learn the lay of the land? I wouldn't be buying anything, I hastened to add, when inevitably Margaret raised an eyebrow at me. Convinced that two thirty-something friends driving a beat-up Dodge minivan were unlikely to be given the time of day by a busy realtor, I suggested we role-play. After some haggling, we landed upon the persona of the "Faziolis"—a recently married Italian-American couple from Chicagoland. It didn't seem to matter that we weren't a "couple," weren't Italian, and weren't from Chicago. So long as the realtors understood I was only browsing—indulging a long-held flight of fancy—my alter ego could avail himself of their services with a clear conscience.

As I look back on it now I realize my presence in the Ozarks required, from the get-go, the construction of a fiction sufficient to drive its improbable plot forward. While Mr. Fazioli, my doppelganger and foil, might be a man bold enough to purchase a second home in the mountains, Mr. Jack never would. Mr. Jack, by contrast, would be obliged to spend the rest of his life in the thoroughly cultivated, carefully sanitized, straight-as-an-arrow Midwest, where

Jefferson's grid of six-by-six-mile townships thwarts the drafting of new life curves. Even as the Faziolis plunged southwestward from St. Louis, deep into the Ozarks, I found myself seized by existential doubts. Wasn't my fascination with southeastern Missouri the equivalent of my grandfather's unsuccessful attempts to gain a foothold in southwest Florida? Wouldn't mine come to the same abortive ends as his kudzu-choked plot in the Alabama lowlands? The definition of home, after all, is predicated on exclusivity—on choice of where one hangs one's hat. To have two homes, to achieve dual citizenship in the sense of true parity and pluralism of roots, must surely be a pipe dream or at least wishful thinking.

Holding joint title as the world's worst liar and also its most atrocious thespian, I dropped the Fazioli bit within minutes of emerging from the van in the lyrically named town of Willow Springs, Missouri, to shake the grinning realtor's hand. Despite my best efforts I had become the mild-mannered farmer's son again, the one who talked a good game about ecstatic life risk but who habitually faltered at the altar. I felt puzzled and a bit let down by this unbidden retransformation, as if Spiderman had turned unwittingly back into Peter Parker or Superman morphed back into Clark Kent at exactly the moment when a superhero, not a pencil-pusher, was needed.

After some coaxing, our good-natured realtor—Sampson, let's call him—drove us down the highway to a town at the Missouri-Arkansas border. We were now nearly 300 miles south of the Mason-Dixon line, deep into the southland that had once so spurred my grandfather's imagination. We met up with the listing agent, Buzz, a late middle-aged man with a military cut who'd taken early retirement and had recently gotten the hell out of Dodge in Memphis in favor of the Arcadian dream of southeast Missouri. Once rendezvoused, the four of us—seller's agent, Sampson, Margaret, and me—headed out for our necessarily short tour of Show-Me acreages with sticker prices less than a Chevy diesel would cost me in the showroom back home. First up was a mildewed, tumbledown shack tucked behind shady hardwoods and plenty of barbed wire—on entry a nonstarter. The next turned out to be a tin-can trailer, what the listing quaintly euphemized as a "manufactured home" on a dozen or so unsurveyed acres on the edge of the Mark Twain National Forest and just a few miles from the Eleven Point River. On the front door was taped a hand-printed sign reminding the realtor not to let the kitten out, and a second, permanent notice to the local fire company enjoining them to save the owner's cats, numbered eleven, in case of fire. The shirtless elderly man who answered the door turned out to be another Ozark émigré from the Corn Belt, and despite the shotgun readied at his bedside, he revealed himself to be a soft-spoken nature lover.

The property took in slightly less than a dozen acres in total—a half dozen wooded acres in a typical Missouri mixture of pine, cedar, and oak—and a few more "open acres" mowed short. Once we were through walking the property line we thanked the owner and headed back to town to compare notes. I'd liked what I'd seen—liked it very much, in fact. Already I felt the first flicker of romantic attraction—that slow, sweet dawning of new possibilities no matter how irrational or imprudent they might be. Still, modesty demanded that I keep the feelings at bay, and to myself.

Sampson's phone rang again as we filled up at the Conoco station in town—a call from yet another Ozark émigré, an Easy Rider divorcé who'd once run a successful, high-end motorcycle design shop and now wanted out. He had set out with his young daughter in their behemoth RV to find the land he had recently acquired near Jolliff Springs, but whose exact location he had since forgotten. Back home in farm country, where open skies and long horizon lines predominated, an inability to find one's compass points, and thereby one's own acres, would be an unpardonable sin, but in the Ozarks such confusions made sense. The roads doubled back here, one bend looking to the newcomer vaguely like the next, one comely swell of oak-punctuated ground as indiscriminately arresting as the rest.

Jolliff Spring, where we were now fixin' to head, wasn't so much a place, we learned, as an amalgamation of the founding family's surname, Jolliff, with the chief geographic asset that had become the remote crossroads' greatest claim to fame, springs. Randolph Jolliff's people had migrated from the aptly named Barren County, Kentucky, well before the Civil War. Not long after moving west to Missouri, Randolph had gotten sick, and in a fevered vision the Lord had told him to go wash his face in the spring he had discovered bubbling forth on his newly acquired 120 acres. That same evening there had been a revival meeting planned at the Jolliff church down the road, and Randolph Jolliff had run from the spring shouting that the Lord had saved him, that he had, in this second home, been born again.

More a point of interest than even an unincorporated town, Jolliff had, since Randolph's unlikely baptism, earned a cataloguing as "Spring" by the U.S. Board on Geographic Names. Now all that remained was a well-kept country cemetery at the crossroads, a collection of graves under an oversheltering oak under whose broad limbs Randolph Jolliff himself was buried in the land he had donated as a final resting place for the bones of his fellow Missouri pioneers. Now, Easy Rider and his daughter needed Sampson and his photographic memory to lead them back to the promised land they had purchased. An hour after we'd met at the gas station, we—Sampson, Margaret, and I—found ourselves playing pilot car en route to the Jolliff Springs crossroads, the RV following close behind.

When finally we arrived, Easy Rider's mammoth Winnebago rolled to a stop alongside us in the middle of a high, dry Ozark pasture—utterly alone save for a farmhouse at the bottom of the hill beyond a copse of trees. The man's daughter, a willowy eleven- or twelve-year-old, wandered off in bare feet to explore her new-found domain. Easy Rider had done well for himself, and had spent his net profit from the sale of his business on this, a forty-acre-or-so patch he and his daughter intended to call home.

Once they were settled, we made to leave, waving back at them. As we bounced through the pocked pasture in Sampson's

SUV, I felt happiness and sadness in equal measure: happiness because the American dream—affordable land, fresh starts—I knew to be alive here on the edge of the Heartland. All it required in these Ozark foothills was a generator and a tin roof under which to lay one's head. At the same time I felt a kind of sadness born, no doubt, of an inherited midwestern predisposition to sociability over abject seclusion. What kind of childhood, if any, would Easy Rider's daughter have here, motherless and neighbored by nothing save old oaks and head-high thistle? I had been a farm kid too, a child of corn and wind, and yet I had grown up surrounded by family who'd sunk the deepest kind of roots, roots that would serve me as wellspring. If I'd needed a context back then to understand my place in the world I would only have needed to drink in the history around me. There in the barns and the timber-frame home my ancestors built with their own hands in the years before Fort Sumter and Southern secession stood the physical reminders of my legacy. By contrast, where would my fellow Ozark émigré, this winsome, coltish thing, catch her school bus? What address would she list when, enrolling in the local school, the administrators inevitably asked? Would she simply point yonder to where her father's mobile satellite pointed toward a chicory-colored Ozark sky? In a world of settled people what would the system do with a wild child whose stake in the world rolled atop four wheels—the proverbial turtle carrying its home on its back?

The next day Margaret and I traveled back to take a second look at the for-sale tin-can trailer Sampson had shown us; Mr. Fazioli—remember him, our foil from the Windy City?—had brewed an overnight enthusiasm for the place that proved infectious. We retraced our steps without realtor assist and when we found the place, drove by it several more times, each literal changing of gears there on Bat Cave Hollow Road—forward and reverse, forward and reverse so as to get a proper view of it—an outward manifestation of an inward equivocation. We spent the rest of the afternoon floating the blue-green Eleven Point River in a rented canoe, mulling it over.

There, carried away by the spring-fed waters, Mr. Fazioli finally bent the ear of the hesitant farm kid who hailed from the state with more of its land under cultivation than any other. Here in the Ozarks, Fazioli pointed out with his usual irrational exuberance, flew flies nearly as big as hummingbirds; here hovered hummingbirds "pert near" the size of songbirds back home. Here lay mile after mile of federally protected forest and national scenic river where everything showed up wilder and larger than its equivalent back in my thoroughly domesticated farm state. I thought of Thoreau's essay "Walking" again—his claim that the future lay "not in lawns and cultivated fields, not in towns and cities, but in the impervious and quaking swamps" read as a condemnation of my homogenized, farm-rooted life to date. I was no more west now, longitudinally speaking, than my home place, but psychically I might as well have been in the mountainous woods and wilds of Idaho or Wyoming. The river's shimmering eddies ran away with me.

It was the ecstatic, irksomely irrational poet those spring-fed currents conjured, unbidden, that day. And the imagination that had birthed the incomparable Mr. Fazioli won out over the staid logic of the plowman's son. Looking back now on that first blush of romantic attachment to a place so like, and yet so unlike, my native state, I see myself careening down the slippery runaway slope that is infatuation, a falling in love not so much with the place itself, perhaps, as with the freedom it represents—the release from ground and gravity.

⟫◆⟪

More than eighty years after my grandfather crossed the high Sonoran Desert into California from Phoenix, it's not just our roads that have been mapped but our genes. Our grandparents' maps lead, quite literally, to our own.

How much, I wonder, of the route by which I came to call home the rusty tin-can mobile home in the Ozarks, did I inherit from my grandfather? Simple math would say 25 percent of my genes came from him, but the math—and the map—of genetics is not so simple as that. Is there a gene for wanderlust? For nostalgia? Or is nostalgia something closer to its etymological root—a sickness—in this case for the past? And if I do suffer from nostalgia, was my grasping at a foothold on the Ozark Plateau a remedy for it—a desperate attempt to cure myself of the homesickness that had kept us rooted in place since before the Civil War? Were the maps my grandfather left me instructions for a potential cure—take one of these and call me in the morning—for the disease of homesickness, or were they merely symptomatic of it?

I acquired my Ozark home away from home by a flight of fancy no more logical or well-informed than those that gave wings to pioneers leaving settled farms in places like Ohio and Indiana and Kentucky to push farther west into the unknown. Hope, of course, stakes its own sizeable claims. California towns may have been named for good times and great fortune—Eureka! But as the pioneers of the Ozark Plateau pushed west they named their new settlements aspirationally and according to visions of better things: Fairdealing, Enterprise, Success, Missouri. The pioneers of my second home inscribed their intentions for civility and blessings in the names of the places they put on the map.

My friend Margaret, first nearly as enthralled as I with the region, has long since stopped loving the Ozarks. She visited just once after our initial river run, a few brief but telling interactions with the locals enough to convince her that the folks who make these foothills their natural home are sexist and bigoted—the worst of the urban North's stereotypes of hillbillies. I couldn't disagree more. I feel a touch of pride when, eating at my favorite Ozark café, I look up from my grilled sandwich and fried okra and there on the wall hangs a gigantic plat map of my adopted county. On it is an itsy-bitsy rectangle of land bearing my name.

Sometimes, when a macabre mood strikes, I think of it, my part of that map hanging there in that smoke-filled greasy spoon, as a kind of tombstone, a way of saying, "Here lies the body." At other, more optimistic times, I think of it as akin to a personal record, a boy's notch cut on a tree he loved to climb. At my most hopeful, I think of a potential familial legacy in the making, a map my own grandson might one day unearth among dusty property tax records in the county courthouse. I can almost hear him mutter there in the county recorder's office deep in the Ozarks in a not-so-distant future, and not entirely under his breath, *I wonder what that crazy son of a gun was thinking?* And yet chances are good he would have been thinking much the same thing. A combination of my mothballed maps, mixed and mingled with his own natal charts, led him here, after all.

He'll exit then, that gumshoe of a grandson of mine, and climb in some beat-up jalopy—he'll be a student, no doubt, flush with temporary curiosity about his forebears—and he will follow the map to the place I once knew as a home away from home. Who knows what we will find there then—a ruined trailer inhabited by raccoons or, more likely, a newer house or mobile home built beside or atop the remnants of the old, suggesting what Ozarkers have always known—that history is as much sediment as sentiment.

Country
Love Songs

Part III

Mona Lisas of the Prairie

To be young, or younger, on the windswept acres of Middle America is inevitably to be haunted by a sense of generational inadequacy. Across the miles an inheritance seems to unite us, the young at heartland: the daunting, haunting, fairy-tale relationships of our forebears. With uncanny gravitas they seem to trump, in advance, any supposedly more enlightened, more educated love we might muster ourselves in a digital age. Our well-rehearsed we-are-not-worthies seem somehow a part of the fabric of our generational hand-me-downs—the unspoken yet certain knowledge that our own lovelights are destined to burn more dimly than the mythic loves of our ancestors.

Years ago, whenever my good friend Mark would come to the end of a love affair, I would be summoned to his front porch to lament the swift souring of his romantic fortunes. Gatorade proved our hard-luck drink of choice, and as we guzzled neon-colored electrolytes he'd retell the rose-colored story of his parents' meeting, who met by happenstance at a far-flung tavern in rural Minnesota and who, a mere two months later, married hastily in the kind of starry-eyed daze baby boomers dread for their own children. Nearly fifty years later Mark's parents are still happily wed.

Back then Mark would wonder aloud why, in his early thirties, Cupid hadn't yet aimed his sharpest and most soulful arrows at him, why his latter-day relationships seemed forever to pale by comparison to his folks' fairy-tale romance. Underneath my good friend's sincere lamentations, however, it seemed to me he possessed a quiet kind of certainty concerning his future. Graduate degree firmly in hand, he would return home to Minnesota, where the family wagons would dutifully circle around him. He would eventually find a local gal, buy a nice house in Apple Valley or Edina, and live happily ever after. Privately, I knew my own return to my rural home, equally as inevitable as Mark's to Minneapolis, promised to be more deeply riven. I would be returning not to a thriving suburban place where a space had been reserved for me, but to a ruin—a hardpressed hometown, a farm with no clear heir, a deeply loving yet darkly troubled father who'd stayed behind to man the fort, draining the resources of the farm even as he dutifully tried to save them.

In my weaker moments I wondered whether my own attraction to my demographically challenged region hadn't in fact morphed into a fatal attraction, one destined not to delight but to dictate life and its possibilities. Lately, I had made myself an expert on studies of rural demographics, most of them substantiating demographer Richard Florida's claim that "people born in disadvantaged locations tend to carry that initial disadvantage across subsequent life stages." Florida quotes fellow geographer Bethan Thomas, as saying that folks born into such an environment will find, at every step along the way their "chances much more constrained" and concluding that "where you live can limit or assist your life from cradle to grave."

And if my relationship to home is indeed a fatal attraction, in opening up the boxes containing the more blessed artifacts of my grandparents' courtship there, am I, in my own way, opening up Pandora's box? Does their kind of platinum golden oldie amount, now that it's gone, to a hard-luck swan song for me and my generation, a tear-in-my-beer country and western? A swan song for our town? For an entire rural region? Are our parents' and grandparents' gold standard ditties better left on the shelf . . . a bottle of good whiskey? And is the singing of such sweet songs bound only to evoke the nostalgic or the melancholic, reminding us of the sobering gap between the greater harmonies of their cultural moment and the lovelorn dissonances of our own—Glenn Miller versus Lady Gaga? Or is singing the golden oldies of our regional and familial Thens necessary in order to hear the historical rhymes with our Nows, turning the old songs into sing-along songs that help sing us home when the light grows dim?

What would happen, we lovelorn sometimes wonder, if we voted for love made local, for that homely, homey place of our birth, for that boy or girl, man or woman, that only seemed inadequate but which our native soil grew for us? And what if the near-mythic relationships enjoyed by our parents and grandparents—those we long ago turned into gold standards to play when our own personal love-lights flickered and grew dim—weren't so destined as we first supposed, but were instead the product of tough, should-I-stay-or-should-I-go-now decisions not unlike our own?

⇒•⇐

Chicago, the lodestar, the place demographers class as one of the nation's urban magnets, its Second City. It remains the place to be, whether your aim is to wheel and deal in profitable pork bellies at the Chicago Board of Trade on Jackson Street, or to woo one of the upwardly mobile young professionals filling the high-rises on Lower Wacker Drive—the tens of thousands who stream out of their office buildings at 5 p.m. to catch the fleet of Metra trains waiting to spirit them away to cozy, steam-heated North Side studios in trendy places like Wicker Park and Wrigleyville. In the heart of the Chicago Loop, two-thirds of the "creative class" boast four-year degrees and they're out to match up in what demographers not-so-jokingly call "the great mating pot."

My friend Mark was born under a prosperous star into an upper-middle-class Minneapolis suburb destined to accumulate culture and capital, in part because his own father left a midwestern farm a generation earlier, found a stellar gal, and had enough horse sense to settle down in a dynamically diverse community. I, on the other hand, drew first breath on a farm outside a blink-and-you-miss-it hamlet that eighty years ago promoted itself as "Pork Center of the World," but that, by 1990, served as Exhibit A in Davidson's *Broken Heartland*—a place where there is no diner or café, no movie theater, no in-town high school, hotel, or newspaper.

Sometimes my own fortunes feel fatally marked by the town and the state I choose to call home, located as they are smack dab in a greater region suffering a brain drain so terrific that at any given time since the 1970s, nearly 40 percent of Iowa's native sons and daughters have been living outside its borders. All of which begs the question, am I from an advantaged place—a place with plenty of land-wealth and solid neighbors and a rich history steeped in black soil—or am I from a place that, judging by the stats, is as poor as many an Appalachian holler? Isn't mine a place of abundant blessings, a land that provides, a fabled and fathomless American breadbasket?

Looking back through my family's letters, I'm surprised to learn that my grandfather Edward Lee Jack, quintessential Heartland farmer and husbandman, once felt the gravitational pull of the city Carl Sandburg famously called "Stacker of Wheat and Hog Butcher for the World." I had grown up living across the barnyard from my grandfather, thinking of him as the consummate rooted soul, the one who'd grown up in a golden agrarian age when, though the work was hard, the choice to stay at home on the family acres proved a no-brainer.

But love stories, I am learning, are never as simple as they are told.

<hr />

A mere few years after listening to the esteemed J. Willard Lampe of the University of Iowa's School of Religion intone his commencement speech for the edification of the go-getters populating Mechanicsville's class of 1935, many of my grandfather's most talented classmates had already succumbed to the pull of the Windy City, establishing what amounted to tiny but high-spirited midwestern "immigrant" communities in Sandburg's City of Broad Shoulders.

Prelude in C-sharp minor by Rachmaninoff had played at my grandpa's baccalaureate service and the Reverend Osborn had reminded his youthful flock to "magnify the Lord" and "exalt His name." Later Mozart's "Gloria" reverberated in the nave of the Methodist Church, and my grandfather and his pals had, apropos to the occasion, sat in the pews basking in the sounds of a choral amen and a postlude of Wagner's "Pilgrim's Chorus." Edward Lee Jack, Julia Mae Puffer, and their good friend and president of the senior class Jim High had, a special to the *Cedar Rapids Gazette* reported, been part of the largest class ever to graduate from the Mechanicsville Consolidated School.

Theirs had been a feted bunch ever since their entry into high school four years earlier. *The Gossiper*, a four-page, back-to-front mimeographed affair that passed during those Depression years for a high school newspaper, reported in "Facts about Your School" in the December 1932 edition, "The attendance this year has increased from 67 to 87. This means that more young people are taking advantage of the opportunity to gain an education. It also must mean that Mechanicsville offers work suitable to the needs of the student." Of the twelve girls and nineteen boys, roughly 90 percent qualified as farmers' sons or daughters. Theirs was a class brimming with confidence, one that envisioned great things for itself, as *Gossiper* editor-in-chief Ella Mae Kiel observed in her editorial: "Who knows but what some of us may hold prominent positions in the county, state, or perhaps national government in the future." The choice of baccalaureate postlude had been apt, as the most gifted among the 1935 graduates of the Pork Center of the World were, then as now, destined to lead pilgrim's lives in places like Minneapolis and Chicago. Their class motto had read, "The door to success is labeled 'PUSH.'"

From the latter of these magnet cities my grandfather's classmate and love interest Valetta May Krumroy penned him a pining letter from LaSalle Street three short years after they graduated

CLASS OF 1935: Top Row: Robert Mullan, Geraldine Cook, James High, Leonard Longerbeam, Evelyn Stiles, William Hass. Second Row: Alberta Boots, Robert Unruh, Lillian Aaron, Jean Thomson, Everette Kline, Wanda Baker. Third Row: Howard Campbell, Alice Gleason, LaVerne Sievers, D.C. Gemberling, DeVere Young, Julia Puffer, Everette Gallmeyer. Fourth Row: Gorman Robinson, Lois Smith, Bernard Eggert, Earl Moir, Wayne Borden, Maxine Unruh, James Ferguson. Fifth Row: Edward Jack, Edith Jack, Linnell Kerr, Dale Warmuth, Valetta Krumroy, Francis Crock.

together. What Valetta May lacked in subtlety she made up for in honesty, opening her missive with an explanation for why she had responded so promptly to the note she'd received only that morning from my grandfather. "As I've said before," she wrote, "If I don't answer right away, I never answer. Am I getting to be a

real old maid? Here it is Saturday night, and I'm at home again." Valetta had time-stamped her reply "Saturday nite" in big bold lines, adding below "11:30 o'clock"—the addition clearly designed to conjure in my grandfather's mind the Hopper-esque image of a lonesome maid on LaSalle Street dreaming of an old flame. Valetta continued her post with the less vexing news of her day:

Valetta Krumroy.

> *Got up early this morning and went to the Loop and bought me a pair of shoes, gloves, hat, and purse to match, and Valeria got two dresses. . . . Gee, Edward, if you ever do come in, I'll treat you even nicer than my guy across the street.*

Valetta next ho-hums her way through a description of her workaday life at Montgomery Ward, wanting her old high school chum to know, one imagines, that she was making it just fine in the big city despite its fearsomeness ("I'd be afraid to even walk down Madison Street") and that my grandfather, should he one day choose to play house with her there, would be marrying an independent working woman, not an old-fashioned schoolmarm or farm wife.

> *I guess I should be thankful I have work, but do I ever hate it. They sure drive you, before you even have a chance to show your own initiative. We have to put out eighty letters an hour, and if we put out more we get a bonus. Some kids earn around $2.50 or $3.00 bonus every week. I usually get around $.47 to $.65. Last week I didn't feel very well, and only got $.11. . . . Every night I come home so tired and worn out I'm usually in bed by 9:00.*

Falling into bed spent after an exhausting day's work was something to which my grandfather, who had by that time taken up farming with his father, could well relate. Modest himself, he appreciated modesty in others, and so Valetta tailored her letters to address her old classmate's likely suspicions that she had, as the agrarian saying goes, gotten too high on her horse. To underscore her humility she drew a sharp contrast between herself and her roommate in Chi-town, Valeria, who, she laments in the last paragraph of her communiqué, "just came in, smelling like a brewery." Echoing another farm-born idiom of the time Valetta May observes,

> *Boy, she is really going to town. Two fellows where she works are pretty nuts over her, and she has another one over at Milford. Her birthday was Friday and she got something from all three. Merle gave her an outfit, and I gave her an Oriental crepe purse.*

At times it proved difficult for Valetta May to avoid sounding sour grapes.

> *I look at her, but I can't see what she has that I haven't got. It used to be me that was always out and she sat home. Now it's the opposite. I'm trying to work on the guy across the street, but am sure I haven't made any progress. Must close and get off to bed. It's after twelve and I'm tired. Have got to get up and go to church in the morning and iron my clothes. Hope by the next time I write I have some new stationery. Maybe I will get a raise (I'll get a kick out the door first), or if they stop raising the rent, we'll be able to afford some of our own.*

She closed there, did this most forward of my grandfather's potential suitors, no doubt entertaining the notion of ending the

letter "love" but ultimately landing, as would any prudent small-
town girl of her time, on the better-safe-than-sorry sign-off, "Sincerely." And, as is so often the case in affairs of the heart, it's the
postscript in which the missive's real message—*Call me, you silly
boy*—gets inscribed. She writes,

> *P.S. My phone number is still Diversy 5320, only
> ask for 1020. Try and come in* <u>*soon*</u>*. That is if you don't
> mind being around a confirmed 'old maid' like me.
> Don't worry I'll be free for years yet.*

⟫•⟪

Somewhere in the midst of my immersion in the "golden oldie"
that was my grandparents' long-ago prairie love song, I'd promised
Claudia, the editor of a local arts magazine, that I would peck out
a column detailing my feelings about my own search for love some
seventy-five years after my grandparents got hitched. My e-mailed
draft to her read something like this:

Last Man Standing

Sometimes, when I look out the window at this small farm
I steward, I realize I am shockingly alone. In my mid-thir-
ties I've become a last man standing—last to bear my family name, the only son in a farm clan whose land has been
in continuous ownership by my kin since 1855. It's a truer
and sadder plot than ever I could have written, and one I
never anticipated in a dreamy boyhood when my people
seemed an abundant part of this prairie, inevitable as the
dandelion, stalwart as the meadowlark.

Were the aloneness I feel simply personal, I wouldn't
trouble you. But it's your loneliness too, deep and black as
topsoil, because as rural America goes, so goes you. I could

feed you the stats, but let's just call a spade a spade: our young don't stay, and if they do, it's straight to an apartment or condo in the city, leaving the country bereft of single twenty- and thirty-somethings.

Call me Chicken Little or Debbie Downer, but where among your many friends and neighbors and associates can you find, say, a young, single professional living alone in the countryside more than a dozen miles from a major city? And what of the future viability of a place almost entirely devoid of young women? We've seen this movie before— Roanoke, the Wild West, the Yukon Territory, all starkly beautiful, perfectly unsustainable places.

Were I to write you a novel of a breadbasket place so fertile the world had never seen its equal, where corn yields 200 acres a bushel and stands in rows straight enough to please any minister, you might believe me, just barely. What if, turning the page, this miracle place of highest literacy and unspeakably fine schooling turned out also to be a place where, in the hinterlands, marriageable women were all but absent—like the land of the Amazons in Greek literature, only in reverse. The scenario thus written seems pure science fiction, and yet this fabulously precarious place exists. I know it because I live in it, and so do you.

Bob Dylan famously sang "you don't need a weatherman to know which way the wind blows," and you don't need a mathematician to dig the demographic equation: Brain drain + Lack of young rural singles = Death for the rural civilization whose survival is every bit as crucial to urban America as the hobbit's shire was to the fate of Middle Earth.

I've lived my thirty-odd years on Planet Rural America deeply and dutifully studying its history and culture, and frankly I'm fed up with the annual Pompeii of historical reenactments, "living history," and small-town fairs that ironically celebrate the very cultural mainstays that long ago passed away into ceremony in much the same way that suburban housing developments are said to be named after the thing they destroy.

My family's seven generations of history here amid the tall corn have made of me, at thirty-ahem, an old man, and my habit of studying our state's history in detail has made me dustier still. But the thing is, by rural America standards, I'm a young 'un, and so are you, and there's something urban America can do to help their country cousins beyond visiting the farmer's market and paying state income taxes; it can acknowledge that folks living twenty or thirty or forty miles beyond the city lights ought to, by rights, have as good a chance at meeting an educated mate at the general store as an urban dude does at chatting up a prospect at Starbucks. Our entrepreneurial spirit has brought us country-dwellers the "wonders" of high-speed Internet and digital cable, but I'd rather see an educated, dynamic, fiercely independent country girl stroll by my rural window than catch the latest episode of *Glee*.

I could continue to stew here in the hills in prideful isolation (I will, and I do), but I'd be fiddling while Rome burned and the old generals expired or abandoned their posts. In the last decade alone I've lost my grandfather to cancer, and two too-young uncles to heart attacks. This winter my sixty-year-old father left for Florida, sick already in heart and body. Their death and disappearance makes me free and bereft, blessed and cursed. I'm left to witness alone many farm mornings and evenings too beautiful to describe except in wish-you-were-heres. Still, I stay here, stand for here, because it's in my makeup, the way a horse lowers its head to stable as night comes.

But here's the thing: so long as we rural and small-town singles draw breath in Grant Wood's America, voting with our feet for what sweetnesses remain, there's a chance fate will find us where we live, and by our own mulishness and vestige of whatever it is that sustained our families here, deliver something like romance, something like manna.

I can do that much . . . put one foot in front of the other, stand my ground, become, as my dad always said, "A jackass in a hailstorm."

Years earlier, I had written poems to stave off the lovesickness I felt at the prospect of a life lived alone and unpartnered on my rural acres—a life so unlike the wedded rootedness of Mark's parents or my grandparents. Not surprisingly, the image of the storm-tossed lover infused them. They were frustrated bits of verse, fragments of love and loss and maddening stasis made up of lean harvests and clenched, raised fists.

Had my grandfather felt a similar desperation back in 1935 as he contemplated the vagaries of courtship in our little town on the edge of the prairie? Did he despair? Did he writhe or otherwise offer prayer? Did he, like Odysseus, contemplate setting sail for some other port on a prairie that seemed as wide and as endless as the sea?

Back home in Mechanicsville, Pork Center of the World, Valetta's letter from 1935 reached my grandfather, her would-be beau, years after he had given up working at the DX Standard station in town and a wished-for life as an over-the-road trucker to reluctantly take up the plow alongside his father.

For his part, my greatgrandfather Walter was proud

W. T. Jack and son, circa 1918.

of this nascent father-and-son partnership, proudly inking the first page of his *Farmers' Account Book* with, "Business Record of W. T. Jack & Son. Breeders of Hampshire Hogs. Record starting Jan. 1, 1922 . . . Our business platform: 'Eat what we can't sell.'" At the time my great-grandfather named his only son full partner in the livestock business, Edward Lee had just turned five years old.

Inside the front cover, father and son would eventually add their signatures over and over, doubtless testing a pencil newly knife-sharpened for the occasion. By the look of their dramatic John Hancocks decorating the page, they might have been practicing for all the check endorsing and sign-on-the-dotted-line wheeling and dealing they hoped to do when, inevitably, their hog-breeding operation hit the big-time. Inside the volume's front cover, the publishers in Hastings, Nebraska, offered "Suggestions for the Use of This Book," which included keeping a breeding record for "the dates on which animals are bred" and the "date of maturity" after successful insemination had been assured.

Meanwhile Walter's son—my grandfather—followed his entre-preneurial nose in a field of a different sort, hoping one day to wed the neighbor farmer's daughter, Julia Mae, who lived just north and east of the home farm, not more than a mile and a half distant as the crow flies. As children they had attended neighboring one-room schoolhouses in Pioneer Township, and they entered the same high school class at Mechanicsville High together. The two families, one fitfully Irish and Welsh, the other mostly German mixed with a chaser of Native American, mixed easily and well at local Farm Bureau suppers and dances, remaining, as farm families did back then, distantly aware of the other clan's well-being.

The Pork Center of the World was indeed a heady place to be back in the spring of 1935 when my grandfather, safely returned from a pneumonia health scare and plenty of senior-year school-work completed from his hospital bed, graduated from Mechanics-ville High and began contemplating the possibilities of courting his neighbor and longtime friend. For her part, Julia Mae had remained aloof throughout much of high school, dating an older boy named

Dale who played in the band at the University of Minnesota while she remained in high school dallying with her friend and fellow classmate Jim High, an intellectual and a thespian who tickled her funny bone and her fancy and who once wrote her asking, "You don't suppose by any chance you could manage to let me slip in a date about next Tuesday evening do you? Will you drop me a line if you can? It's been quite a while," before closing the letter mysteriously, "Write me about that little matter. I do love to be with you. Here's hoping, xxx, Jim."

Dale, my grandmother's first flame, and in uniform no less.

Theirs was a gifted, boy-heavy class and the young woman who was to become my grandmother had her pick of the litter. From her editorial post on *The Gossiper* Julia Mae paid lightly satiric attention to the man who would become my grandfather. Because Edward Lee Jack wasn't an athlete, or a thespian, or even a member of the declamatory squad, she had to be creative in finding ways to slip him into her weekly editions. During the spring carnival issue, she sneaked a reference to her overlooked neighbor into the Sophomore Notes section: "The high school faculty is always on the alert to curb even the minor vices. . . . if you don't believe it, just ask Edward Jack." In an installment called "Can you imagine," the high school editors asked, "Can you imagine Ed Jack as a preacher???" In November Julia Mae composed a little ditty for *The Gossiper* in praise of her classmate's souped-up car, entitled "Ed's Chevrolet." It went,

Blessings on the little car
Gears all stripped and seats that jar
Knocks are many, springs are few
Chassis broken, far from new;
With two speeds, slow and stop,
Cut out open—darn the cop!
Lively pick-up as it whirls
Picks up tacks and pretty girls;
Paint all gone—now girls, don't scoff
You'd look worse with your paint off.

Elsewhere the editors of *The Gossiper* could be counted on to run the quips and comebacks my grandfather launched in class, witticisms that, once overheard, inevitably found their way into the newspaper humor column. In one, the high school biology teacher, Mr. Gemberling, asks, "Edward can you tell me where the dew comes from?" And Edward Lee replies, "The earth rotates so fast that it perspires." In another the school's mathematics teacher, Mr. Peak, asks him, "What is a right angle?" and the class cad responds, "Two straight lines around a corner." Then "Mr. Peak: Is sociology a branch of biology? Edward Lee: No, it is a twig." And so on.

As Mechanicsville's largest-ever class came of age *The Gossiper* faithfully recorded their evolving romantic interests, as couples paired off and broke up, and sometimes found themselves lured away by beauties and beaus in neighboring towns. Editing the news of the sophomore class, Julia Mae tried out a little good-natured innuendo in her coverage of the class picnic: "The sophomores seemed to all be on deck Monday morning after the big picnic out at Aarons pasture. We wonder if all the sophs went home like good little boys and girls."

As members of the class of 1935 earned their driver's licenses, a cheeky competition broke out between my grandparents' native whistle-stop and the nearest town to the west, Lisbon, over the rival villages' ballyhooed belles and beaus. In some ways it was safer to find a sweetheart who lived beyond the close watch of neighbors and classmates who knew all about you and your family. By con-

Edward Lee Jack, circa 1935.

Julia Mae Puffer, circa 1935.

trast, courting in a contiguous town, county, or state afforded the dater a greater measure of exoticness and anonymity. "Just what is all this talk that one hears now and then concerning McVille boys visiting Lisbon quite frequently?" the editors of *The Gossiper* asked. "All the pretty girls of McVille will be grass widows in time to come, as the cream of the high school is slowly but surely lured toward Lisbon." Predictably the McVille girls struck back, reclaiming their supremacy in a quatrain that read, "The Lisbon people had a rooster / They put it on a fence / The rooster crowed for the McVille girls / Because it had some sense."

At times the whole academic enterprise seemed little more than a pretext for the larger and more important task of partnering up with the best prospect those last years of young adulthood might yield up. For all but a few in my grandparents' class, their secondary education at Mechanicsville Consolidated would be their last years of formal schooling, and the adults around them seemed to suggest that they take full advantage by ensuring ample occasions existed for Jack to meet Jill—not just at the usual fairs or athletic events or dances but at special class picnics and carnivals where the community itself conspired to match homegrown sweethearts. The fall carnival, for instance, featured a "Fortune Telling Room" where the boys and girls of Mechanicsville High could pay a nickel to have their love fortunes told. "Why just think of all you fellows that haven't got the jack to get your best girl a diamond," the newspaper advert read. "Well, it won't take long to get that now, so come in and have your fortune told so that you can get that load off your mind."

Courtship too was evolving as the bursting-at-the-seams class of 1935 matriculated. The Jazz Age had come and gone; women had enjoyed the vote for nearly a generation; and an increasing rate of urbanity meant that my grandmother and her girlfriends enjoyed a measure of mobility and potential for selective partnering of which their mothers could only have dreamed. "Women are busy nowadays," the editor of the school newspaper, Ella Mae Kiel, pointed out. "They have very little time to even think about men, let alone drop and sigh over them." For Edward Lee Jack and Jim High the competition had grown stiffer, and in an urbanizing countryside the competition for the local brains and beauties came not just from neighboring corn towns, but from Chicago and Minneapolis.

While Ed, fourth behind top-of-the-class intellectual and thespian Jim High, boasted the fastest car and the quickest draw at the local pool hall, it was Dale—the older boy who'd left home for the bright lights of Minneapolis, Dale the brass in the University of Minnesota band, Dale the business major and up-and-comer—who at first seemed a better candidate to steal my grandmother's heart than the farmer's son down the road with his broken nose and bright blue eyes. "Last night the business school had a party," Dale enthused in a letter to Julia Mae. "I was the play coach. I put on the skit, *The Lighthouse*. Had four boys and a girl in it." He dated the letter one day before his rival Edward Lee's birthday in 1933, but not before tooting his own horn a bit further: "I thought it might be a flop, but I was complimented by a lot of people, even by the big-shot head of the business department." Mechanicsville seemed a necessarily distant reality to Dale, Julia Mae's ambitiously mobile beau, who wrote of liberal Minneapolis parties he attended where folks by the name of Mr. and Mrs. Glasser cross-dressed in each other's clothes. "She was his son," Dale guffawed in his recounting of Mr. and Mrs. Glasser's antics, "and he was Mae West."

In May of 1935 the *Cedar Rapids Gazette* ran the headline "Mechanicsville Class to Give Play Friday" and a short blurb, date-lined Mechanicsville, announced Julia Mae Puffer's starring role as Laura Morrison in the senior class play *Heart Trouble*. The play was a long-standing favorite of Mechanicsville Consolidated superintendent W. B. Hammer, whose endorsement ran alongside rave reviews from other small-town high schools in places like Eldorado, Illinois; Kinsman, Ohio; Atkinson, Nebraska; and Hawley, Minnesota. "This is the second time that *Heart Trouble* has been given under my administration," Superintendent Hammer trumpeted in his nationally distributed blurb. "In both cases, the genuine appeal of the play to adults, its excellent portrayal of the problems of young people . . . plus the change in heart of Laura Morrison, present a plot that holds the attention of actors as well as audience."

Written by Howard Chenery as a domestic comedy, *Heart Trouble* couldn't have been more germane to the senior class of a rural Heartland high school. A staple in the Gateway Series of Tested Plays offered by Row Peterson of Evanston, Illinois, *Heart Trouble* and its ilk had been conceived as pieces of didactic literature for undersized Middle American schools. "The published product," the series editors noted in their foreword, "is therefore not that of the commercial or professional situation, where large theaters, lavish financial resources, paid actors and staff and a highly urbanized, blasé, and jaded metropolitan audience are taken as a matter of course." By contrast, the editors of the Gateway Series of Tested Plays intended their dramas to be earnest, meaningful, and moving—respectful of the rural and small-town communities in which they played. "It goes without saying," they wrote, "that a work so designed is at once adaptable to general community use."

In casting my grandmother as Laura Morrison, director Marjorie Coleman made a choice that foreshadowed Julia Mae's own future. In the stage notes, Laura is described as a "victim of her mother's misguidance. Her repentance is genuine and the final curtain should find the audience quite in sympathy with her." When Laura enters she is described as "dark, and extremely attractive"—a dead

Jim High, class president of 1935, and another of my grandmother's beaus.

ringer for my grandmother. Laura's dilemma in the insular confines of the fictional Midwest burg of Middleville is a common one: she's intrigued by an alluring newcomer to town, Conrad Tyler, an older, more sophisticated man the series editors describe as "smooth-tongued young Lothario with all the accoutrements," but alas Laura is promised to Tommy Caler, "a stalwart youth with no soaring ambitions, but with those substantial qualities which make for solidarity and competence in business life." Tommy Caler, as irony had it, was played by another of my grandmother's real-life pursuers, senior class president Jim High.

In the play Laura, like Julia herself, grows dismissive of her native corn town and its otherwise boorish or boyish lovers. "The town of Middleville isn't very interesting for me," she laments early in act 1, a complaint to which Tyler replies, "These small-town fellows get on your nerves, don't they?" Laura agrees, dismissing the homegrown specimens as "simply hopeless." Laura is the Morrisons' favored child, proud and talented and beautiful and ripe for the nascent brain drain, though that term would not be coined for another decade and a half. Favored by a mother who has aspirations for her daughter to escape Middleville by marrying well, Laura has never so much as joined her more homely younger sister, Patricia (described as "a Cinderella") in the household chores.

As Laura falls head over heels for the more exotic Conrad Tyler, and begins to distance herself from her plainer, younger, hometown crush Tommy, a rivalry between the two beaus mounts until the climax when Laura learns that the smooth-talking Tyler is in fact married, a crisis that galvanizes her retiring father, Fred, to confront his wife. "I don't like it because it's dishonest, Grace," he tells her. "You've got Laura feeling that her chief business is to look pretty!" Finding his long-lost voice, Fred Morrison challenges his and his wife's spoiling of their prima donna child, and points the finger at himself and his partner for making it seem as if the only way young Laura could escape her small-town confines and one day lead the refined, urbane life would be to grow up sufficiently pampered as to feel entitled to something better. "Getting a few slaps on the back for being big-hearted, I tell you, isn't going to do much for our children," Laura's father declares. "You're not a bit too good to wash a few dishes, Laura."

In fact, my grandmother and her most vivacious classmates found themselves in exactly Laura's position—a fact not lost on the superintendent, school board, and play director. The hometown boy Tommy Caler, "honest and forgiving," should be given a chance, their choice of senior play implied, even if he was ostensibly less impressive than newcomer-to-town Conrad Tyler. In real life Julia Mae had faced the same dilemma throughout her senior year. Earlier that autumn she had made the long drive to see Dale's University of Minnesota band march at a rival university's homecoming game. The Minnesota band played "Hail Minnesota," "The Vanished Army," and "His Honor," and Julia Mae fell hard for Dale in his crisp band uniform.

The senior class play went over wonderfully when it hit the stage on the tenth of May in 1935, eleven days shy of my grandmother's eighteenth birthday and less than two weeks before commencement at the high school auditorium. At commencement the first two senior class songs—"School Days" and "Happy Days Are Here Again"—were followed by a song of a more recent vintage choice, "Last Round-Up," whose popular lyrics had been altered by the class of '35 to reflect its unique makeup.

> You're here for your last round-up
> There are nineteen jolly boys here all free from care
> And there are also twelve pretty maidens fair
> All here for their last round-up

Keep a-goin' little senior, keep a-goin' right along
Keep a-goin' little senior, keep a-goin'
Keep a-goin' little senior, keep a-goin' right along
Keep a-goin' little senior, keep a-goin'

You're here for your last round-up
To the far away goal for which you'll have to strive
And there will be no more worries when you arrive
You're here for your last round-up

You've come for your last round-up
You're here all together for the last time here
With your memories which you all hold so dear
You're here for your last round-up.

The choice of song had been apt—an uncanny tune to suit an uncanny class. Debuting in their sophomore year, Billy Hill's dark-horse cowboy jingle had shocked urban record executives, meriting a feature story in the October 23, 1933, *Time* magazine. "A song as simple and unadorned as any piece of folk music set U.S. commercial records last week," the article trumpeted, adding that since its debut at New York's Paramount Theatre two months earlier, the popularity of the runaway hit had "started to get out of hand." The rapid urbanization caused by the Great Depression had caused metropolitan America to grow suddenly nostalgic for its cowboy tunes and wistful prairie love songs.

In many ways, "The Last Round-Up" signaled last call for the agrarian civilization in which the class of 1935 had come of age, and when its slow, mournful chords played in the auditorium, the lines "You're here for your last round-up / To the far away goal for which you'll have to strive" and "You're here all together for the last time here / With your memories which you all hold so dear" signaled a coming diaspora that would send the class not just across the Midwest, but across America.

The graduates in their gowns that May all had high school friends who had long since put the rural Heartland in their rear-view mirrors, especially Julia Mae. A handful of her pals wrote to her from tony Chicago suburbs like Glen Ellyn, relaying the many splendors of the city by the lake. Julia's friend oohed and aahed:

> *It was truly beautiful out there. The lake looked so pretty—deep blue green, with sailboats and yachts here and there on the water, seaplanes, and sea gulls in the day along with white clouds and a grand cooling breeze. That evening there was a dinner party in the Marine Dining Room and later we went out on the outdoor terrace and dance floor which is gorgeous—twinkling blue lights in all the many surrounding trees and darling modernistic flowers and mushroom lamps. Roger Pryor's orchestra was there and they had a cute floor show. We had a grand time.*

Others in my grandmother's army of ardent suitors wrote from the vibrant, varied cities to which Heartland towns exported their finest. Dale wrote from Minneapolis and Everett, a.k.a. "Pokey," scribbled from cosmopolitan Iowa City, whose virtues the *Des Moines Register* had trumpeted in the 1930 headline "Iowa City Now U.S. Literary Center, Suggests E. J. O'Brien, Noted Boston Critic." Lowell wrote from Randolph Field, Texas, where he had become a flying cadet in the Air Force. Lowell's cautionary note put on hold Julia Mae's plans to make a romantic reconnaissance trip of her own down Lone Star way. "Why don't you get your father to take your Texas trip next year?" Lowell asked in his letter. "Then I would have time and equipment to make it worthwhile. Now, about all I could say would be 'Hello-Goodbye.'"

Others in Julia's roving band of high school pals had by that time gotten hitched. Chum Donald Thompson had married lovely Bonnie Bittner in a ceremony by candlelight glowingly reported and by 1937, the twenty-one-year-old, not-yet-spoken-for Julia Mae must have swooned over the lavish descriptions of her friend's elegant betrothal as she read of them in the big-city newspaper, the

Cedar Rapids Gazette: "The bride wore her mother's wedding dress made of white silk crepe, fashioned in tunic style, and trimmed with lace made by the bride's grandmother one hundred years ago. Her tulle veil, falling from a shirred cap, was caught at each side with a tiny lace rosette centered with orange blossoms. She carried a shower bouquet of white roses and lilies of the valley." For their honeymoon, Bonne and Don, whose little sister Jean had played the role of Mrs. Morrison in *Heart Trouble*, had, the wedding announcement crowed, "left Thursday evening for Chicago on a motor trip." For her going away, the new Mrs. Thompson "wore a royal blue tunic dress with gold buttons and gold cord trim. With it she wore black accessories and a corsage of gardenias."

Of the half dozen or so serious contenders for Julia Mae's heart that remained a few years after the class of 1935's graduation, only my grandfather had put down roots in Mechanicsville. High-flying Dale had graduated from the University of Minnesota and returned to the nearby county seat, Tipton, to ply his trade at the bank, but his ardor for Julia Mae had cooled. Where once Dale had painstakingly typed four- and five-page love letters to his best gal back at McVille High, he now answered her queries both belatedly and curtly on too-formal bank letterhead. "Dear Julia," he wrote shortly after April Fool's Day in 1939, "Has been so long since I received your nice letter that I am about ashamed to answer it." He did not close "Love" or "XXX" but merely "As Ever," and the letter's final lines read breezily, "Stop in when you are in Tipton and write if you find a chance. Be good, old kid, and I'll be seeing you." What substance there was to the typed note proved mostly small talk. "S'pose you are all set with a new Easter bonnet and all. Boy, there are some of the craziest hats I have ever seen. Flat tops and tumblers, stovepipes, and what not. The colors are kinda pretty though."

The dark horse in the race for Julia Mae's heart four years after her two-year stint at Cornell College remained Edward Lee Jack. After his wanderlust trips to far-off worlds in places like New Orleans and Los Angeles, Edward had reason to be hopeful. Julia had, after all, signed his senior autograph book "Yours till Niagara

Falls," which counted for something, and in the invisible agrarian order that was then still intact in the small-town Heartland, a union such as theirs would be judged fitting—a sacred meeting of neighbors on equal footing, of good farmers, of land wealth and land ethic—the best kind of boy and best kind of girl the land could hope to produce coming together in holy matrimony.

But the young at heartland are forever throwing a wrench in the no-nonsense dictates of their well-ordered communities, and my grandmother, first-chair violinist and tubist, had not immediately hitched her star post-graduation to Edward Lee or anyone else. She had instead pursued her talents at nearby Cornell College, where she joined the school band, dated plenty, and succeeded in sparking combustion of an utterly nonromantic sort when she blew up the campus chemistry lab. In that first year away from home, she had written how disappointed she had been that Edward Lee, her childhood friend and potential lifemate, had refused a perfectly good college education for an odyssey around the United States doing manual labor. In between relaying news of the college's impending winter musical and two of her most daunting final exams, she mused, "I don't think I will ever forgive you for not coming to college when you had a chance. You would make such an ideal college student. You could still come if you would. My roommate had been out of school for three years before she came to college." Opening the letter at his friend Scoop's garage near Hollywood to confront the plainspoken condemnation from the woman he desperately wished to marry must have rattled Edward Lee profoundly, but there was interest, even admiration for his rambles, in her letter too. Julia Mae closed her reply, "Say hello to Scoop and his mother and give them my love. Write me all your adventures so if I make a trip like that I will know what to expect and what to do. As ever, Julia Mae." His letters to her, more voluminous by far, indicated that he felt she was spreading herself too thin, carrying more for the follies of the academic life than the truer obligations of the soil and its people.

Still, while visions of the distant Julia Mae remained with him in 1936 and 1937, my grandfather was not without other prospects, and he was a practical enough man to realize that pining for a woman who had yet to make up her mind, or whom fate had not yet taken by the hand, constituted a grand waste of time. Unlike his beloved, he did not date much, did not call often on girls or attend many shows, but began making cautious visits to those farm maidens who had earlier expressed an interest in him, including Corinne Robinson, whose folks lived up the road a mile or so and who had written him this after a missed visit, reassuring him, lest there be any doubt of her affections, "When mother told me you came late, I was just sick because I missed seeing you."

Ed and Julia remained passing ships until Julia Mae's older sister Mary—likewise a graduate of both Mechanicsville High and Cornell College—became pregnant with the first of several sons, and Julia's parents' wishes that she be there for her sister coupled with Julia's own rural-born frustrations with the pretense and pomp of college caused her to leave school and return home, where she lived off and on with her sister and her parents until what seemed to all observers like the old maidhood of her mid-twenties.

My grandmother didn't miss the college life much—she wouldn't allow herself to. Writing to a friend she confided, "I have been back to Cornell for a short visit during the time they had the opera . . . and I was so disgusted. I couldn't wait till I got home to forget it again. It seems to me it is much worse." Asked by her chum what news she had of her love life, Julia Mae wrote, "I have been going with a lovely boy that graduated in my class. We have lots of fun but we disagree on almost everything." Still, she did keep up an active, sometimes impassioned correspondence with the college-educated beaus who had already all but asked her hand in marriage—Dale at the bank in Tipton, Jim at Cornell College, and undereducated Edward Lee, her old neighbor and most long-lived love interest and provocation, who had come full circle from his odyssey to the American South and West to farm alongside his father just a couple of miles away from her parents' place.

These three suitors, finalists in the greater prize that was the heart of this most unusual Heartland daughter, orbited around Julia

Mae tightly as any three young men might around a raven-haired, college-educated woman who was already well beyond the "marrying age" and who was wasting away, they presumed, in her folks' farmhouse, waiting for her ship to come in. And though my grandmother was far too busy with farm work for pining, two years out of college had leavened her characteristic high-spiritedness with a touch of sobriety. "A note of melancholy seems to me to run through that letter of yours and, honey, it does things to me," Jim High wrote. "Your letters are much different from home than they were from college. It's not hard to see that either. I was home today, things are sad and depressed in the world outside college, don't you think so? The people here are all so full of pep and sunshine you just can't hardly be in the dumps for long." Her old pal and sometime love interest next wondered aloud about a possible road trip the two of them might undertake to Yellowstone that summer, closing with "Goodbye, Julia. God bless you. You won't be an old maid if I have to come to the rescue."

Though as a liberated woman she cared little for the specter of old maidhood, its very possibility served as a cold reminder of the seeming poverty of a life lived solely for oneself and one's family. Throughout 1939 the letters from Jim, now a junior at Cornell, kept coming. In May the onetime president of my grandmother's senior class captured the flavor of a utopian moment when commodity prices had begun to rebound and the magic inherent in coming of age in an agrarian place appeared as if it had returned to stay. Jim wrote,

> *We're studying in English now about Utopia and other worlds. It's heaps of fun getting others' opinions of what perfection would be. One fellow wanted a world of swing bands and pretty girls with no daily assignments from a textbook. Would you like to hear some of mine? You wouldn't! That's fine, here they are. The country about the size of U.S. and Canada combined. Surrounded entirely by ocean. Located in the temperate*

latitudes with one month of winter and eleven of sum-
mer. Government-controlled business and industry
to eliminate waste or friction. Perfect health through
physical education and scientific discovery. Instan-
taneous death, cremation, a race of evenly distributed,
decided blonds and decided brunettes. Everyone has a
month vacation with pay, too.

A farmer's son, Jim didn't say it in the love letter penned from Cornell College's Altoona Hall late on a Sunday eve, nor did he have to: his own idea of utopia would be marrying one of those "decided brunettes" so unlike Julia Mae, who had yet to decide on Jim or anyone else, though she had decided on one thing: her home would be the Heartland.

As a college man Jim offered many assets my grandfather did not, especially the ready access to culture his status as a liberal arts undergraduate secured. Badly needed on her parents' farm, where her father's health had begun to fail, a youthful night on the town with her old high school chum proved hard to resist. Julia Mae wrote in her journal,

> *Dad planted oats, finished 30-acre field. Eddie*
> *gave me a surprise visit about 9:30. I sort of had an*
> *inkling. I told him about Jimmie + I going to the*
> *opera. . . . I have hurt him by sneaking out. It's the*
> *gypsy in me. Now he doesn't believe me or trust me.*
> *Oh, what a fool I have been. Somehow he gets me. I*
> *just can't seem to get away. I feel like I want to cling to*
> *him. Love? Not again. Or yet?*

But like Laura Morrison, the self-possessed debutante she portrayed in her senior play, my grandmother was growing into a woman capable of taking into account others' feelings, understanding that love meant choosing. Gathering her courage, she wrote Jim,

Greeting card sent from Julia Mae to Edward Jack.

> *We have been going around so much together it would be too much of a shock for the community, and the questions and hints Eddie would receive later would hurt him. I think he loves me. You might imagine what it would be like. So perhaps it would be best not seeing you this vacation. I am really very sorry. You do understand, I hope.*

In an effort to sort out her thoughts, my grandmother wrote to herself,

> *Jimmie wanted a date for tonight or Thursday but I couldn't give him either, and wasn't I glad, for no less than five minutes later Eddie drove in with Helen. We went to town, met Jimmie at Phillips. . . . Eddie in overalls always gets me or anyone for that matter . . . wonder why. I just burn inside when he hugs me. It's so wonderful feeling his warm lips on mine. Dale asked Stella if she knew I was to be married and to whom. Dale, I have always wanted you to love me, but you are so dishonest.*

Julia Mae remained exceptionally patient, knowing on some level that the decision before her—whom to marry—would reverberate for generations. So she made lists of her potential suitors' strengths and weaknesses, lists for Jim and Everette and Dale and Edward Lee. Under Ed Jack's name, Julia scrawled in the heading "Good":

> *Trustful*
> *Honest*
> *Kind*
> *Good financier*
> *Particular about clothes, neat*
> *Fairly good manners, not too embarrassing*
> *Good snuggler*

Under "Bad" she spared no ink, listing some sixteen of my grandfather's most noxious habits, ranging from his enthusiasm for "dirty stories" to his color blindness in clothing, to the usual vices of smoking, drinking, cussing, and lack of church-going. Starred under the list of "bad" were "bad grammar" and "should get nose straightened, tonsils removed." And still Julia Mae wrote,

> *Is it love? Every time he touches me any place I just freeze + grow stiff then when I relax I feel so very good, but yet so bad. When I am with him somehow I don't get enough of him, but I don't know what I want. I just hold my breath to keep from screaming. But what does he have that gets me? Not handsome, little money, bad grammar, socially an outcast, temper, stubborn, no education. We don't agree on anything. He's marvelous.*

"Sometimes I think maybe I could love Eddie," my grandmother mused.

> *I like to have him around so well, but I just
> can't let go because I have planned on a millionaire
> + someone with a profession he loves. Eddie doesn't
> like farming although he probably is a good farmer +
> besides he doesn't like classical music, but somehow he
> gets me. Got a letter from Dale last week + it put me in
> a bad mood for a couple of days. I think he intends to
> marry sooner, but he thinks I am, too. Please don't let
> us make a big mistake.*

As the snow began to melt on the farm in March of 1939, so too did Julia Mae's inhibitions.

> *Eddie came to the church for me. I was aching to
> see him. Just to hear him breathe totally thrills me +
> it is mostly through his mouth and half of his broken
> nose. I had better be careful before I fall madly in
> love. He was magnificent or was it the night? Quiet,
> pleasant, so soft and gentle. I could just scream. . . .
> Did I feel this way with Dale? There is so many ways
> to compare them. I wish we could be together always.
> I wonder if he thinks I really love him. I tell him it's
> an act + it was intended to be. Do such thrills come
> from that?*

Broken nose or no, the love of Edward Lee, neighbor boy and farmer's son, caused my gran to do something completely unexpected—after weighing her lists she up and chose the country bumpkin, the old familiar, the one with the longest and most particular list of minuses by far. "He looked handsome in his overalls. Really he seems so much more adult and less dirty-minded," she wrote in a journal entry remembering the boy from her high school class who reveled in dirty jokes told in dirty pool halls. "I like him like he was tonight. Better than usual somehow. If I don't get to see him every night I feel so blue and lost."

When their good friends Bill and Bonnie Hass married on March 11 of 1939, Julia Mae and Edward Lee waited the customary seven days before paying their old classmate and his blushing bride a visit on their rural Mechanicsville farm. The visit proved infectious, and when my grandmother returned home she scribbled in her notebook,

> *Went to see Bill and Bonnie [Hass] now married a week + a day. Maybe it is the lovely warm spring day or seeing the newlyweds or could it be me. Eddie was so marvelous. I felt the urge so strong that it made me feel like I would faint.*

Nine months later to the day, my grandparents followed their good friends' example, concluding a long and sometimes fraught courtship with a wedding that merited some dozen column inches in the *Cedar Rapids Gazette*. "The bride entered on the arm of her father to the strains of Lohengrin's wedding march," the story in the December 11, 1940, paper read. "She wore an ivory transparent velvet gown fashioned with hip-length fitted bodice and floor-length skirt gathered full. The veil was of white silk net falling from a double ruffle headpiece of net and ending in a train of old family lace. The entire costume was made by the bride herself."

One hundred of my grandparents' friends and relatives attended the wedding "solemnized at high noon," as the newspaper copy put it, at the Methodist Episcopal church in Mechanicsville, in whose very pews my grandparents had listened to their high school baccalaureate service. Those gathered for the wedding five and a half years later heard the sweet strains of Thomas Moore's 1808 tune "Believe Me if All Those Endearing Young Charms" resound in the church nave:

> Believe me, if all those endearing young charms,
> Which I gaze on so fondly today,
> Were to change by tomorrow, and fleet in my arms,
> Live fairy-gifts fading away,

Thou wouldst still be adored, as this moment thou art,
Let thy loveliness fade as it will,
And around the dear ruin each wish of my heart
Would entwine itself verdantly still.
It is not while beauty and youth are thine own,
And thy cheeks unprofaned by a tear,
That the fervor and faith of a soul may be known,
To which time will but make thee more dear!
No, the heart that has truly loved never forgets,
But as truly loves on to the close,
As the sunflower turns on her god when he sets
The same look which she turned when he rose!

Who knows exactly why Julia Mae picked her neighbor Edward Lee, the son of a dirt farmer, the one whose affections she had resisted for nearly a decade. The recesses of a lover's heart forever harbor the greatest of mysteries. Perhaps, on a practical level, distance proved the deciding factor in those days when only the rarest of young women had a car to do with as she pleased, my grandfather living nearer at hand than Jim, some ten miles distant in a college town. Beyond such logistical considerations, my grandparents' union never was logical, and still it sizzled in the high-tension spirit world of the awkwardly matched yet utterly fated.

Post-honeymoon, the two childhood friends settled into quiet domesticity characterized by increasingly chilly distances that my dad later described as a "cold war." My grandmother's decision to choose the life of the farm wife when her heart was that of an artist-rambler, my mom always claimed, perhaps explained her later depression and alcoholism and the pointed, sometimes painful warfare she would engage my more conciliatory grandfather in. My mom's speculations seemed especially apt when once my dad and I, on an errand to locate something for my grandmother in the bedroom she had once shared with my grandfather, opened a bottom drawer in the bureau to find a note—a love note—from my grandmother to my grandfather, Julia Mae to Edward Lee, signed, "Love, Your Enemy."

Still, their union abided and endured and phosphoresced, producing four children and a passel of grandchildren and great-grandchildren. Though she outlived her husband by a half dozen years, my grandmother never stopped talking about the man she wed—not with flattery but matter-of-factly, the way you do with an old friend who has both unintentionally wronged you and loved you well.

Seventy-five years—a lifetime—after my grandparents' soul-stirring union, I too, like my friend Mark, am haunted by the inevitability of their union, wondering what has become of a region whose homegrown courtships and memories seem sequestered in the past, as deeply buried as the Model T or the butter churn. How many of the rural Midwest's college-educated daughters and sons today follow my grandmother's and her sister's leads, parlaying the finest liberal arts education the Heartland has to offer into sacred matrimony with a truly homegrown mate?

Edward Jack, Julia Jack, and their first child, Patricia, circa 1942.

The questions continue to vex long after I box up my grandparents' old love letters and lie awake nights and mull over my own romantic predicament. When I was a boy on the farm and afternoons were long and people still took scrawny, mewing kittens home from the grocery store and fed them warm milk for no good reason at all, love was everywhere, or so it seemed to me. It was in the kernels of sweet corn we ate each night, as it was in the just-right fruit of the pregnant watermelons that volunteered in the patch out back, and in the rain that burst forth suddenly from the dark underbelly of a cloud and broke the drought and brought us such jubilation we wanted to dance right there in the middle of dinner. Back then we didn't try overly hard to name the mysterious force that made things good and right, but we felt its spirit moving all the same, stirring the tassels in the cornfield like the hot breath of some higher power. At night, as the crickets chirped their love and the bullfrogs barked theirs, we fell asleep to swoony men on our radios crooning their hearts out to beloveds whose image swelled and grew until it became the song entire.

Among my grandparents' things, I unearth an old print that I find myself staring at with such intensity that when I close my lids I still see its image burned in my mind's eye. An illustration from

From *Joseph Breck's Annual Descriptive Catalogue of Seeds*, 1886.

an old seed catalogue, I presume, but who can say? It's titled "Angel of Midnight Field Corn." Love must be like that field-corn angel, I think, come in the middle of the night to bring inexplicable gifts to the very people who toil and try each day and night at the impossible task of helping the pollen fall just right. Even in those rare moments when their tired eyelids flutter like butterfly kisses, and their heads loll forward like rag dolls, love descends like manna, like unexpected communion, like an archangel with wings in terrific flutter.

At libraries around the Heartland I've met hundreds like me—searching in old dusty archives, wracking their memories, seeking desperately to recollect the words of their parents' or grandparents' love songs, those golden oldies, as if love was a snippet of a tune carried away by the wind or a face glimpsed long ago in a crowd. And in every dusty library where I keep my own peculiar vigil, I likewise encounter the naysayers and boobirds too, who, when I describe the image to them of a woman fluttering down from the heavens with a fistful of grain and a pixie-dust of pollen, look at me as if I had just pulled a rubber chicken from my messenger bag and danced the tarantella with it.

True love will not bless their gardens, I tell myself, or beat its wings at their front stoop bearing joyful news. Follow love back the way she flew, back down the country road into that dim and flickering past, yours and mine, past fencerows and farmhouses and skies a perfect shade of midnight blue and it's possible to find a boy sleeping under his parents' roof dreaming of a girl, and a young lady sleeping fitfully in a gingham nightgown dreaming of whatever it is young ladies are wont to dream about, then as now.

There love roosts in the trees like a magnificent bird shaking its great wings before alighting to do such good and necessary deeds as happen under the cover of night—blowing the bothersome leaves from the front porch, capping the flowers with brilliant blooms—until the girl and boy wake, rubbing the sleep from their eyes, burning suddenly with the secret knowledge that the whole world depends somehow on their finding one another. They slide their feet into slippers and follow into the dewy morning at an hour they scarcely knew existed, to stare through the leafy canopy to the moon beyond that seems to light up at their affections.

Sometimes, when I begin to doubt the amber glow of my own dim memories, I give in and find myself believing what the naysayers would have me believe—that they were nothing special, a boy and a girl lost to time and stuck in a little corn town others practically tripped over themselves to leave.

Once love has flown and imposters have taken its place, things that once seemed miraculous come to seem ho-hum . . . even hum-drum. And where once we saw the hand of fate disbelievers see only the cold logic of things they call "factors," for want of better. They treat the boy and the girl of their long-agos harshly, call them naive and foolish and silly. Sure, they may trot them out once in a blue moon for a ceremonial trip down memory lane, but they keep them under lock and key at all other hours, storing them on the highest shelf of a faraway closet in a faraway city to aid in their forgetting.

Suffice it to say I feel as if I knew Edward Lee and Julia Mae once when love was new, and a boy and a girl looked at the moon. And try as I might I cannot forget them, or the peculiar music of their laughter, or the little keepsakes they left behind for me to find one day like a bread-crumb trail leading back, or the particular way the light of autumn illuminates them from within when, ruminating late into the night on the farm they made together—I consider what remains of the moon that turns them golden.

Wonder Women

In 1976 America celebrated its bicentennial year, and my own circle of rural women warriors, led by my mother and grandmother and aunts, dressed us kids up as Redcoats and Revolutionaries and loaded us atop a float they'd made with their own hands to pull behind our lawn tractor. It wasn't unusual for the wonder women in our family to whip up a float to advertise our agrarian arts fair, Wind in the Walnuts, but this year was different: America was turning two hundred.

Our Fourth of July parade in tiny, unincorporated Cedar Bluff, Iowa, had become an unlikely national staging ground for feminist protests, and we disco-era kids attended each year expecting to see, at the very least, bra burnings and left-handed political statements made by women who perennially chose this backwater town near ours as a launchpad for their activisms, both because its remoteness offered some small measure of anonymity and because it was just near enough to a gender-liberated university town to make the drive doable. Still, our provincial bacchanal was mostly a best-kept secret until the year five women dressed as Lady Liberty rode topless across their women's rights float, making, they claimed, a statement against pornography and nudity.

———⟡———

"Find yourself a strong woman," I remember my farm elders telling me as a kid growing up in the Heartland. I think what they really

My sister and me in the staging ground for one of our earliest Cedar Bluff parade floats, this one before our "Spirit of 1776" float.

meant to tell me was "find a woman like your mother or grand-mother," for anyone who grew up in midwestern farm country will tell you it takes a love-partner made of strong stuff to endure the inevitable slings and arrows of a life lived from and by the soil.

Lately, though, I'd been wondering . . . did they mean *strong* as in opinionated? Did they mean *strong* as in independent or maybe self-reliant or firm in purpose and moral compass? Did *strong* mean a woman who was to be feared—quite literally *awesome*? I was never entirely sure. It seemed almost required of farm or ranch elders to offer vague chestnuts like these without ever bothering to explain their definitions.

My father always said ours was a matriarchal clan, but it wasn't until I rooted down on my own rural acres that I really understood the truth of his statement. I had been a kid in the era of Lynda Carter's *Wonder Woman*, after all, the late-middle of the sexual revolution, and yet it somehow seemed to me that my father and grandfather—who drove the tractors and plowed the fields—held the reins. When I look back on it now, though, I realize my clan's rural women were the wonder women of our operation.

In 1972, the year the first *Wonder Woman* TV pilot debuted on network airwaves, my grandmother Julia mustered the country women of my family together in a joint venture that made the front page of the *Cedar Rapids Gazette*, where a photo spread ran bearing the caption, "Everybody works who visits the site of Wind in the Walnuts near Mechanicsville. Busy scrubbing the loft of the big red barn are, from left, Mindy Coon, 10, Tasha Jack, age 15 months, and Rodney Sullivan, 6, three of the six grandchildren of Ed Jack."

The truth was my grandmother, rather than my grandfather, was the driving force behind the headline "Art Show on Farm Is Family Project." In a second photo my grandmother smiled demurely in front of an antique stove she'd just wiped clean, the caption billing her as "director" of our enterprise. Datelining his feature, newsman Art Hough began,

> It's only a few miles south of bustling Highway 30 to the site of Wind in the Walnuts, but it might as well be a hundred. Wind in the Walnuts will be a country art market . . . on a farm whose buildings go back more than 100 years. . . . A family project, directed by Mrs. Ed Jack, the diversified art show will be produced under the shade of a grove of beautiful walnut trees and in a big red farm building which has been reconverted from a woodworking shop to what will be a year-round art center.

In those days it was still customary to address the farmer's wife as "Mrs.," as in "Mrs. Ed Jack," but we knew better. Ours was what even then was considered a "feel-good" story about a prairie family who somehow managed to hold it together. "The reason Mrs. Jack calls this a family project is because it is," Hough insisted. "The Jacks' three daughters, a daughter-in-law, and even the six grandchildren are hammering away and sawing, scrubbing, painting, and polishing to get the barn and grounds ready for the public." What

made Hough's story front-page material was the real headliners
in my family: its women. "All of the family, at least the women,
are [rural] artists in their own right," the article trumpeted. Going
on to list my grandmother's cadre of she-assistants, the article
read, "Assisting Mrs. Jack in the art show preparation are the Jack
daughters, Mrs. Charles Coon, Mrs. Robert Sullivan, and Miss
Barbara, and a daughter-in-law, Mrs. Michael Jack. All but the
Sullivans, who reside at 706 Danbury Street SE, Cedar Rapids,
live in the immediate area." The object of the Wind in the Walnuts, according to my grandmother, was "to get people in this
area interested in their own [country] artists." The human interest
story of our farm daughter–led venture was likewise picked up
by the *Iowa City Press-Citizen*, where word of the "first annual
country market" seven miles southeast of Lisbon appeared beside
movie ads depicting the broader gender fires then reaching combustion in the world beyond our barnyard.

My aunt Barb had set a wedding date for the summer of 1975.
My mother, herself a farmer's daughter, had recently returned with
my father to his parents' farm. For a time all of us—grandparents,
parents, aunts, and a passel of cousins—shared common ground. My
grandmother Julia, a farmer's daughter turned farmer's wife, served
as our ringleader and queen entrepreneur, our barnyard Hippolyta.
In the previous decade she'd begun her own ceramics studio, Coral
Gables, in the basement of her farm home, where she taught pot-
tery classes to the women of our rural community. Indeed, our
Queen Bee had turned her home into such a regular community
center and coffee klatch that my aunt Barb hung a hand-painted
placard beside the front door that read "Julia's Coffee House."

My grandmother was omnipresent—the driving force behind
any and all of the farm's operations in an almost subliminal way that
now, nearly thirty years later, I am still sometimes at a loss to explain
to others. Gran was not the gun-wielding, wear-the-pants agrarian archetype who had long ago cowed her husband and subdued
the hired man—a Calamity Jane of the prairies. Nor was she an
ideologue or an intellectual, though she was better educated than

every male farmer in our neighborhood. She eschewed virtually all
the -ist labels, with the exception perhaps of conservationist—one
of a very few mantles she wore proudly. She was avowedly not a
feminist, though she was, paradoxically, feminism defined, owning
and running her own business from her basement, mentoring and
cultivating the talents of her daughters and daughters-in-law, and
embracing her own body in ways her rural community sometimes
found shocking. She was the first and only woman of her era to
mow the farm's generous lawn in a bikini top, a grin-and-bear-it
wardrobe selection that brought her in head-to-head conflict with
my grandfather, who had been raised by a Quaker father and had
come to embody all things modest. Needless to say, Gran won that
battle of the sexes on the farm, and many others that followed. What
she was, in the end, was a guiding spirit, a goddess in the sense that
all actions taken around her had no choice but to accommodate
her sometimes fickle and unknowable wishes. Like our midwestern
weather, she could be punitive where the dreams and schemes of
the adult men in our family were concerned, though she was never
anything but the sweetest and most benevolent of coconspirators
to her grandchildren.

Like many rural women, my grandmother passed away without
much fanfare and with few of the usual patriarchal artifacts marking
time and ownership, though she was an incorrigible packrat. Having lived in the same country ranch house for nearly fifty years, she
had had considerable time to squirrel away emblems and albums of
her past in the home she designed herself to include ample storage
for her most prized possessions: rocks from our family timberland,
seashells from early marital trips to warmer climes, dresses from her
go-get-'em youth, and plenty of what seemed at the time to be
mostly useless bits of paper—most of them the doodles she made
while watching educational television, grocery lists, and receipts.

And yet when the officiant called for the obligatory "family
stories" to be shared on the late spring day of her funeral in the
pioneer cemetery across from the woodland through which she
had joyfully tramped her entire adult life, the request was met with

a silence so deep that even the officiant cleared her throat to remedy the awkwardness. The quiet lingered until finally my eldest male cousin, Rodney, threw in his two cent's worth. Rodney's favorite story was indicative of my grandmother's modus operandi, and involved my father dropping me off early one morning before heading out to our farm fields with express instructions forbidding my grandmother from allowing me to play tackle football with my older, rougher male cousins. As soon as my gran heard the door slam behind him, she had turned to me, Rodney recalled with a chuckle, and told me to go out and play with the older boys, never mind what my father had said.

Beyond my cousin's story, however, there were few if any takers, and our officiant mercifully moved on. It wasn't that there weren't yarns to share about Gran, but that the anecdotes themselves seemed beneath her—could never begin to take the measure of her influence. The offering of quaint little stories about a woman whose presence was so omnipotent struck us as almost heretical, like making small talk with Aphrodite about the surf.

Later, however, my mom was eager to share with me her wholehearted praise for a woman she viewed as a true "free spirit," a country girl and country booster who nevertheless found that the confines of the rural life were "not always where her heart might be at times." *Where her heart might be at times . . .* In the days that followed my grandmother's funeral my mom's words replayed over and over again in my mind until they became strangely self-evident to me. What had I *really* known of the contents of my grandmother's heart? A few months after her passing, under my father's direction, an oversized dumpster arrived in front of my grandparents' now-empty ranch house. Like most rural homes after the death of their last remaining guiding spirit, the house had been left largely untouched since she'd passed, a reliquary and museum to hers and my grandfather's years, until finally my father had had enough. Once the dumpster was in place, he assured me, his sisters—my aunts—would come to do the cleaning and sorting of my grandmother's things, just as he and I had sorted through my grandfather's after his death years earlier. This postmortem sorting of a mother's things was, in my father's eyes, gendered work that modesty prevented him from undertaking. Something about a grown son sorting through his mother's slips and skirts and undergarments struck him as a breach of decorum. My father was not sanguine about the prospects though, predicting that "the girls" would take months to complete a task he might accomplish in a long weekend of dedicated trash-hauling.

For months that fall, my three aunts toiled away in the rooms of my grandmother's largely cloistered life. They would come and go on an irregular schedule—sometimes working together, sometimes apart—all the while making precisely as little headway as my father had predicted. And yet each time I peered into the cavernous dumpster, the junk pile had grown. Had more opportunist extended family members come and dumped their own trash in the oversized bin, or had my aunts made more progress than the still-cluttered rooms of the house suggested?

Once or twice, Aunt Barb called to ask if I might like to join them, and once or twice I went, eager and at the same time reluctant. I wanted more than anything to be the curator of my grandmother's things, having earned her trust over a lifetime as grandmother-grandson confidants. And yet something about the hunting and pecking involved in sorting—dresses ohhed and ahhed at, feminine secrets unearthed—threatened, it seemed, to unman me. So that in the end I felt forced to compromise, playing an occasional supporting role, lingering at the edge of the bedroom door and agreeably serving as an audience for my aunts' exclamations at surprise finds and the impromptu memories they triggered. During those afternoons especially, I often felt a traitor in an enemy camp, a man sneaked into the backrooms and boudoirs of a beauty queen like a soldier smuggled into Troy in a horse.

I was eating lunch with a friend later that fall at our local small-town pizza joint when a call rang in from Aunt Barb informing me that the sorting was finally finished; and that she had left me a few special things, including a sheaf of my grandmother's famous doodles—the ones she had made while listening to Julia Child or watching *Wonder Woman* or Lawrence Welk reruns, or her favorite, *Nature*. Their cleaning had turned up diaries and journal entries—an unexpectedly meaningful harvest Barb told me they would divvy up amongst themselves before (and here she paused) burning the rest.

Burn them? Why on earth, I wanted to know.

There were things, my aunt said slowly, that I did not know about my grandmother . . . things "the girls" had discovered in their cleaning that they thought it best not to share with the rest of the family. Gran had not always been happy, or at least not as happy as we had assumed her to be, Barb hinted, leaving it at that.

Instantly, I felt betrayed, struggling to find the right words exactly, until finally I managed to say, *But I want to know my grandmother.* Barb listened politely and demurred, a firmness in her voice I was not accustomed to hearing.

My father had a theory of marriage for which he used my grandparents as his Exhibit A. Walk into a long-married couple's home, he always said, and look at the decor. Whatever era it came from marked the exact point in time that the couple had "stopped trying," the time limit of their amours preserved in the wall and floor coverings as if fossilized or preserved in amber. When I went back to my grandparents' house in the days after I hung up the phone with my aunt, I looked with my father's eyes—at the mustard-yellow laminate walls in the kitchen, at the coral pink–tiled bathroom, at the well-worn linoleum on the kitchen floor—and I thought, *early sixties.* Even the childhood toys that had kept my father and his sisters occupied during that decade still sat on the shelf of the playroom with the built-in slate blackboard—my father's many childhood trucks and his Magic Mike, the board game called Mousetrap, an early Etch-a-Sketch.

In its way, my father's theory corroborated my mother's about the vagaries of my grandmother's heart and the unspoken quality of her needs. If Gran and Grampy had all but quit in 1963, say, how could I ever hope to know the Gran that came later, after the flame. With the diaries and journal entries burned, what chance did I have, short of a séance, to reclaim, or at least name, the goddess of my past? I blamed myself for not having been more present at the sorting, for missing a once-in-a-lifetime chance to come, finally, to understand my grandmother's innermost thoughts and feelings. I imagined the irreplaceable artifacts of her past going up in smoke, feeling desperate and angry again at the decision my aunts had reached minus the consent or consensus of the family. I had lived by the sword, and now, in ceding the all-important work of sorting and saving to "the girls," it felt as if I was dying by it.

For months I tortured myself over the loss, until I remembered my grandmother's equally valuable keepsake, the one Barb had earmarked to be given to me—the massive collection of daily doodles that documented her life in a voluminous paper trail of sketches featuring everything from the mundane cat-litter reminders to the sublime illustration of superheroes, gods, and goddesses whose preternatural visages stared out from the same loose pages on which my grandmother had scrawled grocery lists featuring Spam and Thousand Island.

Breast-baring and stars-and-bars would seem strange bedfellows, but in America's bicentennial year, these mingled motifs gave birth to two one-hour specials starring former Miss World USA and USO star Lynda Carter. Carter's Wonder Woman costume represented a purposeful hybrid of the Amazon woman warrior—tiara, modified breastplate, bracelets, and boots—and Lady Columbia, the long-standing female personification of America that predated Uncle Sam by at least a century. The raven-haired actress's star-

One of my grandmother's full-page doodles.

spangled getup appealed to the patriotic ethos of 1976, serving as an easy-on-the-eyes antidote to America's painful retreat from Vietnam and the many (mostly masculine) transgressions and trespasses of Watergate. Executive producer Douglas Cramer presented American TV viewers with what he intended from the get-go to be a cultural bellwether—Wonder Woman, the long-legged, ebony-haired, preternaturally athletic Amazon played by Carter. In the series debut, Cramer has Wonder Woman sacrifice the safety and sanctity afforded her on the tranquil, all-woman Paradise Island for a life fighting the evil doings of evil men in a godless capital.

Episode one of the much ballyhooed series opened with hunky co-star Steve Trevor crash-landing into an uncharted tropical isle ruled entirely by women. The hapless pilot is promptly discovered by the gorgeous Amazon princess Diana and her ginger-haired sidekick, Rena. "I've never seen a man in the flesh before," Rena avows, to which the azure-eyed princess replies, "Who of us have?" Princess Diana picks up the unconscious airman easily and, cradling him with superhuman strength, sprints across the island holding the fully-grown man as easily as if he were a child. The camera pans the cliffs as Diana runs with her man-specimen in hand, revealing scores of other statuesque beauties engrossed in their classically agrarian archery practice. Mid-quiver, they call after their handsome princess, "Looks like a man! What is it? Where did you find him?!"

In the next scene, we meet Diana's mother Hippolyta, legendary queen of the Amazons, played by Cloris Leachman, as she confers worriedly with a female attendant. The graying but still beautiful queen is cast to conjure the mothers of the mid- to late 1970s, many of whom had been seasoned campaigners for women's liberation. Conversely, the naive daughter played by Carter depicts the young women like my mother and aunts who had come of age immediately after the sexual revolution and had already, in many cases, taken for granted their mothers' hard work for gender equity.

"A thousand years and man has never discovered us," the queen laments, only to have the headstrong princess object, "But surely some men can be trusted." Reaching out gently for her daughter's hand, the elder Amazon launches into the necessary backstory. "You're too young to remember how we women were slaves in Greece and Rome. I promised myself it would never happen again. We found this island where we live in harmony, peace, and sisterhood. Now we may lose it forever," she bemoans, picking an apple from her bowl in a thinly veiled allusion to Eve. Queen Hippolyta is convinced her daughter will be beguiled by this handsome devil fallen from the sky onto their peaceable island, and that her carefully built separatist she-society will crumble. "I named this island Paradise for an excellent reason. There are no men on it. Thus it is free of their wars, their greed, their hostilities, their barbaric, masculine behavior."

We grandkids watched the episodes of *Wonder Woman* that followed with keen interest, our own Queen Hippolyta sometimes watching intently beside us on the couch as Lynda Carter whirled her way into her superhero personae, twirling like a runway model, but with a more righteous agenda. This was the part we liked best, the strangely erotic spin that transformed the bespectacled secretary Diana Prince into a beautifully formidable superhero in satin tights and knee-length boots ready to go out and kick some bad-guy butt. I was too young then to have even an inkling of lust for Wonder Woman, whom I loved with the same kind of genuflecting, I-am-not-worthy reverence I reserved for my beatific kindergarten teacher, Mrs. Dolan, and for wonder women like my mom and grandmother. But I could tell from the look in the eye of my oldest male cousins as we watched our favorite superhero on the flickering TV screen that their interests were more than platonic. Wonder Woman had something they had been programmed to recognize, it seemed, to value, and to desire, and so their eyes stayed glued to the tube, mesmerized at the strength of the rare beauty before them.

Paradoxically, the most meaningful artifacts of a farm inheritance often arrive in the most humble packages—brown paper bags, cardboard boxes, garbage sacks. My grandmother's sketches and doodles came to me in two oversized freezer bags—likely the same in which she had once packed and frozen our summer vegetables.

More often than not her doodles had been applied to reused envelopes and stationary, my grandmother a believer in DIY and repurposing long before either became hip. Envelopes addressed "Mrs. Edward Jack, Rural Route 1" constituted her favorite canvas, second only to remnants of my grandfather's letterhead from the Golden Harvest seed-corn company he represented. When neither of these preferred media could be found, our goddess of perpetual doodling would choose the back of the typed letterhead bearing fund-raising solicitations from the development office of her small-college alma mater. "These are times of great potential," the solicitations, signed Richard "Joe" Morton, class of 1950, read, "I encourage you to fill out the enclosed reply card indicating how you are willing to assist." My grandmother, who had dropped out of Cornell College after two years that culminated in her accidental blowing up of the chemistry lab, was apparently willing to assist by defacing the letterhead with her usually idiosyncratic and utterly imitable scribble, including, on Joe Morton's letter, the word **TRAMP!** written vertically in the top right accompanied by a picture of a flame and the caption **NEW Start**. Was Mr. Morton the tramp? It seemed unlikely. Perhaps his wife then? Or was my cousin-in-law Danielle, whose name my Gran also scrawled on the college letterhead, the coquette in reference? Surely not. Or had my grandmother simply overheard those fightin' words on one of the sundry radio or television programs she listened to and absentmindedly inscribed them there, beside Joe's name, for the ambiguous amusement of posterity?

The doodles, as they cascaded from the reused freezer bags into my lap, struck me both as impossibly, almost beatifically, random, and as a highly purposeful documentation of my grandmother's innermost thoughts in the decades after she quit keeping the clandestine diaries my aunts had found. A lover of all things ancient Egyptian, my grandmother had left me with an archaeologist's plight—how much intentionality and composition could be assumed, for instance, in the contents of a buried tomb from which two otherwise incongruous artifacts had been unearthed side by side? Had they been buried there together on purpose, divinely arranged for an afterlife of interpretation and demystification, or simply landed there, cheek by jowl, amid the chaotic rubble? Unlike her journal entries, my gran's doodles had never been secret; most days they lay in plain sight in the kitchen beside the butter container or the Tupperware napkin holder atop my grandparents' kidney-shaped 1950s table. There I and my cousins came upon them gleefully, their method so mad and layered—like Van Gogh's or Munch's—that as kids we never thought to divine the meaning of their words and captions, choosing instead to focus on the strange and otherworldly pictures she drew of what could only be called freaks—old men, goat people, fanged fish, criminals and bandits, buildings that looked like they belonged in Munchkinland, crazy superheroes. Looking at them I realize there was far more going on in my grandmother's heart than ever I imagined, some of it more dark than I had been prepared as a boy to see or to know—a farm wife's Rosetta Stone buried right under the whole family's nose.

1. **Personally cold**
2. **Jeoulous** [jealous]
3. **Care**
4. **Mean**
5. **Bored**

This list of attributes adorns one of her first scrawled-on envelopes, followed, in no particular order, by a haphazard scattering of the words **Burden, Aggressive, Best Alone** and then a series of four awkwardly tilted hearts drawn side by side like a garland. On the

left margin, written large in all caps, appears the word **Burn** followed by a question mark; circled below it are the words **Reverse Attack** and **Anger** dusted in brushfire flames.

Are these the only surviving records of how my grandmother was feeling that day, or how she was made to feel by the King

Oberon to her Queen Hippolyta: my grandfather? A grandson's intuition tells me so, the words used here in keeping with the same she let slip in the rare moments when she voiced marital anger, hurt, or frustration to her grandchildren. On another envelope she has doodled up an original design for a lavender blouse with black collars labeled "yarn blanket stitch." Beside the dress she's drawn a motley fool with a bird perched on his head and the word **PROOF** written as a mysterious caption. Was she looking for proof that day—or every day—and, if so, of what, and from whom?

The next sketch she pens on the back of page three of a handout atop which is printed the heading "Why blood pressure is like air pressure in a tire." On it she draws otherworld castles atop testimonials from a Mrs. S. Harar of Sumner, Iowa, and a Miss Williams of Detroit, Michigan, while aiming a giant, unmistakably phallic rocket, poised and ready to launch, directly at the quote, "I received your health book a few years ago . . ." On the blank side of the health digest, my goddess's captions grow even more mysterious—**Killing Frost** penciled in beside the sketch of a heavily bearded

mountain man and **Trapped by Maddness** scrawled written on the left margin.

On her loose-leaf pages, pedestrian events mingle with subliminal feelings. In one, she makes note that Frank (my aunt Patricia's boyfriend) called ("good tan") bordered on the top by a farm scene, and the words **REPULSE, SELF-CENTERED = "I"** and **MOCKERY**, all in caps. On another she sketches an image of a person with a silly flower blooming from a drum major's cap, the words **Mentadent Toothpaste**, and above it, **NO Trust, NO Respect** double underscored. On the throwaway pasteboard portion of a Kleenex box she writes in dramatically outlined letters **Wrong. Ruin!!!! NO trust, Rid, PAIN, iNtERFERED**. Ominously, another of her notations reads,

No WAtER

No Food

no teeth

Elsewhere, and everywhere, she illustrates pictures of alien landscapes seemingly right out of *Star Wars*, accompanied by strange

superheroes—masked avengers and a balding but buff Superman with the trademark "S" printed on his chest. There are doodles naming something (or someone) Ice Man and Australia Girl. There are pitchfork-wielding devils and male seraphim.

Nearly all of the characters Gran sketched are men staring off the page, head-on, with hooded eyes wearing somewhat inscrutable but not altogether unkind expressions; I wonder now if it's because she liked men best or least. Did she find the masculine espe-

cially heroic, demonic, or both? Just what sorts of gods and demons would a farm goddess draw in her spare time, if she had time to spare? On TV in the 1970s, Wonder Woman was a young princess with ample time and leisure, but our wonder woman was a busy mother and a grandmother helping to raise a second generation on a working family farm.

Every superhero needs an alter ego, an alternate identity sublimated, suppressed, or carefully hidden away to prevent breaches of anonymity and the inevitability of attack. And as I look at my gran's uncanny drawings and their sometimes darkly troubling captions, I suspect she knew little of how much we grandchildren idolized her—how much her beauty and strength inspired our every act of imaginative art and play. The words she doodles—**angry, shutout, end, greed, control**—make me sad for the more pedestrian life she lived, or appeared to live, in the eyes of the rest of the world that knew her only as Mrs. Edward Jack, though in our barnyard and in our hearts she reigned supreme.

Doodling comic books began as a hobby for Wonder Woman cre-
ator William Marston, pen name Charles Moulton, whose day job
was a psychologist with a special interest in the contest between
the sexes. For him, Wonder Woman served as the embodiment of
society's inevitable return to a matriarchal order, one in which men
would have little choice but to submit to the "loving dominance"
of women. Originally, he had named his wonder woman Suprema,
reminding his publisher, Sheldon Mayer, "I fully believe that I am
hitting a great movement now under way—the growth in the power
of women, and I want you to let that theme alone, or drop the
project." Elsewhere in a letter to comics historian Coulton Waugh,
Marston confessed, "Frankly, Wonder Woman is the psychological
propaganda for the new type of woman who should, I believe, rule
the world. There isn't love enough in the male organism to run this
planet peacefully." As a scientist, Marston pointed out that wom-
en's bodies contained, as he put it, "twice as many love-generating
organs and endocrine mechanism as the male." If love, compassion,
and sociability were to be the lynchpins of postwar civilization,
he reasoned, women would be infinitely better designed to carry
out that love-agenda, provided they could reverse man's dominance
and subject him to their will. Early in his 1935 book, *Emotions of
Normal People*, Marston recalls a formative childhood experience
in which his mother taught him the wisdom of submitting to her
will. As the story goes, young Bill Marston was being bullied by a
"half-witted boy with an air gun" on his way home from school.
His father, a pacifist, told him never to fight, but his mother told her
son he had license to "go after him" if the bully fired upon him first.
Marston proceeded to back the bully down without so much as a
shot fired, and while he took some credit, "most of it," he reported,
"belonged to my mother . . . because I submitted to her."

Marston's letter to Waugh explaining the origins of his super-
heroine served as an almost exact paraphrase of his earlier psycho-

logical writings. In the letter he explains, "I have given Wonder Woman this dominant force. ... Her bracelets, with which she repels bullets and other murderous weapons, represent the Amazon Princess's submission to Aphrodite, Goddess of Love and Beauty. Her magic lasso, which compels anyone bound by it to obey Wonder Woman and which was given to her by Aphrodite herself, represents woman's love charm and allure by which she compels men to do her bidding." Young women and girls, Marston claimed in a treatise written the same year my grandmother graduated high school, had superior "emotional training," which tended to "enhance their dominance emotion." The effect of this development, he observed, was "beginning to make itself apparent in the emotional training of the younger generation" among whom "adolescent girls and very young women are pre-empting the spotlight of publicity in national sports contests."

"Some girls love to have a man stronger than they are to make them do things," Wonder Woman declares in one of the earliest of Marston's (using the nom de plume Charles Moulton) comics. "Do I like it? I don't know. It's sort of thrilling. But isn't it more fun to make a man obey?" Gloria Steinem, who loved comic books as a girl growing up in the 1940s, recollects in her 1972 introduction to Marston's *Wonder Woman* how she was rescued from otherwise patriarchal realms at the age of seven or eight by a woman who was "as wise as Athena and as lovely as Aphrodite" with the "speed of Mercury and the strength of Hercules." The budding young feminist could relate to Moulton's plots especially, which she described revolving "around evil men who treat women as inferior beings" and who are "brought to their knees and made to recognize women's strength and values." Steinem celebrates the "sweet vengeance, the toe-wriggling pleasure of reading about a woman who was strong, beautiful, courageous." Following Steinem's introduction to Moulton's early *Wonder Woman* strips appears a more academic take by feminist psychologist and psychotherapist Phyllis Chesler. In it Chesler endeavors to explain the historical and mythological roots of Amazon culture, summing up Wonder Woman as a product of a "prosperous, advanced, ordered, compassionate and basically androgynous all-female society" and an example of "the traditionally superior spiritual and altruistic powers of women." Science in Moulton's original Wonder Woman series is not dominant, she points out, but properly "adjunct" to deeper feminine intuition concerning the "supernatural" and "invisible" universe. Wonder Woman's invisible plane and magic lasso are, she asserts, emblems of "historically practiced female magic."

One of Gran's nature women.

Female magic was something my grandmother possessed in spades. Our wonder woman was our barnyard Hippolyta and Amazon princess rolled into one, and spring was her chosen season. In April she took to the fields and the woodlands encircling the farm just after snowmelt, feet stuck into big leather boots, rock pick in hand, sometimes taking us kids in tow. On days when she would leave for the timber, her doodles would grow more magical. One read simply, "Gone on a Dream." Another recorded the name "Gaia Goddess of the Earth." Others showed a series of nature women, often ren-

dered in the nude and always without human companionship, wading into woods or waters.

Her bible for these wilderness rambles was a book called *Wildflowers of Iowa Woodlands* that Dad and my sis-

ter and I gave her for Christmas in 1982, and which she took to more zealously than any present before or since. That winter she set about annotating the book in its entirety, less interested in what the flower looked like than what it could do. In the table of contents, she annotates in red ink any powers ascribed to each root or bloom. Beside violet, corydalis, bittersweet, moonseed, cardinal flower, lobelia, and white snakeroot she noted "poison," and under bloodroot and violet, the toxins' potential as a cancer cure. "The root is poisonous," my grandmother circles in the entry for blood-root. "Like other members of the poppy family, it contains alkaloids closely related to morphine." Dog-earing the page devoted to jack-in-the-pulpit, she likewise underlines in red, "The Meskwaki also used the root in disputes with other tribes. They'd cook meat with the fresh root and abandon it hoping the opposing warriors would

find it and partake of the meal—later to become sick, or even die, of calcium oxalate poisoning." Nightshade she takes special interest in, both underscoring and starring the line, "Numerous cases of animals and people being poisoned by nightshade berries have been reported."

By the time the book reaches the late-blooming woodland flowers of May and June, my woodland goddess's annotations became less frequent, the blossoms of late spring and summer belonging somehow to a sunnier, sexier camp that seemed to catch her fancy less. Queen's lady's slipper, she noted, was said to elicit temper and passion, and even, for those who ate the root, the book warned, "momentary conversion into the satyr condition." Ginseng too, my grandmother's notes reveal, could be used as a remedial agent against impotency. Bedstraw, the authors of the wildflower tome remarked and my grandmother dutifully starred, would, according to legend, bless newlyweds with many children if the couple filled their mattress with it.

Gran's wildflower guide fell to me after her passing, and each spring I pull it from its resting spot atop my grandfather's old desk, thumbing through, conjuring the powerful spirit of my grandmother, her *juno*, from its dusty pages. It's a complicated spirit, one that I love completely without the ability to fully comprehend it, a native spirit, part Sioux from her grandmother, a woman who no doubt would have used many of the same poultices and balms and poisons. Sometimes, browsing through the pages of her bible of the natural world, I feel as if I am reading not of woodland wildflowers but of love itself, its balm and passion and poison.

On one flip through, a typed note on yellow paper falls from the page for the flower called maiden's tears, or catchfly, for its sticky, insect-nabbing secretion. "Silene cucubalus. Silence: Probably from the mythological Greek god Silenus, the intoxicated foster-father of Bacchus, who was described as being covered with foam and slippery. Others believe the origin of the name lies in the Greek *sialon* meaning 'saliva.'" The yellow note addresses my grandfather and grandmother, Eddie and Julia, and, after thanking them for giving the children a happy Christmas, advises, "Please try to be kind to one another. Compromise." And later, "And if you would do me one last favor . . . take a long walk together every day. You'll be amazed at the changes." The note closes with "I love you," and a phone number—a Manhattan area code.

I'm puzzled over the identity of the letter writer who in their note thanks my grandparents for taking care of their "weird dog and those obnoxious cats." My father was the only one in the family to ever have a friend in Manhattan, but he would not have left a weird dog in anyone's care; this writing—the writing of a wise, upbeat, no doubt successfully married man or woman—does not belong to my father, whose syntax I would know at a glance. Whoever it is knew my grandparents well enough to know their native stubbornness, to sense the loneliness that existed for both of them within their marriage. Whoever it is was someone audacious enough to suggest the long walks my grandparents refused to take.

——⇒ ● ⇐——

"Independence Day is an ideal time for our protest," Melissa Farley, one of the day's "bare-breasted women," told the world in a UPI story in 1976, the same year our grandmother took us boys to march in that parade. Farley all but dared county law enforcement agents to arrest her, as there appeared to be no enforceable county ordinance against the baring of bosoms, nothing in jurisprudence to check the advance of these Amazon women from the nearest university town come dressed—or partially undressed—as Lady Liberties.

Writer Mercedes Lackey once wrote in praise of latter-day reboots such as Gail Simone's *Wonder Woman: The Circle*, which featured America's most powerful woman in her full-grown complexity: "Amazon Princess. Warrior, Diplomat, Protector, Healer. And Goddess." She endeavors to explain to a new generation of female readers, in particular, the need-to-know backstory: "Writers and storytellers have had a love/hate relationship with the Amazons ever since misogynistic Greeks created them. . . . In the case of the Greeks, it was hate, because a woman's place in most of Grecian society was locked behind walls for the purposes of procreation. And for the Greeks it was also love, because after denying their wives and daughters freedom and education, the learned men of Greece wondered why they were so dull and imagined something wilder, and imbued it with everything they wanted and feared at the same time."

"I don't believe there's a law that really prohibits it [nudity]," our sheriff, George Miller, told the national press corps when asked just what he intended to do with these wild women. While by his own admission he lacked the grounds to prosecute, our rural lawman wished the provoking, and provocative, city women might take their protest out of his parade, where the Lady Liberties drew, according to a report from yet another national wire service, both "cheers and jeers" from rural spectators. One man "charged at [Melissa] Farley" like an enraged bull, according to a report, only to be restrained by one of the float's retinue of muscular male consort-escorts enlisted to shoulder these modern-day Cleopatras.

I don't think my male cousins and I ever forgot our time as foot soldiers in my grandmother's army during that summer of 1976, nor did we forget the wonder we felt in the regular presence of rural wonder women like our gran, who was every bit as real to us as the land.

Still, as my male cousins and I turned into teens in the 1980s, we inevitably turned toward the masculine. Maybe our defection could be attributed to hormones, or the more subtle propaganda and gender-specific rites initiated by our fathers and grandfathers as they ushered us into the brotherhood of maleness. After a while, Wonder Woman's lasso and bracelet seemed haplessly feminine compared to our BB guns and motorbikes. For a while we toed the line between childhood and adulthood until, at some point, we crossed over from having a crush on *Little House on the Prairie's* girlishly earnest Melissa Gilbert to Bo and Luke Duke's cousin, Daisy Duke, she of the famously plunging neckline and revealing cut-off denims.

The brief back-to-the-land utopian movement of the 1970s, with its nurturer's concerns for child-rearing and seed-saving and organic farming, had temporarily given way to a more intensely commodified, more masculine era on the farm. Still, while my male cousins gradually grew up and married the "strong women" their elders had prescribed, of the wonder women who hammered and painted and built our homegrown arts festival directly into the newspaper's headlines in the early 1970s, only my grandmother and my aunt Barb would stay married to their first husbands.

For years I wondered to what I could attribute all of the leaving. Had the men in these women's lives somehow disappointed or betrayed them? Had the rural life underwhelmed or otherwise alienated? Had the get-big-or-get-out macho farming advocated by then–Secretary of Agriculture Earl Butz finally driven them away from the lifestyle entirely, and along with it the *family* in the mythic family farm? Maybe.

A more likely explanation, I think, is that when the wonder women of my youth found themselves shoehorned into the fitful, sometimes isolating monogamy of rural life, they missed the company and companionship of the sisterhood they once enjoyed, and the life-giving variety of both bullets and bracelets. We boys, I think, understood our wonder women's frustration, though we would have been betraying our newfound membership in the man-tribe to admit it. We were still their fans—still members of their retinue, as we had been (unwittingly) in that topless, stars-and-bars bicentennial parade of 1976—but now we had other kings to serve.

We didn't know it then, but the parade in Cedar Bluff was a turning point; after that time, the women of our family drifted apart, even from one another, as they took jobs in town and retreated further into the pressing needs of their own individual households, the children bussing away each morning to school and returning to the farm in the afternoon, the girls—my sister and female cousins—retreating to the vanities in my aunts' old bedroom to experiment with makeup and early punk rock—we boys, perennially at loose ends, gravitating to whatever, with our newfound power, we could conquer or kill.

Afterword
Why We Come, Why We Stay

Urban America has a love-hate relationship with its Big Empty. On one hand, many urbanites fear it—its inconvenient and often unfathomable spaces, its silences, its blackness. On the other hand, those living amid the noise and bustle of the city often look to the countryside as a place of relaxation and renewal; they need the Big Empty to get themselves sorted, to put themselves right again.

Emptiness is too often associated with cosmic lack, with incompletion, even with death. Ironically, laments of "feeling empty" are often greeted by chestnuts like, "You need to find a quiet space within yourself," or "You need to learn to embrace the quiet . . . to hear your own thoughts." To do that, one must often leave behind the straitjacket of the urban and embrace the open and empty freedom of the rural. And when one acknowledges the need for that openness and freedom, one must also acknowledge the danger to humanity of the disappearance of our rural places.

Out here, in America's big empty, we grow into middle age with an implicit sense of the vulnerability of our place, its fragility born of exceptionality in a world that grows more urban by the day. We understand that in a global economy defined by the free movement of goods, services, and people, the world is choosing, in effect, *against* us, by electing to centralize where we would decentralize. Through an understanding of our economic and cultural

247

vulnerability, we come to understand (better than most) that what is here today may not be here tomorrow, and this knowledge makes us as vulnerable as anyone with an ever-present awareness of mortality. We understand that the roadhouse café that serves an occasional breakfast on the weekends but mostly hardcore drunks at night is unlikely to survive; cheap booze doesn't generate enough profit to keep the lights on and the propane flowing.

The losses we so often experience here—of people, of folkways, of essential and underlying characters—sober us and at the same time make us sweet, more fully human. What is sweetness, after all, but a tender contraindication—an acknowledgment of just how hard life can be, how unsparing, how in need of a light touch. And what is tenderness, in the end, but an implicit recognition that things are prone to break if they are not taken care of?

In the Jazz Age, Homer Croy, of Maryville, Missouri, hit the bigtime, publishing a best-selling novel entitled *West of the Water Tower* that had East Coast literati guessing who the literary genius was who had penned it under the name "Anonymous." Croy had only just turned forty and suddenly the farmer's son from the small farm town in northwest Missouri was an overnight literary sensation.

But not quite. The trouble was, the book's publishers at Harper and Brothers had demanded that Croy withhold his identity; his reputation as a humorist was seen as a detriment to the book's potential sales and its serious content. Critics claimed the writing was so pitch-perfect, so ripe for the historical moment, that it could only have come from the pen of one of the country's greatest writers of the Midwest experience—Booth Tarkington perhaps, or Sherwood Anderson, Harry Leon Wilson, Sinclair Lewis, or Theodore Dreiser. Eventually a friend let the little detail of the book's authorship slip at a party and the world arrived at Croy's doorstep. Once the dust settled, the public discussions over the book's authorship had generated sales in excess of 100,000 copies, and Paramount pictures cut Croy a check for $25,000 for the film rights to the novel—at the time, the largest sum ever paid for movie rights to an American novel.

But the life of a literary sensation and bon vivant can be a uniquely unstable one, and by the mid-1940s Croy had, in many ways, hit rock bottom. He had failed utterly as a Hollywood scriptwriter; he'd had his gas cut off, and finally, he'd had his home in New York foreclosed on. Far worse were his personal losses, including two young sons lost to illness and tragic accident. Amid all the turmoil, Croy's thoughts returned to the small towns and mid-sized farms of the Corn Belt. While as a young man he had craved the sentimental, feel-good stories of O'Henry, as a middle-aged soul he wanted truth, as deep and real and folksy as he could get it. But he didn't want truth garbed even in the benign showmanship of a Mark Twain or a Will Rogers; he wanted it to be as direct and simple as he remembered it from his youth. "I began to try, as I never had before," Croy reflects in his memoir *Country Cured*, "to understand my life and my place in it. . . . I began to appreciate the things that gave me moments of exaltation, a lift, a flash of something spiritual." At his lowest, the onetime humorist made lists of what he called "homey satisfactions" from back in Missouri that together formed a spiritual bread-crumb trail that would lead him back home. To make such gratitude manifest, and to keep himself grounded, he inventoried the core beliefs he had learned growing up in the Midwest:

> I believe that most people do the best they can, considering their limitations and their prejudices and the toll their mental limitations have levied upon them.

> I believe that kindness is just about the finest thing in the world. And, it seems to me that kindness has its roots in understanding.

I believe that most people would rather be kind than
cruel, but that their animal inheritance is just below
the surface and is the cause of much of the intol–
erable ferocity that human beings so often exhibit
toward each other.

I believe there is no secret of happiness and that com–
plete happiness is an impossible goal. But that one
can get a great deal of satisfaction as one goes along
by not expecting too much and by squeezing dry
all the little pleasures.

I believe in the innate dignity of human beings and I
hold this to be one of their finest qualities.

I believe no one is free from worry, and that the
person who is happiest and who accomplishes most
is the one who spends his time and vitality doing
instead of chafing.

I believe that most people hunger for approval as the
roots of a flower do for water.

I believe that praise is just about the most powerful
stimulus in all the world. And, unfortunately, about
the least employed.

I believe that every person is part devil and part
pretty fine, and that we must accept these phases as
they come.

Though advancing years and mounting debts forced him to sell
the Missouri home place in 1957, Croy understood well the artis-
tic gift it had been to him. In a 1957 interview with the Missouri
newspaper where he got his start, the *St. Joseph News-Press*, Croy's
tone turned wryly circumspect, saying, "I made more writing about
the farm than I ever made operating it. I guess I took in the worst
paying professions in the world—farming and writing."

—————≫•◦•≪—————

Out here in the Great Middle, our biggest safety net is one another, and yet the holes in the net are astoundingly wide; the spaces in between us are immense and there simply aren't enough of us anymore to form a secure net, let alone create a cushion against omnipresent loss. There is no planned redundancy here, no understudy, no hedge against loss in the form of a "deep bench" of talented souls willing and able to step up. As in a small classroom, a single absence is felt by all.

From the outside we may appear unchanged, year after year, especially to those who only pass through on the highway and pass over in the airspace above. What you often see from your window is a patchwork prettiness or a Hollywood set. You see the quintessence of the American town: the town hall and post office with park benches out front, the hardware store whose owner can find that doohickey you need, the little ma and pa shop that sells gas and a few groceries, the school with a playground, houses with front porches and tire swings, and that little restaurant with the to-die-for homemade pies. But look more closely and you will see the layer of dust and the signs of strain. The post office may be slated to close; the store owners, faced with competition from the big chains, are struggling to hang on; the gas station is part of a national gas station/convenience store chain; the consolidated school, if the town is lucky enough to host one, serves students from far and wide; and the small number of cars parked outside the little restaurant with the homemade pie hints that it will be leaving us too soon.

Many of the storefronts on our modest main streets change hands every few years. The shops, when they close, tend not to close for long. Some local entrepreneur senses a niche and moves in quickly and quietly, with big dreams and good intentions. They make a go of it for a couple years before the business folds, and the cycle of commercial birth and death begins anew. In that way and others, our lives here become an ecology; as with nature, commerce and community abhor a vacuum.

Those who don't know better say the problem in places like ours is a lack of loyalty or subscription or patronage, but don't believe them. As with most things in the hinterlands, what we lack is not vision or loyalty, but numbers . . . critical mass. We accept that business can never be brisk—even the canned goods with a shelf-life of several years find their way to the "expired" shelf. We live on the hairy edge of expiration dates, and somehow find ways to revel in it.

When you fly over the Great Middle, you see a patchwork of farms, but rural America is not only for farmers. Rural America needs doctors and nurses, lawyers, plumbers, and dentists. It needs teachers, florists, mechanics, and bankers, insurance sellers, appliance repairers, bakers, builders, and bulldozer operators. Rural and small town America has fertile soil for entrepreneurs and dreamers, fertile soil in which to plant roots and grow a family and a future.

Approaching sixty, Homer Croy listed the simple things that brought him greatest satisfaction and sweetness. Not surprisingly, most of the items he counted near and dear dated back to when he was young at heartland, writing, working, and daydreaming on his family's acres in Missouri.

> The whistle of a train at night.
>
> Getting into a bed with fresh clean sheets.
>
> Sitting in front of a fireplace.
>
> Fish jumping in a lake at sunset.
>
> Sitting down to dinner with friends.
>
> A child toddling toward me.
>
> Meeting a dear friend I have not seen for some time.
>
> The welcome from a dog.

The smell of coffee cooking early of a morning.

A walk all by myself at dusk along a country road.

Croy fashioned from his list of gratitudes true talismans to shield himself from what felt like an increasingly urban and craven world. Perhaps in reaction to those changes, he decided to give up trying to concoct the kind of gee-whiz stories Hollywood would buy, resolving instead to become a better documenter of the true tales of his native Midwest and the men and women who call it home. And what he may have foregone in the book sales of his more sensational novels, he surely regained in service to his home place when the Armed Services bought his midwestern memoir, *Country Cured*, for distribution among the many GIs who hailed from the nation's midsection. He writes, "As I began to better understand life, I felt that instead of standing alone, I was part of a vast kinship with all other human beings, and that as I suffered, so they suffered; and as I yearned, so they yearned; and that as I felt defeat, so they must experience it, too." Like Grant Wood, hard knocks in a sometimes hard region may have rendered Croy a eulogist, but one imbued with a spirit of shared sadness, spirit, sweetness, and hard-won hope that made possible a still deeper communion with his readers, and his region.

In one of his lesser-known anthems, Jimmy Buffet compares life to a tire swing. And when I think about Homer Croy and a life invested here in these sometimes difficult hinterlands, I think that Buffet must mean a spin on a tire swing is a lot like life: slow in the beginning, breathless in the middle, and bittersweet in the end, when, inevitably, we're called back in. To be the young at heart here, involved in the ever-widening concentric circles of growing up, rooting down, and seeking ground, is a little like the sweet confusion, the uncanny mixture of dizzying pain and pleasure, of a ride on a tire swing.

To live here is to love here, abidingly but not blindly. It is to be keenly aware of things passing, changing form, moving on, being reborn. To revel in babies, weddings, close games at the high school on a winter's night, close kisses under the sheets, our hearts beating double-time. Maybe as consequence we who live and love here experience disproportionate pleasure in things that cause us to feel our heart beat hard in our chest, these things that bespeak life.

Selected Bibliography

Agnew, Eleanor. *Back from the Land: How Young Americans Went to Nature in the 1970s, and Why They Came Back*. Chicago: Ivan R. Dee, 2004.

Anderson, William. *The Iowa Story: Laura Ingalls Wilder's Life in Burr Oak, Iowa*. Burr Oak, IA: Laura Ingalls Wilder Park and Museum, 1990.

Aurner, C. Ray. *A Topical History of Cedar County*. Vol. 2. Chicago: S. J. Clarke, 1910.

Bly, Carol. *Letters from the Country*. Minneapolis: University of Minnesota Press, 1999.

Bourget, Paul. *Outre-Mer: Impression of America*. New York: Charles Scribner's and Sons, 1895.

Carr, Patrick J., and Maria Kefalas. *Hollowing Out the Middle: The Rural Brain Drain and What It Means for America*. Boston: Beacon Press, 2009.

Cayton, Andrew L., and Susan E. Gray, eds. *The American Midwest: Essays on Regional History*. Bloomington: Indiana University Press, 2001.

Croy, Homer. *Country Cured*. New York: Harper and Brothers, 1943.

Davidson, Osha Gray. *Broken Heartland: The Rise of America's Rural Ghetto*. Iowa City: University of Iowa Press, 1996.

Dell, Floyd. "Chicago in Fiction." *The Bookman*, November 1913.

Fellman, Anita Clair. *Little House, Long Shadow: Laura Ingalls Wilder's Impact on American Culture*. Columbia: University of Missouri Press, 2008.

Florida, Richard. *Who's Your City: How the Creative Economy Is Making Where to Live the Most Important Decision of Your Life*. New York: Basic Books, 2008.

Frank, Thomas. *What's the Matter with Kansas?* New York: Holt, 2004.

Fultz, Jay. *In Search of Donna Reed.* Iowa City: University of Iowa Press, 1998.

Garland, Hamlin. *A Son of the Middle Border.* New York: Macmillan, 1917.

The History of Cedar County, Iowa. Chicago: Western Historical Co., 1878.

Jack, Walter Thomas. *The Furrow and Us.* Philadelphia: Dorrance, 1946.

Longworth, Richard. *Caught in the Middle: America's Heartland in the Age of Globalism.* New York: Bloomsbury, 2007.

Marston, William Moulton. *Emotions of Normal People.* London: Kegan Paul, 1928.

———. *Wonder Woman.* New York: Bonanza Books, 1972.

Martone, Michael. *The Flatness and Other Landscapes.* Athens: University of Georgia Press, 2003.

Randolph, Vance. *Ozark Magic and Folklore.* New York: Dover, 1947.

Sandburg, Carl. *Chicago Poems.* New York: Henry Holt, 1916.

Simone, Gail. *Wonder Woman: The Circle.* DC Comics, 2008.

Thoreau, Henry David. *Walking.* Boston: Ticknor and Fields, 1862.

United Nations. *World Urbanization Prospects, the 2014 Revision: Highlights.* New York: United Nations, 2014.

White House Rural Council. *Jobs and Economic Security for Rural America.* Washington, DC: The White House, 2011.

Wilder, Laura Ingalls. *On the Way Home: A Diary of a Trip from South Dakota to Mansfield, Missouri, in 1894.* New York: Harper & Row, 1962.

Wood, Grant. *Revolt against the City.* Iowa City: Clio Press, 1935.

Wood, Richard E. *Survival of Rural America: Small Victories and Bitter Harvests.* Lawrence: University of Kansas Press, 2008.

Worick, Jennifer. *The Prairie Girl's Guide to Life: How to Sew a Sampler Quilt and 49 Other Pioneer Projects for the Modern Girl.* Newton, CT: Taunton Press, 2007.

About the Author

Zachary Michael Jack is an award-winning author and editor of many books on rural life. Twice nominated for the Theodore Saloutos Award for the year's best book in agricultural history and a national runner-up in his class for *Foreword Reviews* Book of the Year, Jack teaches courses in writing, rural, and place studies at North Central College and is on the board of the Midwestern History Association. The author was raised on a heritage farm on land that has been in continuous family ownership since before the Civil War. His ongoing legacy on the land includes living in and operating farm homes in Iowa and Missouri, states his ancestors helped pioneer. Jack is the seventh generation in his family to make his home in the rural Midwest.